DIVERSIÓN

POSTMILLENNIAL POP

General Editors: Karen Tongson and Henry Jenkins

Diversión

Play and Popular Culture in Cuban America

Albert Sergio Laguna

NEW YORK UNIVERSITY PRESS

New York

NEW YORK UNIVERSITY PRESS
New York
www.nyupress.org

References to Internet websites (URLs) were accurate at the time of writing. Neither the author nor New York University Press is responsible for URLs that may have expired or changed since the manuscript was prepared.

Library of Congress Cataloging-in-Publication Data
Names: Laguna, Albert Sergio.
Title: Diversión : play and popular culture in Cuban America / Albert Sergio Laguna.
Description: New York : NEW YORK UNIVERSITY PRESS, 2017. |
Series: Postmillential pop | Includes bibliographical references and index.
Identifiers: LCCN 2016052430 | ISBN 9781479836017 (cl : alk. paper) |
ISBN 9781479846146 (pb : alk. paper)
Subjects: LCSH: Cuban Americans—Social life and customs. | Cuban Americans—
Florida—Miami—Social life and customs. | Popular culture—Florida—Miami. | Popular culture—United States.
Classification: LCC E184.C97 L34 2017 | DDC 305.868/7291073—dc23
LC record available at https://lccn.loc.gov/2016052430

New York University Press books are printed on acid-free paper, and their binding materials are chosen for strength and durability. We strive to use environmentally responsible suppliers and materials to the greatest extent possible in publishing our books.

Manufactured in the United States of America

10 9 8 7 6 5 4 3 2 1

Also available as an ebook

For Alberto Laguna, Minerva Laguna, Maylene Laguna,
and Sandra Hernández
and in loving memory of
Oscar Laguna

CONTENTS

ACKNOWLEDGMENTS

Writing these acknowledgments has been an opportunity to look back at all it took to get this book done. Although I can provide only the short version of all the people I'd like to recognize, my deepest gratitude dwells between the commas.

Where else can I begin but Jersey? At Montclair State University, Jim Nash, Sharon Lewis, and Leslie Wilson stepped up to support this interesting idea I had about getting my PhD in English. It is at Montclair where I met Patrick Deer, my first advisor in the English department who would later become a good friend and a kind of grad-student life coach when we met again at New York University. Patrick introduced me to Ana Dopico whose "Cubanologies" class opened my eyes to intellectual possibilities that I didn't know existed. If not for those happy coincidences, things would have turned out much differently. Patrick and Ana, *gracias por todo*. Ana's critical introduction to *cubanía* would soon lead me to the door of José Muñoz, who took for granted that he'd be on my exam and dissertation committees. José is the inspiration for this book, not only because of his work on *choteo* but also in how he embodied a kind of critical Cuban *jodedera* that I continue to aspire to. To walk into his office overlooking Broadway and see this man not from Miami, Los Angeles, or New York City but from Hialeah—*agua, fango, y factoría*—meant everything to me. I like to think that he would have thoroughly enjoyed this book. Back in the English department, Phil Harper helped keep me on course. Tom Augst, Juan Flores (QEPD), Elaine Freedgood, Crystal Parikh, and Mary Louise Pratt schooled me at critical moments.

The César Chávez Predoctoral Fellowship at Dartmouth College gave me the time and funding to write, but more importantly, allowed me to develop my work in conversation with Valerie Dickerson, Lourdes Gutiérrez Nájera, Patricia Herrera, Israel Reyes, Silvia Spitta, and Kendra Taira Field. Jobs at Wesleyan University and Columbia College Chicago surrounded me with fantastic colleagues who showed me the ropes as I made the transition from student to faculty member. My thanks to Joel Pfister, Sheila Baldwin, Madhurima Chakraborty, Ken Daley, Sarah Odishoo, Karen Osborne, Doug Reichert Powell, and Pegeen Reichert Powell.

I wrote my second book first. When I arrived at Yale in 2012, my plan was to revise my dissertation. I had been dabbling in studies of play in Cuban diasporic cultural production on the side. Thankfully, Michael Denning and Matt Jacobson pointed out in a conversation about my scholarly plans that I had been doing a bit more than dabbling and that maybe I should write this book first. Mind blown, I got to work. Their feedback on various chapter drafts was indispensable as I revised. American Studies and Ethnicity, Race, and Migration at Yale have been wonderful homes for my scholarship and teaching. The brilliance around every corner is surpassed only by the generosity of my colleagues. Alicia Schmidt Camacho was my first guide when I arrived here and has continued in that role, modeling what's possible when high-powered scholarship and community activism intersect. Steve Pitti has shown support for my work from the beginning and has been a tremendous help as I navigate the profession. Daphne Brooks provided feedback on a late draft and has jokes of her own. Many thanks as well to my colleagues Jean-Christophe Agnew, Birgit Brander Rasmussen, Ned Blackhawk, David Blight, Hazel Carby, Jessica Cattelino, Genevieve Carpio, George Chauncey, Kate Dudley, Marcela Echeverri, Anne Eller, Crystal Feimster, Glenda Gilmore, Jacqueline Goldsby, Ronald Gregg, Zareena Grewal, Inderpal Grewal, Leslie Harkema, Jonathan Holloway, Seth Jacobowitz, Katie Lofton, Mary Lui, Dan Magaziner, Joanne Meyerowitz, Marc Robinson, Paul Sabin, Caleb Smith, Laura Wexler and Sunny Xiang for insight and good conversation along the way. Special shout out to Laura Barraclough, Greta LaFleur, and Dixa Ramírez. What *can't* we figure out over lunch? Academic departments are not run by academics. My deepest thanks go to Jean Cherniavsky, Tatjana Cisija, and Susan Shand for their administrative acumen and warmth. I'm also grateful for institutional support from the A. Whitney Griswold Faculty Research Fund, the MacMillan Center, the Frederick W. Hilles Publication Fund, and the Poorvu Family Fund for Teaching at Yale College.

Some of the best conversations I've had have been with my students: Aleshia Barajas, Michael Bustamante (el paquete!), Cathy Calderón, Melissa Castillo-Garsow, Karla Cornejo Villavicencio, Angie Díaz, Heidi Guzmán, Cristina Moreno, Rachel Pérez, Sebastián Pérez, George Ramírez, Pedro Regalado, Christofer Rodelo, Yami Rodríguez, and Damián Vergara Bracamontes. Their energy and promise are invigorating. When NYU's English department accepted Roy Pérez and me in the same year, José Muñoz christened us the Cuban pandas—brought in as a pair so we wouldn't die. He wasn't far off. Thanks for everything, meng. I must also thank Leticia Alvarado for her close readings of various chapters and for making such a truly wonderful friend in high school. Antonio López and Alexandra T. Vazquez immediately recognized what I was trying to do. Their insights framed by the *cubaneo* that marks this book were not only critically productive, but restorative. José Quiroga appeared at two crucial points in this book's life and provided crucial feedback with his usual grace and fierce humor. Frances Negrón-Muntaner helped me see the bigger picture. I'd also like to thank Julio Capó, Jr., Mario González-Corzo, Lillian Guerra, Jesús J. Hernández, Ariana Hernández Reguant, Erin Heslin, Sallie Hughes, Karen Jaime, Carmen Lamas, Jill Lane, Marisol LeBrón, Iraida López, Lillian Manzor, Monica Martínez, Rory Miller, Ariana Ochoa Camacho, Ricardo Ortíz, Susana Peña, Lisandro Pérez, Eliana Rivero, and Sandra Ruíz. I also appreciate the mentorship and feedback made possible by the *súper buena gente* of the New England Consortium for Latin@ Studies.

Putting this book together meant making connections in Havana and Miami. I am profoundly grateful to the staff at the Cuban Heritage Collection at the University of Miami for their help in locating materials: María Estorino Dooling, Gladys Gómez-Rossié, Mei Méndez, Annie Sansone Martínez, and Rosa Monzón-Alvarez. Special thanks to María who also helped me set up interviews; she is the "fixer" of Cuban Miami. I am likewise indebted to the comedians, journalists, scholars, artists, and business people who took the time in Havana and Miami to share their histories and insights: the Alvarez Guedes Family, Pepe Billete, Iván Camejo, Gerardo Chávez, Manolo Coego, Zulema Cruz, Baudilio Espinosa, Ramón Fernández-Larrea, Angel García, Maribel González, Nemesio González, Carlos Gonzalvo, Pablo "El Pible" Garí,

Alen Lauzán, Los Pichy Boys (Alejandro González and Maikel Rodríguez), Leslie Pantín, Jorge Alberto Piñero (JAPE), Dr. Ana María Polo, Enrique "Kike" Quiñones, Fernando Ravsberg, Octavio Rodríguez, Denise Sánchez, and Elisabeth Sarduy Linares.

Early on, I thought NYU Press would be a great fit for this book. Many thanks to Eric Zinner and the editors of the Postmillennial Pop Series, Karen Tongson and Henry Jenkins, for reciprocating the love. Alicia Nadkarni helped make sure that this book exists as a thing in the world. The anonymous readers dropped the knowledge necessary to make it better. A very early version of Chapter 1 appeared in "Aquí Está Alvarez Guedes: Cuban Choteo and the Politics of Play," *Latino Studies* 8, no.4 (2010): 509–531. Parts of Chapter 2 were published in "Cuban Miami on the Air: Narratives of Cubanía," *Journal of Latin American Cultural Studies* 23, no. 1 (2014): 1–24.

This book wouldn't exist without my having grown up surrounded by some very, very funny and loving people. My father, Alberto, is one of the funniest people I know and a world class *jodedor*. My mother, Minerva, can't tell a joke to save her life but watching her try is enough to get me laughing. My sister Maylene's ebullient laughter and hilarity were a constant reminder that this project was necessary. More importantly, they have always been an unwavering source of love and support. Visiting Cuba for the first time put the sacrifices my grandparents made into clearer perspective, *gracias a* Sergio "Pipo" and Isaura "Mima" Pérez and Ignacio and Himilce Laguna for their courage. I thought of thanking the rest of my family from Union City to Miami with a blanket "thanks" to all the aunts, uncles, and my many cousins. But that doesn't seem adequate, especially when a piece of each of them is in this book. To my cousins who so often made diversión possible: Adriel, Alan, Alexa, Cesar, Danny, Gilbertico, Jackie, Judy, Loren, and Maritzita. And to the *tíos* and *tías*: Barbara, Cuty, Idalmis, Pablo, Maritza, Mirita, Oscarín, and Reina. Our family has sustained serious and untimely losses in the last couple of years: QEPD Pablo Chirino and Oscar Laguna. Here's to the future with Adrian, Logan, Alina, Andrew, Dante, Oscar and those to come. I'm also thankful for my family in Cuba. The Jaén, Pérez, and Perera families embraced me quickly and helped me feel at home in a place that feels both foreign and familiar.

Marriage has meant adoption into the Nuñez and Hernández families. They have welcomed me with open arms, Cuban coffee, and the best *lechón* on the planet. Sonia Nuñez is *la suegra perfecta* helping me with translations at a moment's notice with a side of love. And though I appreciate her help, I'm particularly grateful for her daughter. Sandra Caridad Hernández has seen this book take shape from the very beginning and was there when *diversión* was the last word I would have used to describe the process of writing it. She read drafts and clicked every link I sent her enjoying the funny and enduring lo pesao. She gets the jokes and me. I could go on singing her praises but Graciela had a much, much better voice. I leave it to her:

> Tú me quieres, yo te quiero
> Tú me adoras, yo te adoro
> Me quieres, te quiero, me adoras, te adoro
> Esto es felicidad . . .

Introduction

Feeling Cuban

By not opening with a joke, I heed a valuable lesson learned from the many comedians I write about in this book. Any good joke, like any introduction worth reading, requires a solid setup. Moments of humor will come—however fraught—as I discuss political and generational shifts within the Cuban diaspora in the United States from the 1970s to the 2010s while at the same time pointing out what ludic popular culture can tell us about community formations, performance, and race. But before I can get to these points, I need to provide you with some of the details, the context, that will make the purpose of this book clearer.

Think of it as my own setup.

I grew up in and around Union City, New Jersey, affectionately referred to as "Havana on the Hudson" because of the large Cuban population that settled there in the years following Fidel Castro's rise to power in 1959. My family had all the exile street cred: unfair imprisonments, seizure of property, the high-ranking family member whose loyalty to the Revolution trumped family ties. While these stories framed angry and explicit anti-Castro sentiment, they were largely overshadowed in both frequency and intensity by the ludic in quotidian life. Jokes about bumbling communists. Trips to the bathroom prefaced with "voy a mandar una carta a Fidel" (I'm going to send a letter to Fidel). My grandfather's *guajiro* sayings marked by double entendre and filtered through the symbolic economy of the farm he worked—plenty of *gallos* and *yeguas*. From an early age, this is what it meant to be Cuban in my mind. Not the rumba or roast pork but *la jodedera*, "perhaps our only national sport" as Enrico Mario Santí has suggested—the joking, wordplay, and comic barbs aimed at anyone who needed to get knocked down a peg.[1]

In making my way through the bibliography on Cuban America, I found the affective emphasis inverted. Most scholarship on Cuban America equated exile with melancholy, anger, and bitterness.[2] Where was the focus on the kind of quotidian pleasures that are the reward for a long workweek—the bawdy satirical comedy playing at a local theater in Little Havana, the latest joke about Fidel a friend shares over a *cafecito*? To be sure, life in the exile community wasn't one big conga line down Calle Ocho or Bergenline Avenue. But popular culture was always there to inspire not only the laughter that keeps you from crying but also a ludic sociability that helped shape narratives of a community. Searching for a way to make sense of what felt like a profound disconnect between scholarly focus and lived experience, I started listening to jokes, lots and lots of jokes, in an attempt to laugh my way to greater clarity.

After hours of listening to the comedy of Guillermo Alvarez Guedes—one of the most beloved figures in the history of Cuban popular culture—I came upon a moment from his eleventh standup album recorded live in 1980 that would become the point of departure for this book. Innocently enough, Alvarez Guedes begins the second half of this album with some observational humor about people's obsession with putting on weight. But before he can provide his insight into corpulency, a man in the audience interrupts the crowd's attentive silence by directly addressing the comedian: "¿Y no va a hablar del Mariel?" (Aren't you going to talk about Mariel?).[3] At the time of the recording, Miami was a city in chaos roiled by racial tension and the Mariel boat crisis.[4] Cubans had stormed the Peruvian embassy in Havana in hopes of securing political asylum. In an effort to take control of the narrative, Fidel Castro allowed people to leave via the port of Mariel—in fact openly insisted that anyone who wanted to leave the country could do so. Castro claimed that he was ridding Cuba of its "undesirables"—criminals, drug abusers, homosexuals, and others he categorized as socially deviant.[5] The *Miami Herald*, voice of the white establishment and hostile to the Cuban population at the time, played a key role in disseminating these characterizations. The depressed state of the Miami economy, conflicting opinions about the *marielitos* within the exile community, and the backlash by the white establishment due to the "uncomfortably large Cuban population" created an atmosphere of heightened tension for *all* Cubans in Miami at the time.[6]

So when a man in the audience prompted Alvarez Guedes to address the unfolding crisis in the middle of his set, the air was instantly sucked out of the room, leaving an anxious silence in its wake. The interjection seemed to catch Alvarez Guedes off guard. All of his standup performances were well planned, and this is the only album out of thirty-two in which the comedian can be heard breaking his routine and interacting with his audience in a direct, seemingly unscripted dialogue.[7] After some hesitation, he replied:

> "No chico, lo del Mariel es, no le veo el ángulo humorístico a eso. Eso es muy dramático. Porque están utilizando a los cubanos otra vez, los comunistas. Están aprovechándose. Saben que los que son amantes de la libertad son también amantes de la familia. Entonces están aprovechando esas circunstancias." (No man, I don't see the humorous angle to that. That is very dramatic. Because they are using the Cubans again, the communists. They are taking advantage. They know that the lovers of freedom also love their families and so they are taking advantage of the circumstances.)[8]

Remarkably though, despite the disruption of his usual performance practice, Alvarez Guedes successfully reverses the building tide of tension through a seamless shift back into his comic persona. He ends his commentary on the boatlift with the following quip about the difficult conditions Cubans endured while awaiting passage: "Lo que cobran es una barbaridad para las cosas: un galón de agua diez pesos, una cerveza quince pesos, un filete treinta pesos. ¡Pa' cagar hay que pagar siete pesos allí! ¡Dos pesos por la bolsa y cinco para el que lo va a tirar!" (What they [Cuban price gougers] charge is outrageous: ten dollars for a gallon of water, fifteen for a beer, thirty for a steak. Even to take a shit you have to pay seven bucks! Two for the bag and five for the guy who has to get rid of it!).[9] This unexpected comic shift instantly dispels the unease in the room. All at once and for a full twenty-four seconds after the punchline, the audience communicates its relief with bursts of laughter accompanied by clapping, moans, and screeches of delight that can be heard on the track even as Alvarez Guedes attempts to segue back into his routine. Audience members can be heard exhaling, feeling saved from a potentially unpleasurable turn to the evening. One man lets out a prolonged "ayyyy" as he sighs in comic relief. Another audibly declares, "Está muy bueno," as the men and women around him catch their breath. In a span of fifty-five seconds, Alvarez Guedes successfully reroutes his audience's affective bearing toward Mariel from anxiety to a state of relieved comic pleasure.

When prompted to engage the topic of Mariel, the comedian first responds with a serious, grave tone consistent with exile political talking points and complete with a reference to the family-crushing *comunistas*. Indeed, the initial tone and language Alvarez Guedes deploys in his response are consistent with dominant representations of the exile community. They reflect the Cuban America chronicled so elaborately in the media: rowdy protests in the streets denouncing Fidel Castro and the Clinton administration during the Elián González saga come to mind. It was the Cuban America of presidential elections—an irascible bunch easily provoked, a Republican voting bloc that supports the candidate with the hardest line on Cuba, or put more appropriately, the candidate who can most passionately parrot the same empty anti-Castro rhetoric and punctuate it with a final, triumphant, English-inflected *Cuba Leebray*![10]

But the wheezing of audience members catching their breath and the high-pitched staccato chuckles in response to Alvarez Guedes's comic twist communicate an intensity of experience that demands attention. I imagine people drying their eyes, faces reddening, and doubled-over. There is a choral quality to the laughter, which produces an invitation to the listener that says, "Join us." Though I have heard this recording dozens of times, I cannot help but be affected by laughter's contagious properties. I close one eye, my chest begins to quake, and I become part of the chorus of laughers "responding to an exigency of life in common."[11] This life in common is marked by the shared understanding of that historical moment, the setup and twist, and a recognition of how Alvarez Guedes's performance *feels* Cuban—a feeling triggered by his accent, tone, the words he chooses, and the scatological framework for his punchline. This moment signals to me another way for thinking about the relationship between affect, politics, and everyday life. What if, instead of quickly moving from the humor to the somberness surrounding Mariel, we lingered on that ludic intensity? What if we followed Alvarez Guedes's lead, laughed along with the audience, and listened to the rest of the album? What are the possibilities that arise when we understand this joke not just as an animated interruption in the usual discourse surrounding tense moments in Cuban diasporic history but as an example of the ludic as a consistent strategy for narrating the present and what it means to be Cuban *off* the island?

Diversión: Play and Popular Culture in Cuban America focuses on *momentos de diversión* like the one I have just described—moments of diversion, of play, of laughter—in order to make two primary arguments. The first provides an affective complement to Cuban American and Latina/o Studies more broadly by shifting critical emphasis away from feelings that so often dominate academic conversations around minoritarian experience in the United States—the anger, pain, loss, and disappointment expressed in the first part of Alvarez Guedes's response to the question about Mariel. Though I engage these feelings alongside the ludic, I am more interested in the critical possibilities that arise in the bursts of laughter inspired by a comedian's punchline, a prank call to Fidel Castro, or a foul-mouthed puppet's take on politics. In that laughter, I "hear" the long history of humor as both an object of study in the Cuban intellectual tradition and as a key component in cultural production on and off the island. I can hear a mode of relationality, a ludic sociability, echoed throughout the history of the Cuban diaspora and fostered by the consumption and circulation of popular culture. By paying close attention to that laughter and the language and performance that produce it, I unravel how ludic popular culture "provides emotional 'paradigm scenarios,' inculcating particular ways of feeling, emotive modes that have political and social consequences" as communities imagine themselves over time.[12] And perhaps most importantly, it allows me to get at a basic question that I will address throughout this book: What do ludic popular culture and the feelings it inspires *do* in the diasporic context?

The book's second major argument utilizes a cultural studies approach to highlight the massive demographic and generational shifts within the Cuban diaspora—Miami specifically. South Florida is home to the largest population of Cubans living in the United States. Scholars like Ricardo Ortíz have been right to point out the problematic dominance of Miami in the study of Cuban America.[13] Most scholarship has focused on the exile generation that arrived between 1959 and 1973 and settled there.[14] But Cuban Miami has changed a great deal and cultural studies scholarship has been slow to catch up. More Cubans arrived in the United States between 2000 and 2010 than in any past decade.[15] Together, the US-born and arrivals since the 1990s now represent the majority of the diaspora. But while these cohorts differ from the older exile generation in many ways, there has been little scholarship on how these shifts manifest themselves in quotidian life and cultural production. *Diversión* aims to fill that void.

To make these arguments, I begin in the 1970s and quickly move to the twenty-first century with close readings of a popular culture archive that includes standup comedy, morning talk radio shows, festivals, television, and social media content. Starting in the 1970s with the exile community allows me to push back against the characterization of this segment of the diaspora as mostly melancholic while detailing the established Cuban Miami that later generations will contend with in the twenty-first century. Though the primary sources that I examine have received little attention from scholars, their popularity and status as cultural productions for and by Cuban audiences shed light on how succeeding generations have negotiated their relationships to the United States, each other, and a sense of *cubanía*—a Cuban cultural identity.[16] Despite being a word that suggests a kind of cultural essence, *cubanía* has functioned as a "vague concept, malleable and adaptable."[17] Popular culture allows me to track how cubanía has been formulated in the diaspora in various ways at different historical junctures. Such an approach reveals alternative genealogies of the diaspora and its internal diversity through analysis of artists and popular culture that travel in and between the United States and Cuba. This transnational framework imagines cubanía "as a structure of feeling that supercedes national boundaries and pedagogies" and disrupts the ossified Cold War logic of two Cubas separated by political ideologies and government policies.[18] This logic, long untenable, has been weakened further by the December 17, 2014, announcement regarding the reestablishment of diplomatic relations between the United States and Cuba. In this study, I explain how ludic popular culture has been a means for, and a reflection of, changes that have profoundly affected life on and off the island in the last twenty-five years.

Diversión Defined?

In centering this project on what I am calling *diversión*, I am partici-
pating in a long tradition of examining the ludic in Cuban culture by
island-based intellectuals.[19] This scholarly conversation has often
focused on a term that has accrued over one hundred years of scholarship in Cuba, *choteo*.[20] Choteo can be described as a form of irreverent
humor and mockery common among the masses, articulated through
the idiomatic specificity of Cuban popular culture, and highly suspicious of authority in all forms. The most quoted scholar on choteo,
Cuban cultural critic Jorge Mañach, describes it as "something that all
Cubans have" and a "typically Cuban form of relation" in his 1928 essay
"Indagación del choteo."[21] Since he weighed in on the subject, many critics have invoked the term to describe Cuban cultural production and the
"character" of the Cuban people.

Such essentializing language raises red flags. For one, the attitudes
and practices described above in relation to choteo are not exclusive
to Cuban culture. In fact, critics have explored the similarities between
choteo and other comic forms like Puerto Rican *guachafita* and Mexican
relajo.[22] Others have suggested that choteo can be found throughout the
Caribbean.[23] So what makes Cuban choteo so Cuban? Why has it been
claimed so strongly? In his study of humor in Puerto Rican literature
on and off the island, Israel Reyes explains: "It is true that nations often
claim particular species of the comic as part of their national character,
and Spanish American and Hispanic Caribbean nations are no exceptions."[24] In the early years of the republic, Cuban academics consistently
claimed, cited, and studied choteo as part of a larger intellectual project
and debate geared toward defining what it meant to be "Cuban" in the
newly independent nation.[25] Today, choteo continues to be cited as a
means to describe the Cuban national character. Juan Antonio García
Borrero, writing in 2004, sums up this sentiment succinctly: "Está bien
claro que Cuba sin choteo no sería Cuba" (It is very clear that Cuba
without choteo wouldn't be Cuba).[26]

Academic studies by island-based intellectuals have taken cues for
studying choteo and Cuban humor more broadly from quotidian life
and cultural production. The spirit of choteo was a central element
of *teatro bufo*—a form of Cuban comic vernacular theater that first

appeared in the mid-nineteenth century featuring characters in black-face.[27] An irreverent tradition of political cartooning extending back to the mid-nineteenth century has long utilized choteo to skewer the powerful.[28] It also appears in the work of artists like filmmaker Tomás Gutiérrez Alea and writers Mirta Yáñez, Virgilio Piñera, and Guillermo Cabrera Infante.[29] The Cuban love affair with the ludic also registered on television where, as Yeidy Rivero points out, the first program was a comedy.[30] But while artists and scholars have mobilized choteo and the intellectual history behind it in the service of their own projects, the word itself is rarely used in quotidian life.[31] Instead, *jodedera, dar cuero*, and *relajo* often function as synonyms for *choteo* to varying degrees in everyday speech. Defining the differences between comic forms can be tricky and translation increases the difficulty.[32] What these terms all do is suggest a kind of levity, of not taking people or things seriously, even if they merit just that.

Is it possible to create a typology of ludic terms in Cuban popular culture complete with definitions? Perhaps, but such a project will not be the focus of this book. I am not interested in distinguishing how choteo might be similar to or different from say, relajo. Instead, I choose the word *diversión* as a means to index a host of terms like *choteo, relajo, jodedera*, and *burla*, which populate Cuban scholarly and vernacular expression. At times, I will use certain terms, with qualification, when it is particularly apt in the context of the material I am discussing. *Choteo*, especially, carries a significant amount of weight because of the long intellectual history of the term and its anti-authoritarian bent. But the general attractiveness of *diversión* as this project's organizing logic is its imprecision. Its broadness allows me to stay away from what I consider the less interesting conversation around classification. The discursive latitude of diversión allows me to place a variety of ludic cultural forms into conversation to illuminate the ways in which levity and play broadly conceived have shaped the social in dramatic ways.

I deploy *diversión* on two complementary levels. On the first, I use the term to describe ludic popular culture texts or moments as "archive[s] of feelings" charged with "feelings and emotions that are encoded not only in the content of the texts themselves but in the practices that surround their production and reception."[33] Diversión is the morning radio show you listen to on your morning drive that helps to set the tone for your day. It is the funny meme you circulate among your friends on social media that only they would understand. Diversión is the ridiculous "Cuban" nickname your aunt has given to one of your friends. It is the standup comedy show you attend on the weekend where gestures and jokes intersect to produce comic pleasure. It is born out of the cultural clashes that occur as Cuban Spanish and English meet in Hialeah to produce mistranslations or when you try to communicate the meaning of idiomatic phrases like "le zumba el mango" in English.[34] As these examples suggest, a key component of my analysis will be a focus on language. More committed to wordplay and the absurd than slapstick, an analysis of diversión must be attentive to how language produces comic moments and ludic sociability over time. Diversión is the language used to narrate shared pasts and presents with designs on a potentially pleasurable future.

On the second level, I use *diversión* to describe the performative logic of these cultural forms—not only *what* is said but *how* it is said. As I will highlight throughout the book, *el cubaneo*—the sonic and gestural repertoire of cubanía—goes hand in hand with diversión.[35] The pronounced aural dimension of much of the material under scrutiny here demands that we "listen in detail" if we are to fully appreciate how sound informs the performative palette of cubanía.[36] I am talking about how a laugh can *sound* Cuban to a listener with a finely tuned ear. The sonic logic of diversión is at work when I call out "oyeeeee" with a heavy and exaggerated Cuban accent in the hotel lobby of a busy conference to get the attention of a fellow Cuban American colleague—a kind of hailing through jodedera. Diversión can also be signaled by the body through gesticulation; it is the hand waving and the flip of the wrist that orchestrates the telling of a story. One need only watch a clip of Fidel Castro's marathon speeches to appreciate the relationship between gesture and meaning. Interrogating diversión as a performative form of relation highlights the potential for the kind of intimacy and ludic sociability upon which communal identifications are built and projected. The pain, the trauma, and the melancholy of exile are often invoked to highlight how the Cuban diaspora has cohered historically. In this book, I make the argument that diversión has been just as vital.

The Archive of Diversión

In the previous section I cited the long history of diversión in Cuba as both a cultural practice and academic area of interest stretching back to the nineteenth century. But what about the diaspora? Those who left Cuba? It did not take me long to discover that diversión had been making the trip from Cuba to the United States for over one hundred years. It was always there, hiding in plain sight, molding community formations and the means of sociability alongside the brooding lamentations of exile. Continuing a long tradition of political cartooning on the island, Cuban exiles in New York published newspapers like *Cacarajícara*, which functioned like a nineteenth-century version of the *Onion*, complete with cartoons and satirical commentary directed at Spanish colonial rule.[37] Puerto Rican Bernardo Vega, in his memoirs of life in New York City in the early twentieth century, thought it important to devote time to describe how jokes served as a means to promote ludic sociability among the politically engaged *tabaqueros*, "especially on the part of the Cuban comrades."[38] Scholars like Antonio López and Christina D. Abreu have captured the relationship between race and forms of diversión in New York City from the 1920s through the 1950s through readings of print culture, bufo performances, the Cuban music scene, and social clubs.[39]

When Cubans began settling in the United States shortly after Fidel Castro rose to power in 1959, diversión quickly became a highly visible and popular way for negotiating the new space of exile, developing the emotional tools for managing the strain of displacement, and establishing a sense of cultural continuity across national boundaries. *Zig-Zag*, a wildly popular satirical newspaper that began its run in Cuba in 1938, initially supported the Revolution. But when the paper's humor ran afoul of the government, key players fled to the United States.[40] By 1962, *Zig-Zag* was back up and running in Miami under the name *Zig-Zag Libre*. The new incarnation featured deeply critical political cartoons of Fidel Castro accompanied by drawings and columns addressing life in exile. It would be joined by other satirical newspapers like *Chispa*, *Cubalegre*, *Loquillo*, and *La Política Cómica* among others through the decades.[41]

But diversión was not just a way to articulate political critiques of communist Cuba. It was a crucial means for keeping cultural practices

Figure I.1. *Zig-Zag Libre*, February 16, 1963. Courtesy of the Cuban Heritage Collection, University of Miami.

and memories alive, especially for children born or reared primarily in the United States. In 1964, an event called Añorada Cuba (Yearning for Cuba) debuted in Miami and featured music, dances, and dramatic works performed by the children of exiles. Younger children could enjoy magazines like *Payaso* (1967) and *Revista Cabalgata Infantil* (1972), which billed itself as "The Magazine of Cuban Childhood" and offered Cuban history in digestible tidbits alongside pictures of children exhibiting their artistic talents.[42] *Zig-Zag Libre* held political cartooning contests for children who could draw the best caricatures of Cuban government officials.

Diversión was certainly on the agenda for adults as well. Magazines like *Espectáculos* and *Showtime*, which combined celebrity gossip with nightlife guides, started being published in the mid-1960s. These magazines featured interviews with exiled artists along with articles with titles like "Su artista favorito puede ser un comunista" (Your Favorite Artist Could Be a Communist).[43] But without question the most consistently popular form of adult diversión came in the form of theater.[44] The first play to take up themes of exile was a comedy called *Hamburgers y sirenazos* written in 1962 by Pedro Román and debuted in 1969, but it would not be the last. Over the years, comedies began to dominate Miami's theater landscape.[45] These works were often written, performed, and staged by talent from Cuba who had fled after the Revolution and thus were familiar to many exiles. Because demand was so high, many theaters dedicated themselves to staging comedies, which often included some combination of political satire, physical comedy, and sexual innuendo.[46] But like all successful comedies, the plays spoke to issues facing the community in their moment. Reflecting community frustration with the durability of the Cuban government, Armando Roblán, famous for his impersonation of Fidel Castro, starred in *No hay mal que dure 100 años . . . ni pueblo que lo resista* (1979) (There Is No Evil That Lasts Forever . . . Nor Community That Can Take It), written by famed satirist Alberto González. When Soviet economic support for Cuba dried up in the early 1990s, exiles believed Castro would soon fall. Comic theater again answered the call with plays like *A Cuba me voy hoy mismo . . . que se acabó el comunismo!* (I'm Going to Cuba Because Communism Is Over!), performed in 1990 and starring Norma Zúñiga and Sandra Haydee, two veteran actresses of the Miami stage. These satires were joined by bawdy comedies about impotent men, cheating spouses, and even taxes. Today, the comic theater scene of Miami remains active, though certainly not as lively as it was in the 1970s and 1980s. Radio programs like *Zig-Zag Radio*, *La Fonomanía*, and *La Mogolla* took aim at the Cuban government and the excesses of Cuban Miami alike. Movies such as *Amigos* and *El Super* used dark humor to work through the pain and disorientation of exile. Cuba Nostalgia, La Feria de los Municipios de Cuba en el Exilio, and early instantiations of the Calle 8 Festival celebrated a narrative of prerevolutionary Cuba through the lens of nostalgia. *¿Qué Pasa, USA?*, a bilingual sitcom that followed three generations of the Peña family as they navigated life in Miami, was wildly popular from 1977 to 1980.[47]

I offer this broad overview not to suggest that this book will take an encyclopedic approach to documenting diversión but to communicate its pervasiveness in a number of contexts and to assure the reader that the moments that I have chosen to examine more carefully in the chapters to come are not isolated incidents cherry-picked to fit some contrived scholarly paradigm. Instead, the cultural forms I examine in this book have long been deployed and celebrated in diasporic culture: the

Figure I.2. Promotional material for *No hay mal que dure 100 años . . . ni pueblo que lo resista*, 1979. Courtesy of the Cuban Heritage Collection, University of Miami.

enduring popularity of standup comedy; radio and its ubiquity in the history of Cuban Miami; and the continued staging of cubanía at fairs and festivals, among others. By selecting contemporary manifestations of popular culture practices with a long history in the diasporic context, I am able to examine not only how Cuban Miami has changed but also how the cultural forms themselves have been transformed to meet the demands of contemporary audiences and the potential of technological advances. The spirit of satirical *periodiquitos* of old now inform You-Tube videos and memes produced by groups like Los Pichy Boys, whose content has been viewed millions of times on social media. Counter-revolutionary comedy produced in Miami once circulated in Cuba in the form of books and cassettes passed hand to hand. Now, thousands of gigabytes of content circulate throughout the island courtesy of thumb and hard drives. My analysis of diversión, then, is deeply committed to understanding a changing Cuban diaspora *and* the aesthetic and perfor-mative evolution of the often-ephemeral cultural forms that profoundly shape everyday life.

I will argue throughout this book that this archive of diversión, and its broad impact on life in Cuban Miami, cannot be divorced from strat-egies for capital accumulation. But a crucial distinction is in order. This is not a study of how Cubanness or latinidad more broadly has been commodified for white audiences in the United States.[48] Diversión, as it is conceived here, is not the overpriced Cuban restaurant in your town covered in sepia prints of '57 Chevys and servers in freshly pressed *guay-aberas.* This does not mean that this popular culture functions outside the world of the market. Instead, I argue that analyzing popular culture created by and for ethnic-racialized subjects provides a glimpse into understanding the role capital plays in mediating social relations and cultural production on local and transnational levels: the "selling" of nostalgia in the form of prerevolutionary knickknacks in stores and on-line; the circulation of popular culture between Miami and Cuba and the financial considerations that go into those flows; and corporate media conglomerates like Univision muscling into the local radio market in Miami and their influence on content.

If diversión has been so pervasive because of its resonance among the diaspora and the role of capital, why has there been so little schol-arship on these forms and practices within Cuban American Studies?

This lack of engagement with the ludic can be explained partially by the incongruity it faces when put into dialogue with the "usual" affective registers used to describe the exile experience.[49] Exile is displacement; displacement is painful. The echoes of loss, abandonment, and deracination encoded within the word *exile* and the baggage it carries with it have limited the term's signifying potential. But this equation of exile with loss and its attendant hardships cannot be explained only by how the concept signifies in broader scholarly and popular imaginations. The relationship between exile, affect, and politics must also be taken into account. In the Cuban context, the feelings associated with exile can be invoked to reinforce claims on Cuban American exceptionalism based on political motivations for leaving the island. This performance has been necessary to maintain a claim on the privileges extended to Cuban émigrés: a pathway to legal status through the Cuban Adjustment Act of 1966 and access to federal programs created by the US government to aid those fleeing communism during the Cold War.[50] Of course, I do not mean to suggest in using the word *performance* that exilic affect is somehow disingenuous. Instead, I seek to stress the importance of affect as a means for making claims to the benefits of exile as a category, especially in the context of the Cold War United States.[51] Historically, the Cuban American lobby in Washington and elected officials have worn the pathos of exile on their sleeves while pushing for a more confrontational foreign policy toward Cuba.

I do not seek to delegitimize the many works of scholarship and art that have foregrounded the very real pain of exile to tell the story of Cuban America. That pain, too, is part of this study with diversión serving as a means to process and manage it. But in privileging the ludic, I hope to get at something as prevalent and quotidian as pain—the shared pleasures within a community that play a vital role in representing and shaping the present. The material I examine in this book does not win awards or attract a great deal of academic attention. It cannot be found on syllabi. The archive I have assembled is most often engaged on the living room couch in front of a television, long car rides with Alvarez Guedes albums playing, social media feeds, celebrations with family and friends, or nights out on the town. I have attended the festivals and interviewed comedians and event organizers inside and outside of Cuba. I have spent a great deal of time on Facebook and in the deepest recesses of the Cuban blogosphere, and I have gotten sucked in to an untold number of YouTube content loops. For years, I have experienced these popular culture forms not only as an exercise in academic analysis, but also as a means to make my way through the world, like so many others. This work has brought me a great deal of pleasure through the years but it has also brought me disappointment, even a mix of the two simultaneously. It is this multivalence of popular culture, its ability to bring pleasure as well as "rage, and frustration about its silences, exclusions and assaults," that I take up now.[52]

Arroz con Mango

The archive of diversión detailed above highlights those cultural forms meant to make people feel good through laughter and communal celebrations. But it is crucial to stir the pot a bit and introduce an analytical thread that will appear throughout this study: the role of race and sexuality. Throughout the writing of this book, colleagues—especially those with knowledge of Cuban popular culture—have expressed enthusiasm mixed with a sentiment best captured with a phrase from Cuban vernacular speech: *arroz con mango*. The phrase, which literally translates to rice with mango, describes a messy or complicated situation, a contradiction that produces headaches. For a scholar deeply committed to critical race theory and social justice projects, studying diversión can often result in generous helpings of arroz con mango. Comic tropes around blackness, women, and homosexuality continue to function as reliable, if not tired elements, of popular culture production. The relationship between race, gender, sexuality, and diversión represents a kind of transnational continuity identifiable throughout "Greater Cuba."[53] This most clearly manifests itself in humor that is dominated by men and utilizes representational strategies inflected with racism, homophobia, and sexism. It is in exploring this basic dynamic—that feeling good can come at the expense of others—that we can further grasp the intersecting, and at times contradictory, narratives that affect how communities come to imagine themselves.

I address this dynamic throughout the book, especially with regard to race and the production of Cuban American whiteness.[54] Antonio López has taken up this question directly, discussing how this whiteness has been historically constituted "*at a distance* from the majority of is-land Afro Cubans, yet *in close*, segregated, often conflictive proximity to African Americans in the United States, especially in Miami."[55] Despite scholars suggesting that Cubans paid little attention to African Americans in Miami, the popular archive indicates otherwise.[56] I will show the ways racial codes from the United States and Cuba have and continue to be melded together in a thoroughly transnational sense to reproduce this Cuban American whiteness over time. It is in the realm of the popular that we can see the crucial role race has played in consolidating a Cuban American identity in South Florida.

Focusing on how narratives of whiteness circulate in popular cul-ture is essential for understanding social relations not only among Cuban Americans but across Latina/o groups. While race and ethnic-ity in the Latina/o context is often discussed as in conflict with United States regimes of white supremacy, scholarship has examined the place of whiteness and anti-black sentiment within Latina/o communities.[57] More of this work is necessary. Attention to ludic popular culture, in particular, can provide access to those notions that circulate within a community, unsaid yet understood. Inside jokes and ideas about the other are often invoked under the sign of the comic as audiences revel in having narratives of group identity with wide currency defamiliar-ized through humor. Examining popular forms can be an especially insightful avenue for understanding the ways in which these commu-nities come to understand themselves in a quotidian register and how negative conceptions around race and other ethnic groups structure social relations, even acting as a barrier to broader coalitional politics.

But the point of considering race and discrimination is not to some-how separate "good" diversión from the "bad." As Stuart Hall usefully reminds us, cultural forms are not "either wholly corrupt or wholly authentic. Whereas, they are deeply contradictory; they play on contra-dictions, especially when they function in the domain of the 'popular.'"[58] The binary logic of resistance/suppression does not adequately account for the messiness of, and our complex attachments to, popular culture forms that can produce pleasure, anger, and disappointment, sometimes simultaneously. Keeping this in mind will allow for a more nuanced understanding of how racist jokes can be uttered right after a satirical skewing of Anglo discrimination in South Florida. It can shed light on how blackface representations on Miami television in the twenty-first century reproduce racist tropes from Cuba that hearken back to the nineteenth century but also play a role in unraveling conservative resistance to improved relations between the United States and Cuba.

A critical approach attentive to the contradictions of popular culture moves us away from simply identifying racist representations and toward asking more productive questions. Why have these representations persisted in diasporic popular culture despite profound generational and demographic changes that include not only original exiles and their children, but also Cubans born and raised in a post-revolutionary Cuba that claims to have mostly eradicated racism? Why do US-born Cuban Americans continue to invest in a narrative of a Cuban identity at all? To answer these questions, I will pay special attention to historical context and most importantly, to how narratives built upon whiteness and heteronormativity have circulated and functioned as a means to claim a hegemonic identity in South Florida with its attendant privileges.

But of course, as Hall reminds us, the world is rarely so neat. It would be reductive to characterize Cuban popular culture and its consumption as an orderly two-way street to explain the intersection of popular culture, privilege, and power. Popular culture must, as Richard Iton explains, "be understood as a result of the creative process and its embedded intentions; the potentially quite distinct and even contrasting—but equally creative—use made of them by others; and the feedback mechanisms and interpolative possibilities linking these various stages."[59] Heeding Iton, I make space for the difficult, fraught relationships one can have with dominant narratives of Cuban American identity, especially in relation to race and politics. This ambivalence manifests itself most clearly along generational lines when US-born Cuban Americans, for instance, may revel in the performative aspects of diversión but may not subscribe to conservative politics and racist representations when they do arise. Can one enjoy the *way* a joke is told—the cadence, the words used, the accent, the style of it all—and still feel ill at ease with the punchline? We can laugh, but it does not always mean it feels good. This is the routine dissonance that often frames cultural consumption in quotidian life. These moments can reveal the disidentificatory potential of diversión, the potential for "identification with and total disavowal of the dominant culture's normative identificatory nodes."[60] This disidentificatory mode can have real effects, acting as a means to levy critique and enact a cubanía at odds with the troublesome representations that can creep up in popular culture.

Popular culture can offer communities a mechanism for self-critique without challenging the desire for group cohesion. Here, we once again see the contradictions of popular culture—its potential for reifying and challenging dominant narratives, at times simultaneously. These are the contradictions this book will live in. Engaging moments that can make us uncomfortable but nonetheless offer pleasures lays bare the complexity of our feelings and attachments within an area of cultural experience so often seen as overdetermined, "good" or "bad"—the popular. *A comer arroz con mango.*

Examining the relationship between race and diversión provides a means for understanding how Cubans in the diaspora have imagined themselves in the United States and how that imaginary has had both sustained and integral effects on social relations in South Florida. But this study also seeks to make an intervention in studies of race, sexuality, and ethnicity in the United States more broadly by "diverting" attention away from cultural forms that privilege the pain, anger, and disappointment in the lives of ethnic-racialized subjects. To be sure, scholars in fields like Queer Studies, Native American Studies, and African American Studies in particular have pointed to this imbalance and have shown what analysis of ludic forms can teach us. Sara Warner argues that her focus on "gaiety" in LGBT performance "serves as a rejoinder to the long-lasting romance with mourning and melancholia in queer theory."[61] Glenda Carpio explains that "African American humor has been an underestimated realm of analysis" in her book on black humor in relation to the legacy of slavery.[62] Yet the question remains: Why has so little been published?

The answer lies, in part, in the history of these fields. Race and ethnic studies in the United States as we know them were made possible by the rise of protest movements. Institutional recognition has always been a fight, and maintaining that tenuous foothold in the university has been a constant challenge. This has no doubt affected the direction of scholarship. Focusing on pleasure and play would seem to run counter to the "real" work at hand. As the struggle for representation continues, the need for "serious" scholarship that legitimates the field has inadvertently created an imbalance in how we write about the lives of ethnic-racialized subjects.[63] In Latina/o Studies, a field I am deeply engaged with as a scholar and teacher, popular forms of humor and play have rarely been the explicit focus of academic studies.[64] *Diversión* foregrounds the ludic not only to provide an affective complement to the fields of Cuban and Latina/o Studies but also to better understand the necessarily complicated relationships people have with popular culture representations that capture a range of feelings that frame and enable social relations.

A Changing Cuban Miami

Popular culture circulates and succeeds because of its relationship to time: "The particularity of time in popular culture is that it is momentary, that with all its embeddedness in tradition and the historical past, it is present, it is contemporary, it is always *now*."[65] Concentrating on popular culture from the 1970s to the 2010s allows me to provide the quotidian texture necessary to understand this book's second major intervention: tracing the degree to which the Cuban diaspora has changed over time in relation to politics, feelings toward the island, and the ways in which a Cuban cultural identity is performed publically— especially since the mid-1990s. The *balsero* (rafter) crisis of 1994 was the catalyst for policy agreements between the United States and Cuba that initiated the steady influx of Cubans into Miami that continues today. In 1994, over 30,000 Cubans took to the sea on makeshift rafts bound for the United States in response to the crushing scarcity of the Special Period.[66] In 1994 and 1995, the United States and Cuba agreed to stem the tide of rafters by negotiating migration accords that included a provision that would allow at least 20,000 Cubans a year to migrate to the United States. This agreement fundamentally changed the character of the Cuban diaspora in the 1990s and beyond. According to Jorge Duany, "From 1994 to 2013, the greatest wave of migrants from Cuba arrived to the United States since the beginnings of the Cuban Revolution (563,740 Cubans legally admitted to the United States)."[67] Between 2000 and 2009, 305,989 Cubans migrated to the United States—more than in any other decade in the history of migration between the two countries.[68] This population is larger than the first wave of Cubans who fled between

1959 and 1962 and greater than the number who arrived in the United States during the Freedom Flights of 1965–1973.[69]

With the joint announcement regarding the reestablishment of diplomatic relations on December 17, 2014, the number of Cubans leaving the island by raft or through border crossings (mostly Mexican) without visas has skyrocketed. In fiscal year 2011, 7,759 Cubans came to the United States this way. In 2015, 43,159 Cubans arrived in the country via ports of entry.[70] They are motivated by the same difficulties that have driven Cubans to leave the island for decades: material scarcity, the search for better economic opportunities for themselves and their families, and politics, though much less a direct factor than the latter reasons. But perhaps most urgently, the uptick of migrants can be attributed to the fear that the Cuban Adjustment Act of 1966 that guarantees residency to any Cuban who sets foot on United States soil after one year might be repealed in the face of warming relations.

How has this influx from the island changed Cuban Miami? Trends in polling reveal that time of arrival powerfully affects one's position on Cuba-related politics. By 2008, "only 45 percent of South Florida's Cuban Americans continued to support the embargo. Moreover, sharp inter-cohort differences emerged. Whereas nearly two-thirds of pre-Mariel (1980) immigrants continued to support the embargo, less than one-third of post-1998 immigrants did."[71] Those with a fresher experience of life in Cuba along with strong kinship ties are the least likely to support hardline political stances toward Cuba. Arrivals since the 1990s are more like other migrants from Latin America who come to achieve greater economic stability for themselves and those they left behind. Hundreds of thousands now return to the island every year.[72] Remittances have increased significantly in the twenty-first century with an estimated $2 billion a year flowing from the diaspora to Cuba.[73] Cuba's termination of the much-maligned exit visa and the United States' five-year visa program, both instituted in 2013, have meant more freedom of movement between the two countries. Contact and exchange will likely increase if relations between the United States and Cuba continue on the path toward full normalization.

Some academic studies have called attention to these shifts. Susan Eckstein has studied how more recent arrivals to the United States are transforming life in Cuba today as a result of the "social and economic ties across borders" that have "eroded socialism as the islanders knew it."[74] Chris Girard, Guillermo Grenier, and Hugh Gladwin have chronicled the "declining symbolic significance" of the embargo among Cuban Americans in South Florida.[75] Yet the mainstream narrative of Cubans in the United States as a homogenous group united in its conservative politics has been stubbornly resistant to change despite shifting political opinions among exiles and dramatic demographic and generational changes: "Because exile serves as such a powerful unifying experience for a people, the tendency has been to categorize all Cubans living in exile as sharing the same political identity and political culture."[76]

While arrivals since the 1990s have reached record numbers, the largest cohort of Cubans consists of the US-born—primarily the children, grandchildren, and even great-grandchildren of the original exile generation. Of the approximately 2 million Cuban and Cuban Americans counted in the United States census, 40 percent were born in the United States. Because most US-born Cuban Americans have never lived on the island, cubanía is learned from parents, family, and the anti-Castro media and symbolism that have historically saturated Cuban Miami.[77] Despite this, poll data has shown that US-born Cuban Americans are less committed to hardline stances toward Cuba. The lack of personal experience with the Revolution allows for some emotional distance and, on many Cuba-related issues, a far less conservative approach.[78] This is not to say that one will find many supporters of Castro among the US-born. The Castro brothers, along with Che Guevara, are symbols charged with contempt—the reasons for the "lost Cuba" invoked by older family members, friends, and Cuban Miami's larger anti-communist imaginary. Nonetheless, the US-born generation is more open to dismantling the embargo, allowing travel, and engaging the Cuban government in dialogue than their parents and grandparents.[79] This group has completely fallen through the cracks of contemporary scholarship. Throughout the book, I detail how the US-born are performing and invoking cubanía through diversión and what this means for the present and future of the Cuban diaspora. In this context, the translatability of *diversión* into the English *diversion* is particularly useful as I chart the relationships to cubanía enacted by US-born generations.

Because the majority of Cubans in the United States today is composed of the US-born and arrivals since the 1990s, the term *exile* with its attendant political and emotional baggage fails to capture the reality of the diaspora today not only in Miami, but also in cities like Houston and Louisville, which have growing Cuban populations. For this reason, I use the term *diaspora* when referring to Cubans in the United States generally. I use the phrase *exile community* to reference those who arrived during the earlier waves from 1959–1973. Today, fervent anti-Castro politics, the Republican Party, and conservative positions on US-Cuba relations no longer grip the diaspora the way they did historically. This is the shift I aim to illuminate in my work through an emphasis on how these changes look, sound, feel, and resonate in quotidian life. Statistics cannot fully capture how different generational cohorts interact with and represent each other. Nor can they capture the points of conflict and connection. Diversión will serve as the means by which the statistics come to life by highlighting the multiple narratives of cubanía that are being articulated and the inherent messiness of diasporic formations.

The book proceeds in five chapters. In the first, "Un Tipo Típico: Alvarez Guedes Takes the Stage," I discuss in more detail the career of beloved exile comedian Guillermo Alvarez Guedes. I use his comedy to understand the centrality of the ludic at a moment in the history of the exile community rarely discussed in playful terms: the late 1970s and 1980s. The Mariel crisis, domestic terrorism against alleged Castro sympathizers, and the drug trade in Miami created strife within the community and turned the tide of public opinion against Cuban Americans. The chapter argues that Alvarez Guedes's popular comic performances helped to consolidate a Cuban exile identity premised on whiteness and heteronormativity while simultaneously pushing back against discrimination against Cubans from Anglo Miamians.

In the second chapter, "Cuban Miami on the Air," the book moves to the twenty-first century in order to begin a conversation about a changing Cuban Miami wherein the majority of Cubans is made up of the US-born generations and more recent arrivals since 1994. I historicize the prominent role of radio in Cuban Miami—specifically the conservative genre of exile talk radio—and then devote myself to comedy bits performed on the *Enrique y Joe Show* and the *Enrique Santos Show*. These radio programs sat at the top of Miami's ratings charts throughout the

2000s. Enrique Santos and Joe Ferrero, both US-born Cuban Americans, proudly performed the narrative of cubanía learned from the exile generation through their use of idiomatic expressions, accents, and their famous prank call to Fidel Castro himself. But their satires and pranks also marked a shift in the handling of Cuba-related topics on the air through the articulation of a far less conservative approach that demonstrates how a Cuban diasporic identity need not be bundled with a particular political ideology. Contextualizing these performances in relation to their audience of other US-born Cuban Americans, the corporate investment of Univision in the Miami radio market in the 2000s, and more recent arrivals from the island provides a means to understand Cuban Miami's shifting demographics and media landscape in the 2000s.

Chapter 3, "Nostalgic Pleasures," takes up a concept that has achieved a kind of keyword status in Cuban American Studies: nostalgia. The chapter tracks nostalgia not as an ambivalent sentiment but as a historically public form of diversión, paying special attention to a festival held annually since 1999 in Miami called Cuba Nostalgia. Cuba Nostalgia has celebrated pre-Castro Cuba through a combination of spectacle and consumption. Musical genres popular before the Revolution play while businesses dedicated to selling Cuban memorabilia dot the fairgrounds. With the demographics of Cuban Miami rapidly shifting, I argue that Cuba Nostalgia is not only a means for reveling in nostalgic memories of a pre-Castro Cuba but also a nostalgia for nostalgia—a longing for a feeling that could be counted on to rally a community historically fractured across class and political lines. The event is a kind of monument in motion to an idealized memory of a united, exilic Miami as that generation fades. Through an examination of the event's focus on education and consumption, I theorize the ways in which generations of Cubans intersect and interact with this narrative of pre-Castro Cuba in order to reveal the transnational and future-oriented stakes of nostalgia.

Years before Presidents Barack Obama and Raúl Castro announced the reestablishment of diplomatic relations on December 17, 2014, ties between the two countries had been intensifying due to increased contact between the diaspora and the island. In Chapter 4, "The Transnational Life of Diversión," I examine the flows of ludic popular culture between both spaces in order to elaborate the central contention of this chapter: the movement of popular culture is indicative of the intensification of transnational contact born out of political and demographic changes on both sides *and* a means by which this intensification occurs. The first part of this chapter focuses on the standup comedy of island-based comedians, which appeals to Cubans who arrived in Miami since 1994—a group rarely discussed in cultural studies scholarship on the diaspora—and its racialized and gendered underpinnings. The second half examines how popular culture produced in the United States circulates in Cuba through a phenomenon called *el paquete semanal* (the weekly package). *El paquete* refers to the sale and circulation of media content primarily produced off the island, mainly from the United States. In addition to keeping up with popular American sitcoms and the latest Hollywood blockbusters, television produced by Cubans in South Florida is also immensely popular. People on the island can now watch Cuban artists who have permanently left the island perform nightly on South Florida television. The ubiquitous presence of el paquete and popular culture produced in the United States more broadly across the island are important sites for understanding the social and economic changes occurring in Cuba under Raúl Castro. Looking at the movement of popular culture between the island and the diaspora will also allow me to highlight how intensifying transnational contact, continuity, and exchange are affecting and reflecting the lives of Cubans on and off the island, culturally and economically.

The fifth and final chapter, "Digital Diversión," moves away from examining geographic locales to consider the rising importance of digital spaces in mediating diasporic identities. In this chapter, I seek to trace how cubanía echoes online through close readings of popular, highly circulated forms of diversión such as parody videos and memes. If Web 2.0 is primarily about sharing content, examining widely circulated forms of diversión online is a powerful means for understanding how and why certain narratives of cubanía resonate. Analysis of this content, in turn, illuminates how the circulation, consumption, and experience of diversión online encourages a ludic sociability that helps to structure one's engagement with the world online and off. A wide view of this content online also reveals generational tensions and the continued role of race in the mediation of Cuban American whiteness. To do this work,

I will closely examine the material of a puppet named Pepe Billete and of Los Pichy Boys—two acts whose material has been viewed millions of times through various social media channels.

Diversión is what we share—the pleasures we experience together as we make our way through the world. It is a world filled with fleeting, ludic moments that are too often passed over or forgotten when the next tragedy strikes. By lingering in these moments, these chapters bring together an archive of popular pleasures over time that tell a story about changes within the Cuban diaspora and the practices and experiences that produce narratives of self and community. At its core, this book seeks to inspire what I experienced when I first listened to all those Alvarez Guedes albums for the first time: a sense of critical possibility, complexity, and yes, even a laugh.

1

Un Tipo Típico

Alvarez Guedes Takes the Stage

I don't remember when I heard my first joke by Cuban exile comedian Guillermo Alvarez Guedes. His comedy has always been in my life, hiding in plain sight. I came to this realization early on in graduate school when I sat down to write a seminar paper on exile humor and decided to listen to all of his albums. It was then that I realized that my father, one of the funniest people I know, had been cracking Alvarez Guedes's jokes for years without much in the way of citation—a practice his son will not duplicate in the chapters to come. I didn't grow up with Alvarez Guedes albums in my house. They didn't play in the background of family parties, or on long car rides as so many others have told me anecdotally. His radio show in Miami didn't reach my home in New Jersey. Yet there he was the whole time, appearing in the joke repertoire of family and friends.

As I show in the introduction, there are many examples of diversión from those early years of the Cuban exile community that I could have addressed in this first chapter: the lively theater scene, tabloid satirical newspapers like *Zig-Zag Libre* and *Chispa*, or folkloric events like Añorada Cuba. But Alvarez Guedes is truly the *only* way a book focused on ludic popular culture in the Cuban diaspora can start. What made him so unique was his durability and popularity across multiple generations of the diaspora over a career that spanned over half a century. Best known for his standup comedy, Alvarez Guedes released thirty-two live albums from the 1970s through the early 2000s. These recordings continue to serve as Cuban social and cultural capital. How many times have I heard someone say, "That reminds me of an Alvarez Guedes joke" and then break out into his or her best rendition? The embeddedness of his jokes is so pronounced that I have even heard people use snippets of his material like "tú eres como el tipo del gato" as a kind of metaphoric shorthand to describe a person or situation—in this case a pessimist.[1] This popularity extends beyond his rank and file audience to other professional comedians on and off the island. Every single artist I write about in this book cites him as a vital influence. Starting with Alvarez Guedes, then, also provides a useful point of departure for thinking through genealogies of diversión in the Cuban diaspora.

Though his influence reverberates across generations, this chapter takes a much more focused approach through an examination of his comedy in the 1970s and 1980s. Even then, in those early years of his career in exile, Alvarez Guedes was looked upon as a kind of model exile subject. His standing among the community is best summed up in an article written by Cristina Saralegui for *El Miami Herald* in 1976, years before she built her talk-show empire: "Ahora, Guillermo Alvarez Guedes es EL TIPICO CUBANO EXILIADO (Now, Guillermo Alvarez Guedes is THE TYPICAL CUBAN EXILE).[2] Alvarez Guedes's status as *un tipo típico*—a Cuban everyman—is partially due to his politics, which were in many ways in tune with what Lisandro Pérez has called the "exile ideology." Its characteristics include continuing to attach importance to politics in Cuba; hostility against the Cuban government; conservative, Republican political views; and general intolerance for those whose perspectives on Cuba differ.[3] Informing what it meant to be Cuban off the island, this ideology manifested itself in a "behavioral repertoire . . . ranging from supporting right-wing candidates to opposing publicly anyone voicing sympathy for the Cuban regime."[4] Not content to limit his anti-communist humor to Miami, Alvarez Guedes travelled to Nicaragua to perform a set for the Contras in 1986.[5]

These politics informed Alvarez Guedes's larger performance of exile *cubanía*—a Cuban cultural identity inflected with the politics of the exile ideology. But that was not enough to make him un tipo típico. More importantly, Alvarez Guedes reflected back what his audience wanted to see in itself: a wise-cracking anti-communist with a magnetic affability who could take the turbulence of exile politics and life in Miami and use it as fodder for diversión. Perhaps more than any other Cuban exile artist, Alvarez Guedes insisted upon a ludic sociability that cohered around a narrative of proud, pleasurable exile cubanía mediated through his humor. My research has yet to turn up a negative review of his work. In fact, I argue that people *wanted* to like him and what his humor represented—an almost utopic narrative of a united exile community that people wanted to believe was possible. His stories about "nosotros, los cubanos" (we, the Cubans) were narratives of unity around a broad notion of cubanía and anti-Castro politics, which served as a distraction from the very real tensions within the exile community. Old grudges from Cuba, past and present political affiliations, and disagreements about how best to bring about change on the island were some of the issues that divided the community from within.[6] Disagreement and even violence among exiles convinced of their views as the best way forward for "liberating" Cuba were common. Alvarez Guedes's albums emphasized common ground through hostility toward Castro, shared Cuban cultural characteristics, Cuban-Anglo relations in Miami, and the manner for engaging these topics through the recognizable codes of Cuban speech and humor. In short, Alvarez Guedes's performances and persona were powerful interlocking sites of identification for Cubans looking to affirm their cultural identities *outside* the island in a way that put aside the tensions inside the exile community in a Miami plagued by drug wars, a slumping economy, and anti-Cuban sentiment in the 1970s and 1980s.

Far from simply serving as a cathartic release from the tensions roiling Cuban Miami, Alvarez Guedes's performances illustrate the role of diversión in forging a narrative of Cuban exile identity that privileged whiteness and heteronormativity while simultaneously speaking back to discrimination from Anglo Miamians. It is in the messiness of popular culture, the way a derogatory joke about blacks can exist on the same album criticizing discrimination against Cubans, that we get at the contradictions that structure quotidian life. But before jumping into my close listenings of the material, more background on Alvarez Guedes's performance practice is necessary to understand why he has been such an important figure in the history of Cuban diasporic popular culture.

Alvarez Guedes, "The Natural"

Alvarez Guedes was a mainstay in exile entertainment for decades. He released over thirty-two standup comedy albums, published joke books and novels, and produced and starred in a number of television and film projects.[7] He co-founded a label called GEMA Records, which released the music of celebrated artists and groups such as Bebo Valdés, El Gran Combo de Puerto Rico, Celeste Mendoza, Elena Burke, and Chico O'Farrill. When Alvarez Guedes died in 2013 at the age of eighty-six, tributes and commemorations poured in from Cubans across generations on and off the island. Despite having his material outlawed in Cuba, it has always circulated there clandestinely. High-profile personalities, including comedians, took to the Internet to express their admiration. Island-based Cuban dissident blogger Yoani Sánchez tweeted, "Maestro Alvarez Guedes! Know that here we have continued to listen to you, covertly, all this time!"[8] In Miami, where the comedian spent most of his life, his death took over the news cycle for days, with bloggers, journalists, and television hosts covering his death and legacy, often through tears.

Although he is generally known for his work in exile, Alvarez Guedes got his start in the entertainment industry as a young man in Cuba. Born in Unión de Reyes, Matanzas in 1927, he made his radio debut in 1949 on programs ranging from dramas to comedies. In 1951, he debuted the character that would make him famous in Cuba, El Borracho (the drunk), on the nation's nascent television network, CMQ-TV. Shortly after Fidel Castro rose to power in 1959, he left Cuba with his family for cities with large concentrations of Cuban exiles such as New York, Madrid, and Puerto Rico. He lived in Miami from 1961 to 1968 and settled permanently in the city in 1980, though he performed there throughout the 1970s. He began recording his standup albums in 1973.

Alvarez Guedes performed on television, film, and radio throughout his career, but most people know his performances through his live standup albums. All of these recordings essentially follow the same format. Once his trademark music signals his entrance on stage, he goes right into his material, usually by rattling off a succession of quick jokes. Two-thirds of the way into his performance, there is usually a shift from jokes to a story format marked by observational humor related to social and political issues deemed worthy of attention.[9] There is hardly ever interaction between Alvarez Guedes and his audience (the Mariel joke mentioned in the introduction is a notable exception), but this does not mean that the audience is passive. There are no laugh tracks on these albums. Listening closely will reveal the running commentary of the audience in between episodic, raucous laughter, with approving phrases voicing agreement ("It's so true!") mixing with sounds ranging from high-pitched cackles to deep belly laughs. The albums were recorded in clubs, restaurants, or studios that Alvarez Guedes rented out for that purpose. The audience consisted of people he invited and their friends for a total of about thirty to forty people in all. The result was a profoundly intimate experience for the audience, which in turn is communicated to the listener of the album. The atmospheric applause and laughter audible on more contemporary standup albums is missing here. Instead, the listener can get a feel for the individuality of audience members and their unique-sounding laughs, their particular utterances, and the cadence of their clapping. In the context of the performance, these expressions of joyful approval *sound* Cuban. The auditory experience of these recordings makes it possible to laugh not only at Alvarez Guedes's performance but also *with* members of the audience in a way that heightens the intimacy and pleasure of communal identification that he himself sought to cultivate.

As the description of the recordings above suggests, the album format begs for a consideration of the way the performance *sounds*. Identification takes place on the auditory level: it includes Alvarez Guedes's

Figure 1.1. Alvarez Guedes performing for audience. Date unknown. Courtesy of Cuban Heritage Collection, University of Miami.

routine, the distinctive musical accompaniment, and the audience's reactions. For listeners familiar with Cuban speech (dialect, voice inflection, modes of expression) Alvarez Guedes would be instantly recognizable as Cuban without him ever saying so. His use of pauses in his stories, the way he exaggerates the pronunciation of certain words, and the strategic use of repetition contribute to the Cuban feel of the auditory experience. As he begins to speak, it becomes clear to his audience that he is Cuban, someone who has endured a set of historical circumstances around exile similar to what they have experienced. Confident and convincing in his role as un tipo típico, he offsets the precariousness and impotence of the exile condition through the creation of a stable, relaxed, inviting space where his performance functions as a means for negotiating the at times difficult experience of exile through diversión. The pleasures of group identification and playful narrative technique combine to produce a ludic sociability among an audience now comfortable with temporarily suspending its usual defensive positions regarding Cuba and the complexities of exile life.

While his albums and performances quickly became hits among exiles, success did not come immediately for the comedian after leaving the island. In a 2007 interview titled "Guillermo Álvarez Guedes, El Natural," he describes the difficulty in finding work in the Spanish-language entertainment industry during those early years of exile in the 1960s and 1970s: "To make a living as an actor in those days, you had to be an actor in television soap operas, and to work in television soap operas, you had to have what they called a neutral accent. When they told me that I said, 'What the hell is a neutral accent? I have a Cuban accent; I don't know what it means to speak neutrally.'"[10] This hostility to the entertainment industry's demand that he tame his tongue created the foundation for his career in exile. Throughout this interview, Alvarez Guedes constantly refers to his commitment to performing "naturally"—a performance practice marked by his use of Cuban vernacular, specifically the corpus of "bad words" that he believed to be authentically Cuban and that lend a quality of "realism" to his artistic production.

The idea of a "natural" cubanía followed Alvarez Guedes throughout his career in exile. His fans and Cuban cultural commentators have long used the term to describe him. Carlos Alberto Montaner, a major voice in the exile community, wrote a short piece published on the back of the *Alvarez Guedes 4* album sleeve in celebration of the comedian's "pasmosa naturalidad" (astonishing naturalness).[11] Emilio Ichikawa, journalist and commentator on all things Cuban on and off the island, similarly alludes to the quintessential cubanía of Alvarez Guedes by naming him "nuestro antropólogo mayor" (our great anthropologist), a man who has "penetrated the codes of Cubanity" and who "doesn't fail to measure the psychophysical temperature of the community."[12] After his death, press coverage echoed sentiments expressed by journalists like Wilfredo Cancio Isla: "Guillermo Alvarez Guedes has died, king of the joke and cubanidad. The man who succeeded in reconciling Cubans everywhere, from the island and the world, through the universal language of laughter."[13]

The "naturalness" that commentators have attributed to Alvarez Guedes is due in part to sonic aspects of his performance that I have already mentioned: his accent, tone, and the words he uses. But it is not simply a matter of a one-to-one relationship between sound and ethnic identification. The "naturalness" is a product of *how* he tells his jokes, the particular style and delivery that make it *feel* like a Cuban practice. This practice can be best described as falling under the tradition of *choteo*. Choteo is a form of humor and mockery common among the masses and articulated through the idiomatic specificity of Cuban popular culture. As Cuban cultural critic Jorge Mañach wrote in his 1928 essay, "Indagación del choteo" (Investigation of Choteo), it is "a form of relation typically ours."[14] It is a recognizable, culturally specific form of diversión and interaction that acts as a way to filter serious or distressing experiences in a nonserious, anti-authoritarian, and irreverent manner and thereby also provides an alternative, critically ludic perspective on people, events, and other social and political phenomena that would not otherwise be objects of jest. The "naturalness" of Alvarez Guedes's choteo, then, becomes a way to help make the "unnatural" state of exile bearable in quotidian life.

Alvarez Guedes's diversión, deployed through his use of choteo and overall performance practice, is not the sole reason for his designation as a "natural" performer, "the typical Cuban exile" that Cristina Saralegui described. Implicitly informing this naturalness is his whiteness. Though his fans primarily experienced his comedy by listening, his likeness was never far behind: it is featured on each of his album covers. Encoded within his "naturalness" is a narrative that manifests itself in jokes that assert whiteness and heteronormativity as part of the communal narrative of exile cubanía. In the section that follows, I examine jokes from the 1970s and 1980s as sites for understanding how the Cuban exile community reconciled attitudes about race and sexuality with US perspectives. Though jokes on race and sexuality in no way represent the majority of the content on his albums, when they do arise these comic bits shine a light on the ongoing project to articulate a cultural identity in exile and its normative boundaries at historical moments when definitions and the privileges of whiteness were being hotly contested. What the popular culture archive highlights is that, contrary

Figure 1.2. Guillermo Alvarez Guedes, album cover for *Alvarez Guedes 8*, 1978.

to other claims, Miami's black population was very much on the mind of the Cuban community in these early years.[15]

Negros y Locas

Cubans arriving in South Florida in the 1960s and 1970s had to navigate all the usual challenges people face in a new country. But in addition to addressing the immediate needs of housing and work, they quickly realized that their social positions in Miami would not be the same as in Cuba. Once at the top of the racial and in many instances the class hierarchy on the island, Cuban exiles were subject to discrimination from the Anglo majority despite the initial warm welcome from federal and local governments.[16] Nevertheless, the majority of exiles did not align themselves with other groups facing discrimination in Miami, such as blacks and gays. Instead, they aimed to redeploy their "possessive investment in whiteness" cultivated in Cuba to help define exile cubanía. This narrative of whiteness received support from the media, at least initially. Cheris Brewer Current explains how the US government and media portrayed Cubans to "fit a national ideal of 'whiteness' and 'Americaness.' Thus, in order to fend off widespread objections, the entrance of Cuban refugees was parsed in Cold War rhetoric that stressed their desirable social, ideological, and racialized class traits."[17] Claims to whiteness, then, were essential components for imagining an exile cubanía drawn from Cuban racial ideologies and reinforced by Cold War rhetoric, which together positioned these exiles as white victims of communism.

While discrimination experienced on the ground complicated this narrative of whiteness and privilege, there was little interest in identifying as an oppressed minority.[18] Instead, Cuban exiles drew from a long history of racist and homophobic humor from the island to assist in the crafting of a communal narrative about the place of the exile community in the social hierarchy of South Florida. In the case of Alvarez Guedes, jokes about blacks and locas (gay men) can be found throughout his albums but are most prevalent in material from the tumultuous 1970s and early 1980s—decades marked by racial uprisings and legislation that discriminated against Cubans and Dade County's gay population. These jokes and performances capture the role diversión played in solidifying and patrolling the boundaries of a white, heteronormative, politically enfranchised exile identity while simultaneously demonstrating the transnational melding of Cuban and US racial and sexual ideologies.

It is not surprising that race-based humor has long existed on an island where histories of slavery, colonialism, and capital have always intersected. What is so fascinating is the way in which the themes and ideological preoccupations encoded within Cuban race-based humor reappear in the popular culture of the post-1959 exile community. In her study of blackface performance in nineteenth-century Cuba, Jill Lane explains the ideological projects of *teatro bufo* performances: "This blackface humor works discursively at two levels: it controls and limits the otherwise menacing significance of blackness at the same time that it renegotiates the meanings of whiteness in a colonial hierarchy that privileged Spanish peninsulares (literally, 'peninsulars,' those born on the Iberian peninsula) over white criollos."[19] Though historical circumstances in colonial Cuba and Miami in the 1970s were of course markedly different, Lane's description of how blackness operated discursively within the context of bufo is relevant here. Like nineteenth-century bufo, Alvarez Guedes's race-based material functioned as a means to negotiate Cuban whiteness and its relationship to blackness. I read his jokes as part of an ongoing project for negotiating Cuban whiteness in the context of US racial politics at a time of great anxiety about blackness in Miami and a moment when Cuban racial self-definitions were under fire from Anglos wary of the Cuban influx into South Florida.

The first joke I consider, from *Alvarez Guedes 2* released in 1974, speaks to the kind of humor inspired by racial politics in the United States:

> A black guy commits a traffic violation in Alabama and they condemn him to die in the arena with the lions. He only ran a red light but they condemned him to die with the lions. They take him to a stadium and they bury him in sand up to his neck. Twenty thousand blond, green-eyed spectators fill the stands. They release the lion and it quickly attacks the black guy who can't defend himself because his head is the only part of his body above the sand. But when the lion gets close enough, the

black guy bites the lion's leg. The twenty thousand spectators stand up and scream: "PELEA LIMPIO NEGRO HIJO DE PUTA!" (FIGHT FAIR YOU BLACK SON OF A BITCH!)[20]

In this joke, Alvarez Guedes positions the audience to see the racial drama of the United States from an outsider perspective with Alabama as the symbolic site. And it is not the only joke where he does this. Throughout the 1970s and 1980s, he sets three more jokes, in addition to his other race-related jokes, in Alabama. As in Cuba, racism against blacks is fodder for humor. In this particular joke, the black man is the silent victim whose last-ditch effort at resistance is read as consistent with stereotypical understandings of uncivilized blackness. The fifteen seconds of uninterrupted laughter following the delivery of the punchline signal the audience's enjoyment and alignment with a comic perspective that routinely uses racist violence as a means to entertain.

Jokes about blacks in the United States would be familiar to a Cuban audience well-versed in race-based humor from the island. But there is more to these jokes. When I began to listen Alvarez Guedes's race-based humor on its own, I could not shake the sense that they sounded familiar, American even. I began to search the "dirty jokes books" that became so popular in the United States in the 1970s and 1980s. And then I found it. A version of the Alabama joke above can be found in Larry Wilde's 1975 *The Official White Folks/Black Folks Joke Book*.[21] I have also found two other jokes from Alvarez Guedes's albums that correspond with material in Blanche Knott's best-selling *Truly Tasteless Jokes* series.[22] In every case, Alvarez Guedes performed the joke before the publication date in the above-mentioned books. But these joke books include little original material. Instead, authors compiled jokes that they had heard independently or, as in the case of Blanche Knott, that were sent to her after she put out an open call for material in *Truly Tasteless Jokes Two*.[23] My sense is that it is quite unlikely that Alvarez Guedes was sending his original jokes for consideration in these books. Completely fluent in English, the comedian was likely adapting jokes he had heard or read for his routine—a practice he would freely admit to.[24]

These joke books were equal opportunity offenders. Larry Wilde, who has penned dozens of these joke books, has dedicated collections to specific races and ethnicities.[25] The formula in the *Truly Tasteless* series was to include jokes on a host of different groups in each installment including: Black, Jewish, Polish, WASP, Handicapped, Homosexual, Dead Baby, and for those who like a mix of ethnicities in their jokes, a section called "Ethnic Jokes, Variegated," among others. Tellingly, Alvarez Guedes never included a Polish or Italian joke on his albums.[26] Such jokes would have been foreign in the context of Cuban Miami. Jokes about blacks would be familiar from Cuba and thus enjoyable for his audience in a way jokes about other ethnicities would not have been. Through humor, Alvarez Guedes and his audience could align themselves with the white racial gaze of the United States through a detour into the race-based humor of American popular culture of the 1970s and 1980s.

Is it possible to read the Alabama joke more generously? To give it the benefit of the doubt as an indictment of the violence inflicted upon black bodies in the United States? While it is important to leave that possibility open, historical context makes such a reading less convincing. Alvarez Guedes invites white Cubans to laugh at the racial politics of the United States at a moment when anxiety about blacks in Miami was high. Bruce Porter and Marvin Dunn detail what they call thirteen separate racially charged "miniriots" in 1970s Dade County—violence that reached a climax with the uprising of 1980, sparked by the acquittal of four white police officers in the beating death of a black man named Arthur McDuffie.[27] These uprisings were rooted in the long history of discrimination, unequal power relations, and segregation in Miami and would have been visible to the growing Cuban community. The vast majority of Cubans in Miami at the time this joke was performed in 1975 identified as white and had little interest in casting their lot with the black communities of South Florida and the challenges they faced. Blacks in Miami quickly found cause for resenting the Cuban community. They watched as white Cubans began competing with them in the labor market. The generous benefits and programs instituted to assist Cubans fleeing communism added to this ill will.[28] While the black community took up the Cuban question frequently, Guillermo Grenier and Max Castro show that the Spanish-language press did not reciprocate this attention. Instead, negative attitudes toward blacks in Miami manifested themselves in more specialized and ephemeral media channels like radio, tabloid newspapers, and of course, jokes.[29]

In one such example on *Alvarez Guedes 16* (1984), the comedian makes a joke about blacks in Miami in the context of growing bilingualism in the city:

> Bilingualism is becoming so entrenched in Miami that even delinquents are practicing it. The negritos that go out to mug people, los negritos, los negritos americanos, have figured out that Cuban women hide their rings and money in their bras. And now when they mug them and take their purses they say ¡TETA! ¡TETA! (TIT! TIT!)[30]

Negrito, the diminutive of "negro," literally translates to "little black." In Cuba, it can be used as a term of endearment within and across racial lines, but as Lane observes, it is impossible to separate this use from the way it has been used condescendingly toward black Cuban men.[31] In this particular joke, there is little affection in the use of the term. Instead, "negrito" functions as a means to soften the very real and direct target of blacks not in faraway Alabama, but in Miami. Black uprisings in response to decades of institutional racism in Miami in the 1970s and 1980s would have certainly informed the telling and reception of this joke. Given the heightened discussion around black criminality due to the uprisings, the use of the diminutive "negrito" is an attempt to bring some playfulness to the tense topic of black crime in the early 1980s while simultaneously reinforcing commonly held attitudes about blackness.

I am also struck by Alvarez Guedes's need to clarify that he is talking about "negritos americanos." On the recording, it sounds as if he catches himself in some kind of error, reflected in a momentary stutter and in his repetition of "los negritos americanos." Only four years had passed since Mariel and consistent with his larger practice of avoiding topics that have divided the Cuban community, he may have wanted to make sure that his audience knew that he was not referring to Afro-Cuban marielitos in Miami who faced discrimination from Anglos and white Cuban exiles. On the other hand, these "negritos americanos" are fair game and are quickly aligned with audience expectations about blacks being violent and out to victimize white Cuban women. In this joke, racist attitudes toward blacks in Miami at a moment of profound racial tension mix with the long history of equating criminality with blackness in

Cuba.[32] This joke in particular functions as a way to address that racial tension while simultaneously asserting whiteness by situating Cubans as victims of aggressive, unruly blacks.

Alvarez Guedes's jokes about race relations in Miami dramatize a clear understanding of the racial hierarchy at work in the city and the nation more broadly, as well as where Cubans should belong in it—above blacks. As the years pass, this is what precisely what happens. Cubans in Miami make large gains in political and economic power, often to the detriment of the black community.[33] Cubans eagerly claimed whiteness and its privileges as the organizing racial logic of exile. To do this, they forged a narrative about blackness through the perspective of US *and* Cuban racial ideologies while simultaneously cultivating whiteness as an essential component of exile cubanía. Adding to the pleasure of these jokes is a kind of comfort in knowing that although Cuba and the United States are very different, some things are consistent. Blacks are targets for humor in Cuba in a manner that aligns with racist humor conventions in the United States, as the joke set in Alabama suggests.

There are important differences between Alvarez Guedes's treatment of blacks who are explicitly defined as Cuban in his jokes and "los negritos Americanos." Black Cubans are often represented in the way they would have been in bufo routines: as wise-cracking, playfully sneaky, and articulating a desire to be white. But one joke in particular captures an important pattern that will play out as this book moves through the decades and I shift my focus to more recent migratory waves. The pattern lies in how groups that would normally be discriminated against or looked down on by white Cuban exiles (blacks, gays, more recent arrivals from the island) become protagonists in political rhetoric and popular culture forms when they can be used symbolically to criticize the Castro government.

A joke on *Alvarez Guedes 22* titled "Vendiendo negros" (Selling Blacks) captures this practice. It starts with a prologue of sorts: "When the Revolution arrived, as you all know, they said it was to benefit blacks and yet they have been the most harmed. For example, young blacks are sent to Angola to fight and they are killed. So the truth is that blacks have been the most harmed in Cuba."[34] Alvarez Guedes goes on to explain that blacks leaving Cuba pose a real threat to the Castro government's rhetoric of racial equality on the island. If they leave, he reasons, it must be seen as a condemnation by the very group the government claims to have helped the most. After these prefatory remarks, we get to the joke, which features a black Cuban man and his family at the airport waiting to leave the island for the United States. There, the black man faces constant harassment from a Cuban government official who is trying to dissuade him from leaving by criticizing US imperialism and the country's treatment of blacks. In a final attempt to convince him to stay, the government official says, "'Blacks in the United States aren't worth a thing!' To which the black man responds, '¿Quién te ha dicho a ti que yo voy a vender negros allí?'" (Who told you I was going there to sell blacks?)[35]

Racism against Afro-Cubans *within* the Cuban exile community is rarely, if ever, explicitly addressed in popular culture. But if racism can be used as a tool to detract from the narrative of racial equality under the Revolution and its policies more broadly, then it is fair game. To be sure, the Cuban Revolution has failed to address a multitude of issues involving racial discrimination as multiple scholars have pointed out.[36] But to suggest that Afro-Cubans have endured the most harm under the Revolution is consistent with the general refusal within the exile community to acknowledge any accomplishments under Castro. White Cuban exiles who arrived before Mariel were quick to use the boatlift as proof of the failures of the Revolution. But the symbolic "victory" of Cubans fleeing the island during Mariel did not lead to better treatment of marielitos, especially black arrivals, once they settled in Miami. This population routinely suffered discrimination on the basis of race, sexuality, and a perceived lack of anti-revolutionary fervor.[37]

What this joke does is "sanitize" blackness for symbolic use in order to criticize the Cuban government. Small details matter. For instance, the black man in the joke is leaving the island *with his family*. He has not taken to the sea as other Cubans of color did during the chaotic boatlift. Instead, he waits for his flight to Miami at the airport—an orderly departure. Like the narrative of his white countrymen before him, this black Cuban male is leaving the island with a family unit because of government persecution, complete with a plane ride. Besides the anxiety about blackness, exiles found the number of single young men arriving during the boatlift troubling—a reversal of the narrative of family-driven migration and the sense of responsibility and wholesomeness that goes with it. In addition, the black man's snappy comeback to the Cuban official's warnings about racism in the United States seems to reinforce the conservative position that claims of racism are exaggerated and an excuse for those unwilling to work hard.[38] The protagonist of this joke is simply a white Cuban exile of a different color whose race provides an avenue for attacking the Revolution in a way that is consistent with broader anti-Castro rhetoric.

The pattern of politically expedient critique also arises in how the exile community seized upon the Cuban government's treatment of gays. Néstor Almendros's 1984 documentary, *Improper Conduct*, captures the experiences of homosexual men sent to labor camps called Unidades Militares de Ayuda a la Producción (UMAPs) (Military Units to Aid Production). Public figures in the exile community celebrated the film for its exposure of the repressiveness of the Castro government and as an opportunity to "shake up the conscience" of liberal supporters of the Revolution in Europe and the United States.[39] Homophobia has a long history in Cuba before and after the Revolution. As Emilio Bejel points out in his study of homosexuality and nationalism: "Homophobic discourses articulated as part of modern national precepts have been publicly expounded by Cuban nationalist leaders from the earliest days of modern Cuban history. Their discussions have often defined the homosexual body, implicitly or explicitly, as a threat to the health of the body of the nation."[40] Of course, the powerfully ingrained homophobia in Cuba did not disappear when Cubans moved from the island to Miami. Although *Improper Conduct* was celebrated, attitudes toward homosexuality in the exile community were less than hospitable. Ricardo Ortíz and Susana Peña have shown that homophobia in Cuba in the 1970s and 1980s was mirrored in the exile context.[41] Like jokes about race, jokes about sexuality combined common social attitudes from Cuba and United States to consolidate a narrative of white, heteronormative exile cubanía and the social privileges encoded therein.

On Alvarez Guedes's albums, the topic of sexuality comes up in the figure of *la loca*, literally "crazy woman." Susana Peña describes locas as "flamboyant, gender-transgressive male homosexuals."[42] Locas serve as a popular, recurring topic throughout Alvarez Guedes's repertoire.[43] In his material from the 1970s and 1980s, they frequently appear in jokes meant to prompt audience laughter through an audible performance of effeminacy and cartoonish representations of sexually aggressive locas with their insatiable and uncontrollable desire for men. The following from *Alvarez Guedes 3* captures the essence of his loca material:

> The police arrive to raid una fiesta de locas and they surround their house with police cars and a patrol wagon. When they have the house completely surrounded, una loca comes out of the house like a shot running [*makes cartoonish running sound*] and bam! gets into the wagon. The cop asks, "Why did you come out alone and get into the wagon by yourself?" To which la loca replies [*effeminate voice*], "Porque el año pasado me tocó ir de pie" (Because last year I had to go [to the police station] by foot!)[44]

The setting of the joke betrays its historical context. With police round-ups of gay men in Miami in the news, Alvarez Guedes signals a situation that would be familiar to his audience. The comedian even uses the word "raid" in English suggesting that this term would be understood by his predominantly Spanish-speaking audience. With state-sponsored violence not being funny in and of itself, the comic pleasure hinges on the cartoonish depiction of la loca. Alvarez Guedes produces this caricature by manipulating his voice to resemble the sound effect of a cartoon character running quickly (think Bugs Bunny) complete with the "bam!" when la loca gets into the police wagon. The next comic layer comes when the joke moves to unsettle the expectations of the audience: Why would the "guilty" loca willingly get into the police wagon? Alvarez Guedes supplies the answer by adopting an effeminate voice and lilt that his audience would immediately recognize. The punchline builds off of the cartoonish representation up to that point. This is not la loca's first run-in with the law. La loca simply can't help being loca. Flamboyance (conveyed in Alvarez Guedes's loca ventriloquism) and the repetition of the "illegal" behavior of attending a party with other locas suggest that the desire for pleasure and the company of men trumps the *unpleasure* of yet another visit to jail. This loca does not resist state violence; it is the accepted cost of effeminate, same-sex desire. In this narrative, la loca is asking for it.

If this joke were made by a Cuban drag queen or queer performance artist, it might be possible to read it as resistance to the criminalization of queer sexualities in the United States.[45] But alas, this is not the performer or the audience. Instead, this joke and others are in keeping with how queerness has traditionally entered and been consumed in popular culture on and off the island—as a kind of abstract entertainment, pure surface, and a convenient source for a quick laugh.[46] This kind of humor is so ingrained that it is possible to discern laughter from the audience on the album even before the punchline is delivered. The mere mention of "una fiesta de locas" was enough for some members of the audience. This abject image of la loca, legible only through sexuality deemed aberrant and thus comical in its incongruousness, was and continues to be a regular feature of Cuban humor on and off the stage. It is a critical thread that I will examine throughout the book.

Problems arise when la loca ceases to exist only for entertainment and becomes "real," a political subject who demands rights and fair treatment and actively campaigns against state-sponsored violence. As with jokes about race, jokes about sexuality can be read in the context of the Cuban community forging a normative narrative of exile cubanía. In January of 1977 a group of gay activists organized under the banner of the Dade County Coalition for the Humanistic Rights of Gays to lobby for a change in the county's human rights statute that would ban discrimination on the basis of sexual preference. Though the amendment passed, it quickly drew the ire of conservative groups in South Florida. Anita Bryant became the face of the backlash leading an organization called Save Our Children, Inc., created to rally support for the effort to repeal the anti-discrimination amendment.[47] In a shrewd political move, Bryant and Save Our Children made an aggressive push to enlist the support of South Florida's growing Cuban community. All accounts point to Cubans as strong supporters of Bryant's efforts.[48] In June of 1977, the anti-discrimination amendment was repealed in a landslide referendum.

There is little doubt that the rhetoric of Save Our Children, communicated in the organization's very title, would strike a chord in the exile community. Many were concerned in the 1960s and 1970s about the Americanization of their children and their exposure to counterculture movements dedicated to questioning the racial, gender, and sexual dynamics of US society.[49] By invoking "the children," Bryant and her organization hit a nerve. The mobilization of the Cuban vote against this issue would serve as an example of what was possible when the community voted as a bloc—a prelude perhaps to the Cuban political dominance of South Florida that would begin to develop in earnest in the 1980s.[50] Only seven years after Cubans in Miami rallied behind the Bryant initiative to repeal the anti-discrimination act, they stood up and applauded *Improper Conduct* for its condemnation of the Cuban government's treatment of sexual minorities.

There are perhaps less obvious reasons for this preoccupation with sexuality and masculinity. The hypermasculine posturing of the exile community and its resistance to a gay rights agenda can be read partially as a response to a certain crisis of masculinity stirred by the profound impotence felt as a consequence of the consistent failure to effect political change in Cuba. The terrible rout of CIA-trained Cuban exiles during the Bay of Pigs Invasion is the most visible example of this impotence. But in truth, Fidel Castro's vitality and carefully curated masculine image— his green fatigues signaling readiness for battle—served as a constant reminder in those early years to the exile community of who "the real man" was. The need to constantly assert a strong, masculine presence was thus extremely important to the exile community, as was displacement of that failed masculinity. Satirical Cuban exile tabloid periodicals often represented Fidel Castro as a woman in the service of amorous Russians.[51] Raúl Castro, followed by rumors of closeted homosexuality since the early years of the Revolution, is consistently represented as una loca in political cartooning even today. It is telling that the government official most often imagined as una loca is the official with the most symbolically "masculine" post as head of the Cuban Armed Forces. Choteo becomes a way to displace failed masculinity onto the communists while consolidating its antithesis in exile—a white, potent masculinity emphasized in popular culture and politics.

Like his jokes about race, Alvarez Guedes's material about sexuality is a meaningful site to pause and consider the ways in which Cubans combined and reconciled social codes and attitudes on the island with those of the United States. Choteo's long history as a popular and quotidian strategy for narrating Cuban national identity and its racial and sexual preoccupations surfaces in the exile context to do similar work. But as I explain in the next section, the articulation of exile cubanía with a claim on the privileges of normative whiteness in the United States did meet resistance from Anglo Miami.

Cubano-Americano Tensions

Alvarez Guedes's comedy was not just a means to claim an abstract, privileged whiteness. Instead, exiles were invested in a distinctly *Cuban* whiteness that also resisted Anglo assimilationist paradigms. Built into the rhetoric of exile is the notion of forced departure and the fantasy of return. These two elements of the exile narrative strongly informed the desire to maintain Cuban cultural characteristics and the performances of cultural nationalism that permeate Alvarez Guedes's comedy. Unsurprisingly, this led to tensions between exiles and the Anglo majority throughout the 1970s and 1980s in Miami. It is out of these tensions that one of Alvarez Guedes's most popular and recurring targets for the anti-authoritarianism of choteo surfaces, "los americanos."

Exiles arriving in the first two waves of migration during 1959–1974 enjoyed a warm welcome from the US government. Aside from hoping that the physical movement of so many Cubans would destabilize Castro's new government, the United States held up the example of the exodus as proof of the evils and failures of communism. This helped to supplement the aggressive, anti-communist propaganda effort in the Americas during the Cold War. To drive the point home, Cuban success in the United States would prove that the American capitalist system was superior to communism. For these and other politically expedient reasons, Cubans were granted refugee status and received a number of benefits in the form of federal assistance.[52]

On the local level, Cubans received a great deal of support from the city of Miami. This is especially true in regard to language policy. Max Castro identifies the three most significant policies regarding language laws as the implementation of "bilingual education in the Dade county public schools in 1963, the declaration of Metropolitan Dade County as officially bilingual and bicultural in 1973 and the creation of *El Herald* in 1976."[53] The fact that these laws existed is quite extraordinary, and they helped facilitate, to some degree, the transition from Cuba to the United States. At the very least, the policies adopted in Miami were symbolic of a certain degree of cultural tolerance.

But the welcome from the federal and local government did not always coincide with life on the ground. María Cristina García explains that locals resented Cubans both for the financial assistance they received from the government (often more than citizens) and for their "boisterous" behavior.[54] Adding to this resentment was the creation and sustainment of a Cuban ethnic enclave,[55] which reduced the pressure to assimilate. As the size and economic power of the community grew, so did resistance and opposition to what many non-Cubans in Miami referred to as the Cuban "takeover" of the city.

The frustrations of "native" Miamians reached a boiling point in 1980 with the circumstances surrounding the Mariel crisis. The *Miami Herald* railed against President Carter's weak, undefined policy regarding Mariel and the exile community's desire to facilitate the exodus and the subsequent resettlement of refugees in Miami. Editors at the paper used Castro's characterization of the marielitos as social misfits to justify their aggressive stance toward the new arrivals and the exile community more broadly. Alejandro Portes and Alex Stepick define the perceived threat to the establishment this way: "first as an economic cataclysm, given the depressed state of local industry and the negative impact of the inflow on Miami's status as a tourist destination; and second, as a direct threat to the establishment power structure, given the addition of many thousands to an already uncomfortably large Cuban population."[56] In the time leading up to and after the boatlift, the *Miami Herald* actively played up these threats and effectively agitated the non-Cuban population in Miami.

With the white establishment bent on asserting power in a time of rapid change, the modern English-Only movement was born in Miami with an anti-bilingual referendum. It passed, and in November 1980, the ordinance changed the policies of biculturalism and bilingualism in Dade County instituted in the early 1970s.[57] Much as it did in the repeal of the 1977 amendment prohibiting discrimination on the basis of sexuality, Miami had taken one step forward and two steps back. But these direct attempts by the *Miami Herald* and local government to limit the power of the Cuban community did not achieve the desired effect: "Instead of subduing the Cubans, the hegemonic discourse of the *Herald* and its allies transformed the exile community into a self-conscious ethnic group that organized effectively for local political competition."[58] By the mid-1980s, Cuban-born politicians held important government posts on the local and state levels. In 1981, the influential Cuban American National Foundation (CANF) was founded with Jorge Mas Canosa at the helm.

With all these events roiling Miami, Alvarez Guedes performed regularly, cementing his reputation as un tipo típico. Much of his comedic production during this time addressed the hot-button language issue and the general culture clash well underway in Miami. As the inflammatory rhetoric and tension between Anglos and the exile community escalated, so did the tone and aggression of Alvarez Guedes's material. Choteo's anti-hierarchical strain became a means to confront Anglo political power while simultaneously attempting to consolidate an exile cubanía founded on national characteristics, anti-Castro sentiment, cultural expressions, and, as discussed previously, whiteness and heteronormativity. Directing some aggression outward toward los americanos created a welcome respite from the infighting, while the tried and true strategy of identifying an outside threat served to buttress a communal narrative of the exile community as being free from internal conflict.

Clases de Idioma Cubano

Language has always been Alvarez Guedes's favorite topic. One of his most popular running gags, titled "Clases de idioma cubano" (Cuban Language Classes), began in 1974, when Miami was still officially a bilingual city. The albums that include these Cuban language classes always feature them as the last track. The reason is clear: they absolutely bring the house down. He prefaces his first "class" on *Alvarez Guedes 2* with the following justification as to why they are necessary in the first place:

> You all know that Miami has been officially declared a bilingual city. The Americans have declared it officially but I think this bilingualism exists only on our part, the part of the Cubans because those Cubans who are here can get by (*se defienden*) in English. But on the part of the Americans, the same thing doesn't apply because among the poor Americans, it is extremely difficult to find one that speaks two words of Spanish. Because of this, I'd like to dedicate this part of the album to the Americans, to give them a class on Cuban language. . . . These classes will help us understand each other better.[39]

The key phrase in this excerpt is "se defienden" translated idiomatically as "get by." In this context, the invocation of the verb *defender* is a common way to refer to one's tenuous grip on a foreign language. I retain the Spanish phrase in my translation in order to explore the resonance of the word in relation to Alvarez Guedes's treatment of cultural and political exchanges between los americanos and the exile community in all his Miami-related material. In this "class" and the jokes regarding language that I take up below, an economy of defense ("defender") is always working as subtext. The use of choteo to narrate the politics of language in Miami amounts to a form of defense for a Cuban community that feels a certain degree of vulnerability as a result of exilic displacement and the challenges posed by a sociopolitical landscape scripted in English. As the political tension in Miami mounts, the signification of defender in Alvarez Guedes's performances will shift to meet the escalation of anti-Cuban rhetoric.

Alvarez Guedes's introduction to his Cuban language class sets up one of the defining features of choteo's political potential as expressed by Mañach. In his essay on choteo, he describes the playful point of view on the intractable realities of life as choteo's *tendencia niveladora* (leveling tendency)—the ability to create a narrative of experience that "levels," or balances, the uneven power dynamics of the social milieu through the language of choteo. Choteo subverts the dominant model of immigrant assimilation in the United States by suggesting that Cubans are in a position to pity those "poor Americans" who cannot speak Spanish. Instead of interpreting the decision to make the city of Miami officially bilingual as a benefit to Cubans, Alvarez Guedes understands it as an almost matter-of-fact, logical unfolding of events. Cubans "se defienden" in English but now the Americans must fulfill the literal meaning of what it means to live in a bilingual city where *everyone* speaks two languages. In the narrative of the Cuban language class, the burden of cultural assimilation and understanding, usually carried by the incoming population, is transferred to the established community through choteo's leveling tendency.

Once he has finished his introduction, Alvarez Guedes begins his class by asking his audience to forgive him for speaking in English so the Americans can understand him. Of course, his audience is composed of Cubans who feel most comfortable speaking in Spanish. But imagining an audience of americanos allows for a comic reversal of the classic teacher-student dynamic at work in the encounter between "native" and immigrant. Under this logic, the newly arrived must learn the language and customs of the United States with a certain amount of deference to those who were born citizens. By putting himself in a position to teach los americanos of Miami, Alvarez Guedes reverses the logic of this dynamic and places power into the hands of the Cubans. His English is accented but syntactically flawless as he explains two "Cuban" words that he will teach, *mierda y comemierda* (shit and shit eater, idiomatically, asshole). He then goes on to explain how phrases in English like "go to hell" can be translated into Cuban as "vaya a la mierda." "Teaching" Cuban phrases that have a distinctly popular, vulgar resonance to los americanos and equating them with English phrases makes the language of political power legible to those Cubans who may feel intimidated by the privileged position of English in Miami at the time. Alvarez Guedes's use of the familiar language of choteo creates the opportunity for a pleasurable encounter with the *unfamiliar* dominant language.

The notion of familiarity warrants further discussion in relation to how choteo brings about pleasure for the audience. Besides already being familiar to many exiles who followed his career in Cuba, Alvarez Guedes's jokes and stories create a safe space where anxieties generated by the experience of exile can be managed pleasurably. The choteo that describes the relationship between Cubans and americanos is an explicit reminder of those common denominators of cubanía that Alvarez Guedes constantly tapped: we are different, special, and one way to articulate that is through diversión as a recognizable form of relation. Every time the audience laughs, applauds, or silently awaits the next joke, they ally themselves with Alvarez Guedes's perspective—a view that values, champions, and furthers the cause of the exile community. Alvarez Guedes's comic persona assumes the mantle of "defender." The humorous, playful language functions not only as mode for reimagining the difficulties associated with exile but also as a means to create an active, critical, political consciousness united around a cultural identity threatened by American assimilationist paradigms.

As the years went by, Alvarez Guedes continued to release albums annually and remained committed to addressing the relationship between los americanos and Miami's Cuban community. What changed was the boldness of the humor as the political climate in Miami became more hostile toward exiles. What started as a Cuban language class for "poor Americans" who can't speak Spanish evolved into a defiant, almost brash assertion of cultural difference. Take "Viva la diferencia" (Long Live Difference) featured on *Alvarez Guedes 10* (1979). Alvarez Guedes opens this story by saying, "Los cubanos se han cagado en el melting pot" (Cubans have shit on the concept of the melting pot), and follows with a list of examples detailing how Cubans have resisted the call to assimilate through the maintenance of distinct cultural characteristics.

"Shitting" on the most recognizable metaphor for American assimilation constitutes a defiant assertion of cultural legitimacy and resilience. The constant use of abject imagery in much of Alvarez Guedes's comedic performance is consistent with literary critic Gustavo Pérez Firmat's theorization of choteo's scatological mode. According to Pérez Firmat, the abject language of choteo is consistent with its peripheral relation to centrist discourse. As such, choteo is "a movement toward or assault from the margins."[60] With Cubans on the margins of Miami political power in the 1970s and early 1980s, Alvarez Guedes's comedy represents a desire to reimagine the power relations within the exilic space and to bring the margins to the center. At the same time, the jokes about negros and locas represent how in that move to the center, blackness and homosexuality were rendered abject and placed on the margins.

Choteo's assault from the margins becomes more pronounced on *Alvarez Guedes 11*, recorded in the chaotic year of 1980. The tension of the anti-bilingual referendum combined with the fallout from the Mariel crisis spilled over into the material on this album. Unlike the more covert aggression of "teaching" words like "mierda" and "comemierda" to an imagined American audience on *Alvarez Guedes 2*, the material on this album addresses the contentiousness in Miami much more directly. In "De ayer a hoy" ("Yesterday to Today") Alvarez Guedes discusses how Miami has changed since Cubans first arrived. He focuses again on language, explaining how speaking Spanish in Miami used to be equivalent to saying a vulgar word and citing instances when Americans would insult Cubans for not speaking English. The theme of reversal, putting the Cubans into the position of power via the humorous narrative, continues but in a much more aggressive way. He suggests that the Americans are now "trained" and are accepting of Spanish. Within this narrative, Spanish has replaced English as the dominant language. This dominance is communicated most effectively when Alvarez Guedes focuses on the reach of the Cuban community into the realm of business. To illustrate his point, Alvarez Guedes describes how he went into a pharmacy to ask for change for a dollar in order to make a phone call. He asked in English, to which the clerk responded in Spanish, "Now you want too much my brother. Now you want people to speak English here and everything."[61] The prevalence of Spanish within the economic sphere symbolizes the growing strength of the Cuban community. Cuban-owned businesses and other entrepreneurial ventures had been climbing steadily, and this humorous example not only serves as a rebuff to demands to speak English but also demonstrates the successful evolution of the Cuban enclave system in Miami standing in direct conflict with American demands for assimilation.

After giving a variety of examples as to why Americans have to learn Spanish to do business in Miami, Alvarez Guedes reaches a conclusion:

> With the Cubans coming from Mariel, with those coming from the North fleeing the cold, and the Central and South Americans that are constantly arriving here, this [Miami] is going to be ours! The few Americans left are going to have to go to hell. We are going to open a relocalization center to send them to whatever city that speaks English.[62]

Amidst raucous laughter, he then goes on to explain that while Spanish is on top, it must be instituted in everything. He makes fun of those people and business names that mix English and Spanish together and then closes with his utopic vision of Miami:

> I always say that Miami will not be perfect until the day that a Cuban police officer arrests an American for a transit violation. The Cuban police officer takes the American to a Cuban judge and when the judge says, "Guilty or innocent?" and the American tells the judge [*in badly inflected Spanish*], "Yo no hablar español" the judge says [*angrily*], "Oh, you don't speak Spanish? Well, to school you go, damn it! Six months until you learn!"[63]

The "perfect" Miami that Alvarez Guedes envisions is met with laughter and applause from the audience because of the irreverent attitude and subversive rhetoric directed toward those in power—both hallmarks of choteo.[64] But the approval that the audience's reaction signifies stands in direct opposition to the anxiousness felt by Cubans and non-Cubans alike throughout 1980. Even in the context of Mariel, when Alvarez Guedes recorded this joke, his desire is to unite by including the marielitos in the narrative of the exile community despite the negative press surrounding them. Discussing the relationship between americanos and Cubans during this period through choteo is a way to filter this social anxiety and consolidate the exile community while simultaneously lodging a critique against the language politics in Miami in the early 1980s through choteo's leveling tendency.

At the same time, Alvarez Guedes and his audience are coming to grips with the reality of exile and the gradual loss of faith in the narrative of return. The inability to participate or contribute to the sociopolitical reality of life in Cuba necessitates a certain shift of psychic, social, and economic resources. Miami must become home; what could not be done in Cuba will be attempted here. Imagining South Florida through the narrative form of choteo is just one step toward making Miami "home." With the subversive, humorous perspective that choteo affords, the struggles that arise out of dealing with a now hostile establishment in Miami can be confronted through a ludic lens that produces pleasure, if only temporarily, within the context of Alvarez Guedes's performance.[65]

In 1982, Alvarez Guedes released his best-selling and certainly most unique album titled *Alvarez Guedes 14: How to Defend Yourself from the Cubans*. What makes this album so exceptional is that it is the only one he released that features him performing primarily in English. The album is a mixture of an expansion on his Cuban language classes and some old material from previous albums translated into English.

With Spanish becoming nearly ubiquitous in Miami, Alvarez Guedes suggests that non-Spanish speakers must be able to "defend" themselves by learning some key phrases. The meaning of the phrase "se defienden," used earlier to articulate how Cubans in Miami described their tenuous grip on the English language, completely changes in the context of this performance. The repeal of Miami's status as a bilingual city moves Alvarez Guedes to reconsider his earlier, playful utopian idea of a city where everyone speaks English and Spanish. On this album, non-Spanish speakers are identified as those who need to "get by" and "defend" themselves by learning Spanish. If they do not, they risk being unable to navigate a Miami that has undergone radical change with the influx of immigrants from Latin America, most specifically Cubans. The text quoted below is from the very beginning of the album when Alvarez Guedes first greets his audience:

> I've been watching very closely what's been happening in Miami lately and I believe that something has to be done in favor of those who can't speak Spanish in this area. They have to learn to defend themselves. They have to learn Spanish because they need the goddamn language. They need it. It is the only language you hear everywhere. I don't care where you are. Wherever you are, in Miami, there are Cubans. . . . Sometimes we take advantage because since we know that you don't speak Spanish, we talk of you [sic] in front of you and you don't know it.[66]

He follows this up by imagining situations in which an americano would have to defend him or herself from Cubans. Every example describes the americano as being on the outside looking in and incapable of understanding when Cubans are talking badly about him or her. Choteo has changed the stakes of the game through a clear inversion of power relations. Cuban culture on this album becomes center while the non-Spanish speaking americanos are marginalized by their inability to understand what has been classified as "foreign" for so long.

This positing of Cuban culture as moving from minor to major indicates a shift in how "defense" has evolved in Alvarez Guedes's repertoire. In the first Cuban language class, "defender" was invoked to describe one's ability to at least "get by" in English. The covert aggression of this first class used choteo to "level" the linguistic power relations in Miami by creating an imagined scenario wherein Spanish was an important, equal part of the "bi" in "bilingual" city. As the political situation in Miami became more intense with the Mariel crisis and the anti-bilingual referendum, "defense" took on a more military connotation—defense as offense. These narratives stress how the Cuban and Latin American presence is a powerful force politically and economically by pointing out the pervasiveness of Spanish throughout the city. Alvarez Guedes goes on the attack on these albums, using choteo to speak out against the Anglo establishment, the example of Mañach's "inflexible authority" attempting to discredit the community. On *How to Defend Yourself from the Cubans*, the Cuban community, and by extension, Spanish, is positioned as dominant. In these narratives, the burden of defense is now upon los americanos in a Miami where Cuban culture has become the center and English is becoming more and more marginal.

Adding to the comic effect of this album is Alvarez Guedes's articulation of Spanish. When he uses Spanish, it is only to "teach" his "American audience" how to use certain vulgar words to defend themselves from Cubans in the situations mentioned above. But when he does explain how to fire back against these Cubans, his Spanish is inflected with an English accent. He mispronounces words, puts the accent on the wrong syllable, and generally sounds like the stereotypical gringo attempting to roll a pair of "Rs" with little success. In contrast to the gringo-inflected Spanish, Alvarez Guedes's speech reflects a relative mastery of English. To perform in English to an audience that understands the jokes as they shift from English to Spanish is to enact the community's attempt at mastering the codes of the dominant culture while simultaneously retaining culturally specific forms like the Spanish language and choteo as powerful, pleasurable ways of narrating experience.

Although the performance is all about displacing the need for defense onto los americanos of Miami, teaching an "American audience" how to defend themselves against the linguistic threat of Cuban Spanish is, once again, a form of defense for a community at a particularly hostile moment in time. National poll results after the Mariel crisis showed the country's extremely low opinion of the Cuban community in the United States.[67] The repeal of bilingualism laws, together with the negative views of the Cuban community, created a need to perform a certain brand of cultural solidarity and even superiority. *How to Defend Yourself from the Cubans* is one example. It performs cultural nationalism in English with a heightened sensitivity to the play between American and Cuban culture. The performance on this album demonstrates that despite learning English and assimilating in some respects, exile culture is still dominated by cubanía. By performing his mastery of English and simultaneously invoking the familiar language and codes of choteo, Alvarez Guedes makes a defiant statement against American assimilation models and stresses the vitality of the exile community.

Alvarez Guedes's choteo and unmistakable popularity provide a means for understanding the ways in which the exile community narrated itself *for* itself during the tumultuous 1970s and 1980s. In a time of domestic terrorism in the form of bombings and threats, generational shifts, political infighting within the community, and the most intense anti-Castro sentiment, diversión played an instrumental role in establishing the "common ground" of exile cubanía. Alvarez Guedes's material in the 1970s and 1980s reveals the utility of popular culture for "analyzing the consciousness of the past."[68] His performances and his widespread appeal reveal how the community made sense of its place in Miami's social hierarchy through a ludic discourse that combined the racial and normative sexual ideologies of Cuba and the United States to inform a narrative of exile cubanía. The history of choteo and its racial and sexual preoccupations on the island aligned with social hierarchies and discriminatory rhetoric in the United States and provided a convenient transnational continuity for exiles getting their bearings. When Anglos in Miami attempted to enclose the exile community in the realm of "otherness" and its attendant disenfranchisement, the community answered with a brash assertion of a Cuban cultural identity that simultaneously insisted on the privileges inherent in whiteness and heteronormativity. This manifested itself in popular culture and as the 1980s progressed, increased visibility and power in local and then national governments. Alvarez Guedes's vision for the "perfect" Miami where Cubans dominated was not far off.

* * *

One of my favorite possessions is a 1983 talking Alvarez Guedes doll. He hangs out in my office, and students and colleagues alike get a kick out of pressing his stomach and hearing him belt out foul-mouthed phrases like "¡Ño! ¡Desde que llegaste lo único que haces es hablar mierda!" (Damn! Since you got here all you do is talk shit/nonsense!). Here, he is surrounded by the many books that have helped me theorize his comedy. But perhaps no study has been more crucial in that regard than José Esteban Muñoz's *Disidentifications: Queers of Color and the Performance of Politics*. Through a reading of queer performance artist Carmelita Tropicana, Muñoz explains how choteo has "disidentificatory potential" in the way it can "mediate between a space of identification with and total disavowal of the dominant culture's normative identificatory nodes."[69] Alvarez Guedes jokes don't always make me laugh, and much of his material on race and sexuality puts him at odds with my politics. But the way he tells all his jokes, the way he mobilizes choteo through language, tone, timing, and delivery, have always been a source of pleasure and an influence on my own "performance" as a public speaker. As Carmelita Tropicana and Muñoz show us, these things do not have to be at odds. It is possible to disidentify with exile cubanía, "not rejecting it and not embracing it without reservations," in order to produce alternative visions of cubanía, community, and the world.[70] I explore this potential in more detail in the next chapter with the work of two US-born Cuban Americans who mobilize choteo to both identify with their parents' generation and criticize the political orthodoxy of exile cubanía.

2

Cuban Miami on the Air

But radio in Miami will continue to be, without a doubt, its
most faithful reflection and even if it's shouted or preached,
applauded to insanity or thrashed verbally in opposition,
one must recognize its unique and predominant role, the
mirror that reflects us, the exponent of our idiosyncrasy. It
is clever, controversial and vigorous radio just like the Cuba
that witnessed our birth and it's reborn here now.
—Heberto Padilla, *El Miami Herald*, 1986

Famed Cuban poet Heberto Padilla's praise for radio in the pages of *El
Miami Herald* not only highlights its powerful role in the city's media
landscape in the 1980s but also gestures toward radio's significant place
in Cuban culture historically.[1] Since the first radio broadcast in Havana
in 1922, radio has played a prominent role in Cuban cultural life on and
off the island.[2] When Cubans began leaving for the United States after
the Revolution, they brought their love of radio with them. Those well
versed in Cuba's radio industry were able to redeploy their talent and
skills in the exile context. The result was the beginning of a vibrant radio
culture in Miami, which continues today. Currently, Miami is the third
largest Latino/a radio market in the United States—a statistic powered
in large part by the city's Cuban population. But does radio continue to
provide a "faithful reflection" of the Cuban community, as Padilla suggests? Has it ever? How can listening to radio programming that features
Cuba-related content in South Florida in the first decade of the twenty-
first century help us understand Cuban Miami in new ways?

Radio's popularity across decades and generational cohorts makes
it a particularly productive site for understanding shifts within Cuban
Miami over time. Historically, radio has been the most effective means
for communicating the exile ideology through a consistent message of
anti-Castro politics and condemnation of those seen as sympathetic to

the Cuban government. But with generational turnover and increasingly moderate stances on Cuba by more recent arrivals and US-born Cuban Americans, the narrative of cubanía on the radio shifted to stay relevant and profitable in the 2000s. It is in the beginning of the twenty-first century that popular culture in Cuban Miami begins to tilt markedly away from the preoccupations of the older exile community to serve the needs and interests of younger generations.

This chapter privileges the generational position of US-born Cuban Americans through an analysis of immensely popular morning radio programs that aired throughout the 2000s called the *Enrique y Joe Show* and the *Enrique Santos Show*. Hosted by Enrique Santos and Joe Ferrero, the children of Cuban exiles raised in the United States, the shows targeted a younger, Spanish-speaking audience on stations that played contemporary salsa, merengue, and reggaeton. But music was never their primary draw. Audiences tuned in for the diversión that framed their daily performances. Santos and Ferrero combined elements of English-language "morning zoo" radio shows such as prank calls, musical parodies, interviews, and the like with a deeply Cuban performance practice. Their word choice, slang, and accents reflected the vernacular of Cuban Miami. In addition, their enactment of diversión through the recognizable irreverence of choteo signaled a particular *way* of joking that was legible to their audiences. Familiar comic tropes, Cuban wordplay and puns, and vocal cues created a sense of intimacy with their audience and served as a kind of invitation to join in the jodedera every morning. This mix of Cuban and mainstream US cultural elements reflects not only the generational position of Santos and Ferrero but also the flexibility of diversión to address the needs of a changing present.

Unsurprisingly, the performative repertoire of diversión employed for these radio shows shares many similarities with the standup of Alvarez Guedes discussed in Chapter 1. Santos and Ferrero learned what it meant to enact cubanía from the older generation the comedian represents. But their performances are not carbon copies of material from the 1970s. As in the previous chapter, here I will employ a practice of close listening in order to get at the complex generational dynamics at play in Cuban Miami in the 2000s. This approach reveals the role of diversión as a disidentificatory practice that allows Santos and Ferrero to revel in aspects of exile cubanía while simultaneously framing the perceived limits of the politics encoded therein. Further complicating this investigation of narratives of cubanía on the air will be my analysis of the role of multimedia conglomerates like Univision in determining which voices and narratives the public hears in the first place.

Radio and Politics in Cuban Miami

From its early beginnings in Miami, radio by and for Cubans has had a political slant regardless of whether the broadcasts were directed toward the island or those living stateside. Radio transmitted from Miami to Cuba has been at the forefront of attempts to destabilize the Cuban government. Radio Swan, widely believed to be financed by the CIA, became active in 1960 and transmitted anti-Castro political viewpoints into the island. During the failed Bay of Pigs invasion in 1961, Radio Swan broadcasts served as a "call to arms" for Cubans to rise up and rebel.[3] Exile groups with their own radio equipment complemented this covert, government-sponsored radio offensive by taking advantage of the short distance between South Florida and Cuba to transmit their own messages over the ether.[4] The Cuban government retaliated with its own political propaganda over the airwaves and by attempting to jam, with some success, transmissions to the island.[5]

In 1983, a lobbying push from the Cuban American National Foundation led by Jorge Mas Canosa, the radio offensive against Cuba received public government backing with the Reagan administration's support of Radio Martí. Still active with the help of government funding, Radio Martí has a mission to provide "objective" news and information to Cubans on the island with the hopes of promoting "the cause of freedom" in Cuba.[6] Over the years, the Office of Cuba Broadcasting has been criticized for mismanagement and an inability to live up to its stated goals. A 2010 report to the Committee on Foreign Relations of the US Senate cites poor journalism, a small audience on the island, Cuban signal jamming, and corruption within the Office of Cuba Broadcasting for its failures. With diplomatic relations between Washington and Havana restored, the future of the station is uncertain.

At the same time that broadcasts were being transmitted to Cuba, radio was thriving in Miami. For members of the exile generation arriving in the 1960s and 1970s, radio quickly became "the medium of choice" for news and entertainment.[7] Established by station owners, staff, and on-air talent who fled soon after the Revolution, radio stations and programming took on a distinctively Cuban flair. Stations modeled themselves on the radio culture in Cuba before the Revolution in order to attract audiences with programming that sounded familiar. As the Cuban population in Miami exploded in the second half of the twentieth century, so did the number of Spanish-language media outlets catering to their needs. The number of newspapers, television, and radio stations steadily increased, and by the late 1980s, there were eight Spanish-language radio stations serving the greater Miami area.[8]

In those early years of exile, radio programs sought to demystify life in the United States by explaining new laws and customs. Stations paired discussions of quotidian concerns with a healthy dose of political commentary in ways that proved instrumental in consolidating the political and affective coordinates of exile cubanía. As María Cristina García explains, "Cuban radio reflected the more conservative views of the community. Editorials were staunchly anti-Castro and anti-communist, opposing a political rapprochement with Cuba and the lifting of the US trade embargo, and supporting émigrés' paramilitary campaigns against the Cuban government."[9] As a mode of communication, radio creates a sense of community, "a strong collective sensibility," strengthened further by a shared set of circumstances.[10] These circumstances—exilic displacement and the existence of a common enemy embodied in the person of Fidel Castro—have been mobilized in media serving Cuban Miami over time to strengthen the notion of a community unified in politics and feeling.

Despite the sense of a unified community relayed on the air, radio in Miami has been a contested site for the dissemination of opinions related to Cuba and local concerns. Proponents of the exile ideology used broadcasts to slam *dialogueros*—those willing to open communication with Cuba—as communists and agents of the Castro government. Attacks in the media were supplemented by physical violence, as María de los Angeles Torres explains: "Terrorism as a form of activism became ingrained in the political life of the exile community. Having gained control of the Miami media, many businesses, and the electoral arena, hard-line exile forces sought to impose a single, rigid anti-Castro viewpoint, using intimidation and violence to silence their opponents."[11]

Radio personalities who condemned this violence became targets as well. In 1976, a car bomb maimed Emilio Milián, a broadcaster who criticized violence committed in the name of Cuba.

In the early 1990s, those sympathetic to engagement with Cuba through dialogue saw the fall of the Soviet Union and the disastrous effects it had on the Cuban economy as an opportunity for change on the island.[12] Once again, radio served as a bully pulpit rallying listeners against dialogue "almost round the clock" at a moment when many believed Castro was most vulnerable.[13] With this sentiment in the air, supporters of the exile ideology successfully lobbied Congress to tighten the embargo, and in 1992 the Cuban Democracy Act (also known as the Torricelli Act) passed. Congress intensified sanctions again in 1996, when President Bill Clinton signed the Helms-Burton Act into law.[14] In 2000, Miami gained international notoriety for the Elián González saga and the heavily contested Bush-Gore presidential election. The scholarship of Susan Eckstein and Isabel Molina Guzmán reveals that Miami's Spanish-language media largely supported the family's asylum claim on Elián's behalf.[15]

But as this book repeatedly asserts, it was never all doom and gloom, fire and brimstone on the Miami airwaves. Guillermo Alvarez Guedes enjoyed a long radio career. Old episodes of *La tremenda corte* (The Outrageous Court) produced in Cuba before the Revolution featuring comic superstar Leopoldo "Tres Patines" Fernández continue to be aired today. *Zig-Zag*, a satirical newspaper famous in pre-Castro Cuba and relaunched in exile, had its own radio program transmitting humor for Cubans in Miami *and* on the island.[16] When radio programs took aim at the corruption within the exile community through the lens of humor, they themselves could become targets. Veteran satirist Alberto González learned this lesson with a radio show called *La mogolla* (The Muddle) that got canceled on more than one station in the late 1980s and early 1990s for angering Miami power brokers.[17] Meanwhile, other radio personalities like Los Fonomemecos (Miguel González and Gilberto Reyes) and Eddy Calderón, popular in the 1990s and 2000s, utilized forms of diversión that were politically "safe" in targeting Fidel Castro and the Cuban government more broadly.

The exile ideology continued to dominate throughout the 2000s, especially on AM talk radio. But cracks in this pattern of radio programming began to emerge in the first decade of the twenty-first century due to the massive demographic shifts that have been underway in Cuban Miami since the 1990s.[18] The Cubans who began pouring into Miami after the 1994 *balsero* crisis were far less interested in the bluster and political positions that characterized most of talk radio in the second half of the twentieth century. While arrivals from the 1990s onward reached record numbers, the largest segment of Cuban Miami still consists of US-born Cuban Americans—primarily the children, grandchildren, and great-grandchildren of the original exile generation. Because most US-born Cuban Americans have never lived on the island, opposition to the Cuban government is learned from parents, family, and the anti-Castro media and symbolism that saturate Miami. Despite this education, poll data has shown that US-born Cuban Americans are less committed to the exile ideology.[19] The lack of personal experience of the Revolution allows for some emotional distance and on many Cuba-related issues, a far less conservative approach.[20]

Although US-born Cuban Americans constitute 40 percent of the Cuban diaspora in the United States, little has been published "beyond demographic surveys and sociological profiles" on this group, as Alexandra T. Vazquez points out.[21] I see two reasons for this. First, adherents to the exile ideology have historically held positions of power and have served as "gatekeepers" who use political influence and cultural institutions to forward their agenda while marginalizing more moderate voices.[22] Second, this generation gets lost in the mix when the topic of Cuba arises. They do not participate in Cuban cultural or political institutions to the same degree as their parents or grandparents, and they consume most media in English.

To address this gap in scholarship, I will privilege the cultural production of US-born Cuban Americans Enrique Santos and Joe Ferrero through an analysis of their top-rated morning-drive radio programs, which aired throughout the 2000s on two different Miami radio stations. Their success can be attributed to both their role as generational intermediaries in tune with shifting demographic changes and their audience's desire for a daily dose of diversión every morning during the workweek. Performing mostly in Spanish, they used Cuban slang, wordplay, and the recognizable comic irreverence of choteo to lampoon their many targets. But examining diversión in the context of their shows also calls to mind the ways in which cultural practices can change and shift in response to other cultural influences. Though diversión as a Cuban comic sensibility and a performance practice contributed to the legibility of these shows to the audience, the best way to describe them would be by way of comparison to the popular "morning zoo" radio programs in English. Their shows drew heavily from this genre and included all the usual features: prank phone calls, celebrity gossip, a crew of complementary personalities, musical parodies, interviews, quick segments of news and traffic, and comedic skits.

Examining how Santos and Ferrero deploy diversión provides a means to understand how the narrative of cubanía has shifted in Miami. For a long time, that narrative of what it meant to be Cuban was dominated by the logic of exile and its hardline politics, anti-Castro rhetoric, and commitment to the cause of a free Cuba. But despite being a word that suggests a kind of cultural essence (the "ness" in Cubanness), cubanía has long functioned as a "vague concept, malleable and adaptable."[23] The performances of Enrique Santos and Joe Ferrero highlight the malleability of cubanía as US-born Cuban Americans remain committed to a Cuban cultural identity but significantly less engaged with Cuba as a political topic on a daily basis.[24] Through its deployment of diversión, the show successfully unbundles hardline exile politics from Cuban American identity while retaining cubanía. The targets for their choteo-inflected performances that I will examine include Fidel Castro *and* what they perceived as the excesses of exile cubanía, namely an obsession with Cuba and its politics. The bicultural sensibility that marks the experiences of Santos and Ferrero thus shaped their deployment of diversión both explicitly in terms of how they framed issues and implicitly in terms of their performance practice.

It would be naïve to suggest that the performance of cubanía on the *Enrique y Joe Show* is simply a product of a younger generation's rising up and taking its turn on Miami's airwaves. Instead, the *Enrique y Joe Show* must also be placed in the context of the companies that own the stations from which they broadcasted, especially media powerhouse Univision. In greater Miami today, Univision owns four radio and two television stations.[25] In putting questions surrounding performances of cubanía on the radio alongside the corporate strategy of Univision, this chapter will also contribute to scholarship in Latino/a media studies and more specifically, Spanish-language radio.[26] According to Mari Castañeda, "Spanish-language radio grew nearly 1000 percent since 1980, and industry analysts predict that the sector will continue to grow well into the next decade."[27] Arbitron's *Hispanic Radio Today 2011* states that "radio's reach among both English-dominant and Spanish-dominant listeners sits between 95% and 96%."[28] In South Florida, the third largest Spanish-language radio market and the place where Spanish is an unavoidable aspect of the sonic landscape, these figures merit increased attention.

While research conducted by scholars outside of the media industry has helped to clarify the growth, relevance, and commercialization of Spanish-language radio, there has been far less scholarship devoted to analyzing specific program content.[29] I will expand this area of Spanish-language media studies by analyzing radio sketches and performance practices that speak to the broader generational, demographic, and political shifts within the Cuban diaspora in the twenty-first century.

"¡Cayó Fidel Castro!"

Enrique Santos and Joe Ferrero got their start together in 2002 on El Zol 95.7 in Miami.[30] From the beginning, the duo used the irreverence of choteo to cultivate an atmosphere of diversión, but not just by telling jokes and engaging in observational humor. Like Alvarez Guedes before them, they tapped choteo's flexibility, as defined by Roberto González Echevarría: "Rhetorically, choteo can take the form of saying the opposite of what one means, of indulging in paronomasias, amphibologies, double-entendres, parodies, and mockery of any and all kinds."[31] They put this flexibility to work most notably in a series of prank calls that put them in the international spotlight. In January of 2003, the duo was able get through to Venezuelan president Hugo Chávez by using a soundboard featuring prerecorded snippets of Fidel Castro's speech. When they finally got Chávez on the line, they dropped the act and quickly began hurling expletives, including calling him a terrorist and a murderer. Those wary of Venezuela's increasingly cozy relationship with Cuba celebrated the prank. It would take only a few months for the duo to top themselves.

In June of 2003, Ferrero and Santos successfully got through to Fidel Castro himself. If the call to Chávez attracted attention, pranking Castro inspired nothing short of a frenzy in Miami. To execute the prank, snippets of Chávez's voice were used to create the impression that the Venezuelan president was on the line. Because the soundbites of his voice were limited, Joe Ferrero played the part of Lieutenant Camilo, an aide to Chávez charged with establishing communication with Castro. Ferrero did most of the talking, while a crew member used a soundboard to strategically place the word "sí" and the phrase "yo le estoy oyendo" (I can hear him) in the voice of Chávez to serve as a form of validation to fool the many Cuban officials that stood between them and getting Castro on the line. Once connected to Castro directly, they dropped the ruse and the call reached its climax:

> FERRERO AS LT. CAMILO: Your agents that were with you in Argentina must make an extensive and detailed search. And the people that are responsible for this must be held accountable. Do you understand that this is a top priority?
>
> CASTRO: I am informed and absolutely in agreement.
>
> SANTOS [*jumps in, previously unheard voice*]: So are you satisfied with the shit that you have done to the island, assassin?
>
> CASTRO: What?
>
> SANTOS: Enrique Santos and Joe Ferrero from Miami, El Zol 95.7. *Caíste* (you fell for it) just like Hugo Chávez.
>
> CASTRO: What did I fall for, *comemierda* (literally shit eater, idiomatically asshole)?
>
> SANTOS: Enrique Santos and Joe Ferrero from Miami.
>
> CASTRO: What did I fall for, *maricón* (faggot)?
>
> SANTOS: All of Miami is listening to you.
>
> CASTRO: What did I fall for, *mariconzón* (big faggot)?
>
> SANTOS: What do you have to say?
>
> CASTRO: *Ni cojones* (literally, "no balls," meaning "nothing").
>
> SANTOS: What do you have to say?
>
> CASTRO: I haven't said anything. *Vete para el coño de tu madre* (Go screw your mother).
>
> FERRERO: All of Miami is listening to you, Fidel Castro.[32]

After this thirty-second exchange, Castro hung up, triggering screams and applause in the studio. On the recording, one person can be heard saying "Oh my God" in a state of disbelief while another proclaims "¡Cayó Fidel Castro!" Excitement spread quickly throughout Cuban Miami. Local callers demanded that the station replay the call over and over again.[33] When the Federal Communications Commission ordered the station to pay a $4,000 fine for airing Castro's voice without his permission, the duo rallied community support and collected the fine in pennies from their listeners.

My first experience with this prank call came on YouTube. I had a basic understanding of what was going to happen. Santos and Ferrero were going to call Cuban government offices and eventually get through to the man himself and likely let him have it. Despite having this knowledge beforehand, I noticed that my heart was beating faster and faster as they got closer to getting Castro on the line. This feeling could be partially attributed to what radio offers as a medium, a sense of co-presence and intimacy through listening, which invites the audience to feel "there" in the world of this sonic exchange with Santos, Ferrero, and thousands of other listeners.[34] Even though I was not experiencing the call live, I felt that co-presence and intimacy with a community of listeners who shared an understanding of the uniqueness of this moment, as I did, but perhaps more importantly, had an inescapable acquaintance with the historical and affective underpinnings of exile cubanía. Pranking Castro was an attack not just on the man, but on the public persona he masterfully and meticulously crafted over the years. His personal life is rarely a topic of conversation in official channels. He has fashioned himself as father of the nation "married" to Cuba in complete and total service to the Revolution. But this was another Fidel, a Fidel the diaspora had never seen, so clearly off his game, so obviously lacking the upper hand—a position he enjoyed almost exclusively in his dealings with the diaspora.

For the majority of listeners, this is the closest they ever got to Fidel Castro. Santos and Ferrero served as the mouthpieces for a community that had wanted to give Castro a piece of its collective mind for decades. The emotionally charged message that has permeated protests against Castro in the streets of Miami, denunciations of socialism over Cuban coffee, and decades of political agitation through clandestine activities and federal legislation, was, for once, directed successfully at the man himself in this prank phone call—simply unprecedented. While Santos and Ferrero did not unleash a tidal wave of expletives upon Castro, they did manage to call him *un asesino*, a murderer. But that is not the most satisfying aspect of the call. The most striking moment in their exchange comes when Castro himself serves as an unwitting participant in his own comic undoing.

Castro's realization that he has been duped sparks a tirade of curses and expletives. He has been brought down to the level of the man on the street through his use of words like *coño* and *maricón*, which are more reminiscent of a typical *viejo malhablado* (foul-mouthed old man) than a man known for soaring oratory and marathon speeches. This incongruity, from podium to prank call victim, is what generates the laughter and excitement among listeners. Yes, there is a satisfaction in directly calling Castro an assassin who has "turned the island into shit" but the true pleasure lies in listening to him undo his own persona through a kind of auto-choteo. Instead of sounding like Fidel Castro, the articulate revolutionary leader, he sounds much more like a confused old man unable to respond intelligently—an old man who must resort to homophobic insults and "your momma" invective in order to mount any kind of rhetorical offensive. Castro comes to resemble the very caricatures that notable comic impersonators like Armando Roblán and Eddy Calderón have performed for decades.

The excitement this prank produced also reveals a sad reality. The pleasure experienced is commensurate with the frustration felt after decades of conflict between Castro and the exile community. It underlines the sense of impotence, the inability to create change. This is the closest the exile ideology was ever directly communicated to Castro in such a public manner. This symbolism and its importance to a community perennially frustrated by the inability to effect real change in Cuba come across in the raucous response in the studio after Castro hangs up and a voice exclaims, "Cayó Fidel Castro!" (Fidel Castro has fallen). The prank call segment of this show was referred to as *caíste* (you fell for it), meaning that the victim of the prank call "fell" for the ruse. The verb *caer* when used to describe Fidel in this instance also resonates with the "fall" of a dictatorship. In this context, "cayó Fidel Castro" refers to his falling for the prank and resonates with how the verb *caer* and its past tense form *cayó* have been deployed, in a hopeful manner, for decades.[35] This is as close as the community ever got to witnessing

Castro's fall, a prank call on a radio show segment called *caíste* that lasted all of thirty seconds.

Santos and Ferrero received an outpouring of love from the exile community. They had tricked Fidel, yes, but the fact that they executed this prank as the sons of exiles must have been particularly sweet. They were able to relay a message that parents and grandparents of US-born Cuban Americans have repeated for decades: Fidel Castro is un asesino. Their sonic encounter with Castro was not born out of a desire for increased understanding represented in the generation of young Cuban Americans who traveled to Cuba in the 1970s as part of *el diálogo*. The prank was combative, consistent with exile cubanía as a structure of feeling vehemently opposed to the Cuban government embodied in the figure of Fidel Castro. It would seem that Santos and Ferrero have internalized the political tenets of exile cubanía. Mission accomplished.

Radio Maní

The above prank call and other performances of solidarity with elements of anti-Castro exile cubanía do not tell the whole story about how they mobilized diversión on the show. As discussed earlier, US-born Cuban Americans are generally less invested in the exile perspective that has characterized what it means to be Cuban in South Florida. Coverage of Cuba-related issues on the show focused primarily on high-profile events with a great deal of symbolic value: rumors that Fidel Castro had died and controversial events like Colombian rocker Juanes's 2009 performance in Havana. The show did not attend to the minutiae of political news out of Cuba, which has been the foundation for AM talk radio stations like Radio Mambí, La Fabulosa, La Cadena Azul, and La Cubanísima. On these stations, callers expressing a viewpoint out of step with the hardline would often be dropped or insulted in order to reinforce an "ideological homogeneity" on the air.[36]

Self-righteous hosts feverishly performing their commitment to the struggle against Castro on the air? Aggressive jabs at those deviating from the exile ideology? An unwavering dedication to the Cuba question for decades? What could possibly be more ripe for parody at a moment when the theatrics of anti-Castro rage were becoming less relevant? On a number of shows in 2009, Santos and Ferrero employed choteo in their satirical parody of the most visible AM station espousing hardline exile politics: WAQI Radio Mambí 710AM. At the time, Radio Mambí operated under an all-news format and focused primarily on politics in Cuba and Miami. The director, Armando Pérez Roura, embodied the station's political leanings. A fixture in the Miami media landscape as a journalist, radio personality, and editor since the early days of exile, Pérez Roura continues to rail against the Castro regime and anyone perceived as "soft" on communism to this day.[37] His short biography on the Radio Mambí website ended with the following: "Armando Pérez Roura feels at peace with his conscience because he has never stopped fighting for Liberty and Democracy in his homeland, CUBA, and wherever tyranny arises."

In 2009, the *Enrique y Joe Show* frequently parodied Pérez Roura and Radio Mambí with a recurring segment called Radio Maní, which featured a character also named Armando. The segment begins unannounced with a classic, dramatic news-radio musical cue, and as the music plays, a deep-voiced announcer introduces Radio Maní as "the best of Miami's morning"—the same tagline utilized by Radio Mambí. As the music winds down, the announcer introduces the director of Radio Maní, Armando.

The decision to title the satirical parody of Radio Mambí as Radio Maní prepares the audience for the choteo that marks the segment. The deep-voiced announcer and dramatic introductory music signal the target: the serious and authoritative tone that has defined Miami's exile media landscape for decades. While these elements situate the listener in the world of exile media, the title of the show initiates the wordplay that characterizes the Radio Maní segment. The word *mambí* refers to those Cubans who fought against Spanish rule in Cuba's wars of independence in the second half of the nineteenth century. Radio Mambí transfers the legacy of Cuban freedom fighters to those who wish to liberate Cuba from Castro. In changing the title of the show to Radio Maní, which literally means "Radio Peanut," the *Enrique y Joe Show* comically interrupts the metaphor of war and exile activism. Bilingual listeners could connect *maní* to *peanut* and all of its idiomatic connotations of negligibility and unimportance in English. More significant for understanding the choteo is the word *maní* and its multiple resonances in Cuban vernacular expression. First, *maní* is slang for money. The show repeatedly represents the Armando of Radio Maní as corrupt and willing to engage in the drug trade and *la payola* (pay for play on his radio segment) in order to line his own pockets.[38] But perhaps more strikingly, the word *maní* can also be used to describe someone who is insane.[39] Radio Maní portrayed Armando's mercurial tone and singular focus on Cuba as excessive to the point of madness. The parodic approach of this segment thus highlights those characteristics that structure the legibility of exile politics and make them "comically visible" in order to provide a starting point and throughline for satirical critique.[40]

Armando (voiced by Joe Ferrero) is playing a part and thus participates fully in the satire, not unlike Stephen Colbert in his "conservative" commentary on *The Colbert Report*. As Geoffrey Baym observes, shows like *The Colbert Report* function as a means for "critically confronting the 'aesthetic totalitarianism' of right-wing political communication that privileges affective spectacle over rational argument."[41] Radio Maní segments operated similarly by providing an opportunity to crystallize and engage with the conservative politics that have traditionally dominated Miami's Spanish-language media discourse. The result is a comic defamiliarization of a discourse so ingrained within the fabric of South Florida media that it goes relatively unnoticed. Sound is crucial to the production of this defamiliarization. Whenever a caller or a character like Armando articulated anti-Castro commentary or intense cultural nationalism, the show played a sound clip of a young child screaming "¡Cuba Libreeeee!" to signal a historical obsession with Cuba in Miami so extreme that it lends itself to comedy. When obscure slang or unintelligible Cuban accents found their way onto the air, they had a clip ready featuring a woman's voice with a distinctly non-Cuban Spanish accent saying, "¿Estás hablando en cubano? No le entiendo nada" (Are you speaking in Cuban? I don't understand a thing you're saying). Clips like these demonstrate how part of the project around the representation of cubanía on the show was to point out its excesses in South Florida—a point perhaps easier to make for the bicultural, US-born Santos and Ferrero.

But the parody goes beyond signaling the excessiveness of Armando with a soundboard and clips at the ready. The humor is born out of his *performance* of those politics, his ventriloquism of exile cubanía through the ludic logic of diversión. Ferrero's mastery of Armando Pérez

Roura's delivery—the dramatic pauses, the choice of words, the peaks and valleys of tone to communicate just the right amount of emphasis and outrage—displays his fluency in the ideological, affective, and performative spectacle of exile cubanía and radio culture in Miami. As a caricature come to life, Radio Maní's Armando provides an opportunity for thinking about how more moderate US-born Cubans represent and imagine exile politics for a seemingly sympathetic audience drawn in by the comic performance and its promises of pleasure.[42]

Radio Maní segments never began with a warning. Upon hearing the introductory music signaling the beginning of the segment, the crew would feign surprise and audibly groan at the prospect of having to deal with Armando. Armando would not acknowledge his less-than-enthusiastic reception and instead would go on with his segment, usually beginning with a news story that he found particularly infuriating: Obama's politics, the sorry state of the youth in the United States, or anything related to Cuba. Then, without fail, Armando would be sidetracked by questions from the crew meant to incite a hyperbolic performance of his obsession with Cuba:

> MIKEY MACHETE (CREWMEMBER): Armando, are you going to Premio Lo Nuestro (Our Awards)?
>
> ARMANDO (VOICED BY JOE FERRERO): No, I'm going to *premio lo mío (my awards)*. [*Crew laughs.*] I don't waste my time on those silly things.
>
> MIKEY MACHETE: But Armando, you have to go there to represent the exile community!
>
> ARMANDO: No, I go only to those places where the liberation of Cuba is discussed.

From the very beginning of the segment, Armando is treated as an annoying, yet entertaining interruption in the crew's day. In keeping with his character, he has no interest in attending an awards show that caters to the latest musical acts and a decidedly younger demographic in a pan-Latina/o framework. In fact, when it comes to song, Armando affirms his love for the musical embodiment of *la Cuba de ayer*, Olga Guillot, a popular Cuban singer of boleros who lived in Miami and actively voiced her opposition to the Castro government. Beyond musical considerations, the event is not of any interest to Armando because he goes only "where the liberation of Cuba is discussed." For Mikey Machete to demand that he attend the show as a representative of the exile community, tongue firmly in cheek, is to emphasize how younger Cubans perceive Armando and his generation as out of touch with happenings in Miami that are in no way related to Cuba, Miami's ever-evolving popular culture scene, and an increasingly heterogeneous Latina/o community.[43]

The reference to Premio Lo Nuestro also reveals the increasing synergy across Univision's media platforms. After a public falling out with management at SBS-owned El Zol in 2007, Santos and Ferrero signed with Univision to fill the morning drive slot on 98.3 *La Kalle*. Plugging the awards show produced by the parent company comes with the territory. As a music awards show produced and disseminated by Univision, the show's title, which translates to "our awards," is consistent with the company's strategy to consolidate latinidad into a single cultural formation—the inclusive logic encoded in the word *nuestro* (our). The show represents Armando's Cuba-centric vision as being inconsistent with the forward "progress" of popular culture and less explicitly, as being outside of Univision's broader narrative of pan-latinidad that receives particular emphasis on nationally syndicated programming like Premio Lo Nuestro. In this quick exchange, it is possible to discern Univision's strategy for the *Enrique y Joe Show*: to target an audience attracted to the performance of cubanía to varying degrees but also fluent in the increasingly pan-Latina/o narrative in South Florida propagated by Univision.[44]

While the segment portrays Armando as out of touch, the staged spontaneity of Radio Maní nonetheless dramatizes how his perspective manifests itself in Miami's media. Like the Radio Maní segments that begin unannounced, the politics Armando represents always seem to be in the background, ready to burst out and take command of the narrative of Cuban Miami at any time despite more widely held moderate positions. Though the crew expresses annoyance when Armando "interrupts," he always gets to have his say. This functions as an integral part of the humor; Armando is allowed to say his piece. But this also indirectly speaks to how the viewpoint Armando represents has historically forced itself upon Cuban Miami and the city through Spanish-language media. As Ian Hutchby explains in his analysis of confrontational exchanges on the air, interruptions are often about asserting power on talk radio especially in what he calls "asymmetrical encounters."[45] In the world of Radio Maní, the crew subverts the "asymmetrical" power dynamic in Miami's media landscape through a less-than-deferential parody of Radio Mambí that demonstrates how its politics are increasingly unpopular in Cuban Miami yet remain influential.

Given the dominance of the exile ideology across the media landscape, it is not surprising that Santos and Ferrero channeled the irreverent and anti-authoritarian logic of choteo to frame this critique. As Narciso J. Hidalgo explains, choteo is "an antidote for society when institutions display an incapacity to be in accordance with the character and needs of the people."[46] While exile politics does not represent an institutional form of authority per se, its ubiquity in the media landscape has had a profound effect on how businesses, politicians, and other public figures have presented themselves in order to avoid the tag of *comunista*. Criticism of the exile ideology is not new, but the irreverent, public nature of its performance demonstrates the decreasing relevance of those politics in a moment of generational turnover, as well as the commercial viability of this more moderate demographic for a corporate entity like Univision interested in profits over politics.

The notion that the exile ideology is disconnected from the future of Cuban Miami and the majority of its members is most powerfully conveyed in the constant emphasis on the advanced age of the exile generation during Radio Maní segments. After Armando explains that he does not attend events unrelated to Cuba, another crewmember chimes in to enable the next "act" of the performance, which will extend the metaphor of advanced age and outdated politics.

MIKEY MACHETE: But Armando, you have to go there [Premio Lo Nuestro] to represent the exile community!

ARMANDO: No, I go only to those places where the liberation of Cuba is discussed.

CREWMEMBER: Mikey, the bus from the León Medical Center doesn't go that far!

OLD CUBAN WOMAN [*interrupts Armando; sounds old and feeble, and has a strong Cuban accent*]: Armando? Armando? Where are we going for the protest today?

CREW: [*Group laughter.*]

ARMANDO: We are going to go directly to any military base to protest against Obama.

OLD CUBAN WOMAN: [*in a weak feeble voice*] I want to thank [inaudible] for lending me a rocket.

CREW: [*Howling laughter.*]

ARMANDO: It's always good to be armed, Miss. I'm happy.

OLD CUBAN WOMAN: With this rocket we are going to liberate Cuba!

CREW: Ohhhhh! [*Laughing, whistling and clapping in unison.*]

OLD CUBAN WOMAN: Armando! On this trip, I'm going with you but get that other old lady away from me because on the last trip [on the bus] she was farting the whole time.

CREW: [*Laughter continues.*]

Mentioning the León Medical Center would likely strike a chord among listeners in the greater Miami area. The León Medical Group provides healthcare and assistance to Spanish-speaking Miami, strategically targeting the elderly population receiving Medicare benefits. León has been aggressive in courting Miami's rapidly aging Cuban population by placing strong emphasis on the Cuban heritage of the company's owners. Cracking a joke about León paves the way for the Old Cuban Woman, a character voiced by an unidentified crewmember. In an exaggerated, feeble voice and Cuban accent, she asks Armando about the site for the next protest. Here, the image of exiles in a constant state of agitation and protest manifests itself in a character who seems to protest as part of her day—a routine cemented by old age. The protest will be against Obama but no specific issue is mentioned; it is protest for protest's sake. If protest was once a popular and visible means for performing exile cubanía, the show seems to suggest that these public acts of discontent are exhausted. Organized protest on issues related to Cuba is a genre of public performance so worn in Miami that it has become almost devoid of meaning—a part of the sonic and visual landscape of the city. Because of this exhaustion, part of the humor is that the listener does not need to know *why* they are protesting in order to get the joke. It is business as usual. The humor of the Old Cuban Woman's presence culminates in her proud admission that she is armed with a rocket that will liberate Cuba. The aggressiveness of the rhetoric, juxtaposed with a voice that conjures up an image of an old, frail Cuban woman, creates an incongruous, comic image. Public protest as a performance, so often aligned with images of youthful idealism, is absent, and thus adds another level of comic incongruity.

But the image of the rocket also summons memories of a not-so-distant past when terrorist tactics were used in Miami to intimidate those who publically deviated from a hardline stance on Cuba. This use of choteo to narrate the Old Cuban Woman and her symbolism of Miami's more violent past stands in stark contrast to the explosions, attacks, and threats that were attributed to exile paramilitary groups and occurred in both Miami and Cuba, creating an atmosphere of tension, intimidation, and fear, which was often reinforced in Miami's radio culture throughout the 1970s and 1980s.[47] In 2009, violent tactics once prevalent in past decades were transformed into an opportunity for diversión.

Reinforcing this depiction of the Old Cuban Woman is her simultaneous concern about the protest, rocket, and a woman who sat next to her on the bus trip to the last demonstration who cannot control her "farts." With that complaint, we begin to hear another sound effect in the studio of a loud bus engine idling in the parking lot of the León Medical Center. Now dependent on a bus from an elderly care center to transport them to the protests that have played such a large role in their civic lives, the show's audience is left with a narrative that attempts to represent hardline exile politics with a slew of images and sounds connecting those politics with infirmity, frailty, and abjection. This focus on the body, particularly on what Mikhail Bakhtin calls the "lower stratum," is a vital aspect of choteo.[48] Like Alvarez Guedes's use of choteo to "shit" on the American melting pot paradigm, this parodic representation of Radio Mambí functions as a critique from the more moderate segments of Cuban Miami. Reducing these protestors and the politics they represent to their material and frail bodies drains the inflammatory rhetoric of all its seriousness and thereby challenges the hegemony of the exile ideology.

Can an argument be made against the Radio Maní parody as political critique? Is it simply poking fun at the advanced age of an older generation that continues to protest, perhaps heroically, against the Castros? A close listen suggests that the political critique embedded within Radio

Maní is sharp, historically informed, and attentive to contemporary tensions within Cuban Miami. As Armando takes calls from an audience that expresses either mock solidarity or incites him into a performance of rage, we begin to hear a pattern in these exchanges that indicates a popular understanding of the limits, excesses, and even hypocrisy of exile politics:

CALLER: Armando, I have fifteen boats for the liberation of Cuba.
ARMANDO: Ok, good.
CALLER: Hey Armando, apart from that, are you coming to pick it up? You know, the *perico* (cocaine)?
ARMANDO: [*whispers*] We'll talk about that later.
CREW: [*Erupts into laugher.*]

As parody, Radio Maní exposed how "institutional forms are revealed to be masks," how "power and status are shown to be acts," and how none of these is above laughter and its critical potential.[49] Through the above satirical exchange, the show shines a light on the accusations of corruption that have plagued individuals and organizations championing the exile cause. As a principal gateway to and from Latin America, Miami has always served as an important access point for the drug trade, but was especially active in the 1970s and 1980s. Though many benefitted from the Miami drug trade, it is believed that some militant exile groups financed their operations through narcotics trafficking. At the very least, the exchange above suggests that the rumor would be familiar to listeners.[50]

Much like protest, corruption has been a feature of life in Miami for decades. Ann Louise Bardach puts it rather bluntly: "The depth and breadth of corruption in Miami is unparalleled in the U.S."[51] Enrique Santos and Joe Ferrero are well aware of the relationship between the righteous rhetoric of public figures in the exile community and the headlines exposing corruption in Miami's newspapers. The choteo-inflected approach to representing Radio Mambí creates what Robert Hariman in his discussion of parody calls a "public consciousness . . . by exposing the limitations of dominant discourses: it counters idealization, mythic enchantment, and other forms of hegemony."[52] The show repackages the narrative of fighting for Cuba's liberation—for decades the dominant, idealized discourse rarely questioned on Miami's radio waves—to show that the lofty message of freedom was at times sustained by activities that were legally and morally suspect. By articulating this on the air, Radio Maní effectively puts this well-known history on the table for *public* engagement through a recognizable, popular form of relation among Cubans, choteo.

Shortly afterward a second caller utters a simple phrase to stoke the fire of Armando's self-righteous pride in his exile cubanía:

> CALLER: *¿Asere, que bolá?* (Hey, what's up man?)
> ARMANDO: Don't talk to me in that language. I'm not a *balsero* (rafter). Don't disrespect me. The Cubans of today got it all wrong. [*Getting louder.*] I'm one of the old guard Cubans who respects his race and his language!

While this moment inspires laughter from the crew in the broader context of the segment's satire, this exchange also reveals the tension between older members of the exile generation and more recent arrivals. As Susan Eckstein explains, "Exiles looked down on the New Cubans, as they had on Marielitos. . . . Exiles considered the most recent newcomers, like Marielitos, guilty by association."[53] The "association" Eckstein pinpoints is with the Castro government, or put more colloquially, *comunismo* as a general way of characterizing all that is wrong with Cuba. The phrase "Asere, que bolá?" has a long history on the island, but widespread colloquial usage of the term exploded after the Revolution.[54] Armando connects the phrase with the term *balsero*—a shorthand for anyone who has arrived from the island since the rafter crisis in 1994. In this skit, these words quickly distinguish the speaker as a more recent arrival and thus subject to what the show's talent and producers see as the prejudices of many members of Armando's generation, who regard them as less Cuban when measured by the standard of exile cubanía.

If, as mentioned previously, choteo acts a form of parodic irreverence that "counters idealization," the ideal in question here is an exile cubanía that positions itself as *the* acceptable narrative of Cubanness outside of Cuba. The caller's three-word performance of the phrase "¿Asere, que bolá?" demonstrates the evolution of cubanía on the island and in the diasporic context. You can *hear* the difference between Armando's tone and inflection and the caller's voice and choice of words. On the show, the only way to differentiate callers and characters by way of age or generation is by listening closely to accents and word choice. If the Old Cuban Woman's voice is performed as frail and her body is described as being in a state of deterioration, it is possible to read her character as a critique of the hardline politics she so aggressively advocates. When the caller chimes in with "Asere, que bolá?" in a heavier, faster Cuban accent, he immediately distinguishes himself from Armando's exile cubanía and the "old guard" of Cubans he represents while simultaneously triggering the expected angry reaction from Armando. Through the performative logic of diversión, Santos and Ferrero were able to capture the generational nuances of Cuban Miami and the tensions they produce, in part, as I have argued throughout, because of their status as US-born Cuban Americans who "learned" the narrative of exile cubanía but who grew up in a rapidly changing Cuban Miami.

Though seldom discussed publicly, generational tensions make themselves known in passing comments about the more recent arrivals "as different" from earlier generations, tainted by their upbringing under the Revolution. On the *Enrique y Joe Show*, this issue received public attention through the more palatable narrative logic of diversión. Later in 2009 on his own show, Santos would create a forum to directly engage these fault lines in the context of another high-profile moment in the history of Cuban Miami—Colombian rockstar Juanes and his concert in Havana.

Rockstar en La Habana

In September of 2009, Juanes announced plans to perform in Havana as part of his "Peace without Borders" concert series.[55] A follow-up to the first installment on the Colombian-Venezuelan border, the event was intended to transcend the political and engage the Cuban people culturally through a musical "message of love and peace." Hardline exiles were not feeling the love, though, and took to the airwaves to voice their discontent.[56] In the weeks before the concert, a Cuban exile group called Vigilia Mambisa organized a provocative protest that made news around the world. At the height of its spectacular excess, protesters burned t-shirts and even rented a steamroller to destroy Juanes merchandise.[57] Across the street from the protests, Juanes fans, many of them Cubans who had arrived after 1994, held a much larger counterdemonstration in support of the singer and his decision to perform on the island. At one point protesters from each side came to blows.[58]

The episode of the *Enrique Santos Show* produced after Juanes's concert aimed to dissect the details of the event, complete with special guests, interviews, and the perspectives of the crew.[59] Though the tone of the show was heavier than usual, people were clearly drawn to the periodic laughs that it promised in a Miami convulsed by protests, counter-demonstrations, and constant news coverage. It was also a place to hear a different perspective on the event, one that defied the discourse on other talk radio programs. Santos himself believed that the concert was a step in the right direction, despite voicing skepticism in the days before the performance. He declared that under the circumstances, Juanes did the best he could. The perceived political nature of the songs Juanes performed combined with his exclamation of "¡Cuba Libre!" twice at the end of the concert helped change Santos's opinion along with that of many other Cuban Americans in South Florida.[60]

In an attempt to gauge his audience's opinion, Santos took a poll of his listeners and asked them to weigh in on the concert. The result, although by no means scientific, was that most callers featured on the air said that it was positive, with only a few saying Juanes did not go far enough to condemn the regime. It is impossible to know how many callers to the station were actually in favor or against the concert because of call screening, but the fact that those who supported the concert were overwhelmingly featured on the air suggests that the show was well aware of its audience base and how best to appeal to them. With few media outlets for those less conservative on the topic of Cuba to express their views, the *Enrique Santos Show* provided its audience with "a sense of power and participation" in order to "achieve greater levels of listener loyalty."[61] To get a more thorough explanation of the negative perspective on the concert, or perhaps to construct a forum for lively debate, Santos invited Miguel Saavedra of Vigilia Mambisa, who was the leader of the anti-Juanes demonstration, to express his views in detail on the show.[62] After Saavedra's many allusions to communist conspiracies, Santos lost his temper and accused him of making the exile community look ridiculous on a national level by fighting other Cuban "brothers" on the streets of Little Havana.[63] To provide a contrasting view to Saavedra, Santos put more recent arrivals on the air to react to the Juanes concert.

According to Bendixen polling data, the largest difference in opinion regarding the concert was between post-Mariel Cubans and those who left Cuba before 1980.[64] The following conversation between Zenaida, a more recent arrival, and Saavedra is particularly revealing of not only the markedly different political positions of these two individuals, but also of the segments of Cuban Miami they both claim to represent in their use of "we" in their exchanges. Close listening to the conversation enables an understanding of the broader tensions and shifts at work in an increasingly diverse Cuban Miami.

ZENAIDA: Miguel Saavedra, as you know from the conversation you just had, is crazy. He is frustrated. Like they say in Cuba, Saavedra, your carnival is over. Things can't always be the way you want them to be. This is a new generation with new ideas. If people don't think the way you do, then they are communist. *You* are the communist who wants to divide people. Everything has to be your way. When Los Van Van came, you did the same, screaming "prostitute" and a bunch of other insults at people. You are an instigator.

SAAVEDRA: Let me ask you something, *muchacha* (girl). What do you do for Cuba? What do you do for Cuba? All you do is criticize the patriots. Is that all you do? You have the system stuck in your head, what the communists taught you. That's why you criticize the patriots. Join the cause! Help out! [*Talking at the same time, inaudible.*]

ZENAIDA: What happened to you people [exiles] happened.

SANTOS: Speak one at a time so we can understand what you're saying.

ZENAIDA: What I'm saying is that he suffered what he suffered, and everyone knows it. We sympathize greatly with everything that has happened but we have to start slowly . . .

SANTOS: But excuse me Zenaida, he suffered what he suffered? No. He continues to suffer, I believe, he and millions of Cubans.

ZENAIDA: Juanes is more of a hero and patriot than Saavedra who stands in front of Versailles [*iconic Cuban restaurant in Little Havana*] to instigate and break CDs. Fidel is laughing in Cuba! We have to start like Juanes, little by little. It's not a war. It's not about picking

up and going over there. What happened at the Bay of Pigs and all
that stuff is in the past. All those things are in the past. This is a new era.

SAAVEDRA: No! We are still wounded by those events!

This exchange between Zenaida and Saavedra demonstrates quite
powerfully the clash of viewpoints along generational lines. As a modern
day *dialoguera*, Zenaida shares much with Cubans who have advocated
for a more diplomatic, direct approach to US-Cuba relations. She is not
fearful at all at the prospect of sharing her political opinions. In fact,
she implies that she is in the majority and that Saavedra's exile ideology
is on the way out. Her use of "we" along with her declaration of a "new
era" seem to encapsulate her generational cohort—more recent arrivals
who are much more acquainted with contemporary life in Cuba. While
she does acknowledge the pain suffered by the earlier exiles, she adopts
a more casual "what happened, happened" attitude. Other callers echo
it, though perhaps more sensitively. Tony explains that he sympathizes
with the older exiles and *los fusilados* (those who were executed by the
Castro government) but he stresses the importance of "one Cuban family" across generations and the need to move forward.

On the other side, Saavedra is unwilling to even entertain Zenaida's
perspective. His reaction reveals a condescending attitude toward more
recent arrivals. First, he addresses Zenaida, an adult, as *muchacha*, a
"girl." While this is evidence of Saavedra's *machista* posture, it is also an
indication of how he feels about newer arrivals and younger Cubans who
advocate a more moderate approach on issues related to Cuba. For him,
they are naïve—hence the infantilizing *muchacha*. Saavedra's comments
reinforce this point. He explains that Zenaida has been raised under the
dictatorship and still has "what the communists taught [her] . . . stuck
in [her] head." This is a common criticism levied against the newer generation of Cubans in Miami.[65] The idea is that they came of age under
Cuban socialism and do not have the perspective necessary to see what
needs to be done. They are also criticized for their apathy in relation
to political activism once in the United States, as indicated by Saavedra's rhetorical question, "What do you do for Cuba?" His anger only
increases when Zenaida firmly locates the failures and strategy of events
like the Bay of Pigs in the past, while her apparent dismissal of them
contributes to Saavedra's conviction that these Cubans are different and

not interested in truly bringing about change in Cuba despite his genera-tion's less than sterling track record in that regard.

Although members of Zenaida's generation are more intimately ac-quainted with life in Cuba by virtue of their more recent migration, older exiles often see this as more of a liability than an advantage. Work-ing under this logic, these more recent arrivals could not possibly have something useful or nuanced to contribute to the discussion unless they are aligning themselves with the exile ideology. This would seem to invert a paradigm within Latina/o studies about authenticity in which those with the closest or more recent ties with Latin America are more "culturally authentic" and thus privileged to speak on matters of lati-nidad or in this case, cubanía. Older generational cohorts of the exile community wave the banner of "authenticity" in order to "police insider status" and its privileges within the "ethnic formation," excluding newer arrivals and the US-born with divergent opinions.[66]

Santos, acting as a generational intermediary, finds problems with both of their positions. He is quick to offer a defense when callers like Zenaida and Tony fail to comprehend that they are asking Saavedra and those sympathetic to his viewpoints to abandon the political, so-cial, and affective dimensions of their exile cubanía. His interruption of Zenaida's passing acknowledgement of the "sufferings" of the exile generation is an example how US-born Cuban Americans can invoke the emotional and political stances of their parents in regard to Cuba.[67] When other callers insult Saavedra and his politics, Santos defends the pain and suffering felt by the exile community. But he doesn't let Saa-vedra off the hook either. Smashing compact discs and burning images in effigy, Santos argues, makes the Cuban community in Miami look foolish. Perhaps more telling is Santos's frustration with Saavedra and others who refuse to engage in dialogue with those who think differ-ently. Santos, though socialized within the exile ideology, has enough critical distance from Cuba to listen to other opinions, to change his mind, and to be critical of exile cubanía.

Although this short conversation in the middle of a four-hour show that airs daily is a drop in the bucket of Miami's media landscape, it strikes me as a powerful moment when the tensions and attitudes that mark how older exiles and more recent arrivals see each other bubbled to the surface in popular culture. For strategic economic reasons, shows looking to entertain and attract the largest audience possible stay away from what divides Cubans and focus on topics that appeal broadly. These tensions are nonetheless part of the public conversation and arise around discussions about reforming the Cuban Adjustment Act of 1966, which grants residency to Cubans after one year in the United States. Critics believe more recent arrivals are violating the spirit of the act by returning to the island frequently, suggesting that reasons for leaving were more economic than political. As a result, figures like ex-Congressman David Rivera and Representative Carlos Curbelo have called for tighter restrictions on travel to the island for those who have received residency under the Cuban Adjustment Act.[68] But this public conversation arises only in the staid language of politicians; it does not capture the underlying tensions and subtext. The alleged "abuse" of the Cuban Adjustment Act is perceived, on a more urgent level, as an "abuse" of the category of exile and its political and cultural dimensions. The debate over "exile" status—permanent residency and a path to citizenship—addressed in the Miami media is an example of how some members of the exile generation and the politicians that cater to them are trying to police the boundaries of "authentic" exile cubanía as the community evolves.

In 2009, the *Enrique Santos Show* represented the messiness of navigating the generational shifts in South Florida on the part of US-born Cuban Americans. On the one hand, there is a deep connection to exile cubanía as a structure of feeling, which is marked by deep antipathy toward the Castro regime, pride in one's Cuban identity, and the sense of Cuba as a paradise lost. On the other hand, the excesses and staleness of exile politics, as the show's parodies and polls indicate, suggest exhaustion and a desire for a new way ahead. Of course, this paints too neat a picture. Luckily, the complexity of popular culture as a site where multiple and contradictory perspectives are voiced points out just how muddy the waters are. Throughout the show in 2009, I noted a number of moments when post-1994 Cubans in Miami like Zenaida were the butt of countless jokes. Santos and his crew would refer to them as *balseros* and connect them with the perceived "low-class" *chusmería* that has marked the working class city of Hialeah in the popular Cuban imagination.[69] These representations, popular among the US-born, can be partially attributed to attitudes passed down by older family members and the way the cubanía of these newer arrivals fails to measure up to the exile narrative of what constitutes "authentic" Cubanness. These newer arrivals are not Cuban *like us*. Difference, a powerful engine of all comedy, helps to fuel these representations.[70]

Santos's performance also says something about the "radio world" that he created on the air—the "boundaries and rules centered around the persona of the presenter."[71] Throughout all the jokes and parodies launched against Cubans across the generational spectrum, he did stress the need to hear everyone's opinion. That might seem like a utopic desire, but it is also a question of audience and Univision's desire to appeal to those uninterested in the usual Cuban radio fare. Jokes about more recent arrivals might be enjoyed by the US-born who tuned in while the openness and embrace of more moderate political perspective on Cuba might have endeared him to an audience of post-1994 arrivals searching for an alternative narrative of Cuban Miami and more willing to question hardline politics. This ludic promiscuity, combined with the recognizable repertoire of diversión, made the show viable across generations and demographics.

The Future of Cuban Miami on the Air?

In Miami's more turbulent past, support for an event like Juanes's performance on the air might have been met with demonstrations, denunciations from prominent politicians and media figures, and perhaps even violence against the offending station. Things had changed considerably by the late 2000s. Multinational media conglomerates have moved in and are more interested in the bottom line than local politics. For Univision, supporting Santos and Ferrero was a calculated move attuned to the shifting demographics and opinions of South Florida's Cuban and Latina/o community. Though I focused primarily on Cuba-related material, prank calls and humorous commentary on life in Miami helped to broaden the appeal of the *Enrique y Joe Show* and the *Enrique Santos Show* among young Spanish speakers across ethnic groups. But this does not mean that Univision abandoned the hardline Cuban exile audience. Univision also owns Radio Mambí, the station targeted by the *Enrique y Joe Show* in their "Radio Maní" parody. By exercising a two-pronged strategy that emphasizes a pan-Latina/o narrative *and* bundles Latina/os and the Cuban community into particular "segments" that can be more easily packaged for the advertising industry when appropriate, Univision can extract profit without having to be overly concerned about alienating parts of the Cuban community. Cubans unhappy about the changes in Miami can find solidarity and solace on Radio Mambí where Univision's corporate machine has advertisers and content lined up waiting for them—though the amount of this content wanes with each passing year.

While Univision's role in Miami's radio culture must be taken into account in order to understand the business interests that shape and make broadcasts possible, the crew's satirical presentation of Armando as a corrupt, Cuba-obsessed relic increasingly out of touch with younger generations begs for a moment of reflection on the cultural history of the airwaves in a community that has always taken its radio consumption seriously. The heavily disseminated narrative of Cuban Americans as obsessed with and intransigent on Cuba—best captured by Miguel Saavedra and Armando's proclamation of "Cuba first, Cuba after, Cuba always" as his sign off line on Radio Maní—no longer holds true for a significant portion of Miami's Cuban community. Poll data, academic studies, and the quotidian texture provided by popular sites of consumption like radio demonstrate how current and future generations continue to reconfigure what it means to be Cuban off the island. The performances on their shows suggest that more moderate political opinions do *not* mean a diminished sense of cubanía. To the contrary, the mastery of an identifiable comic mode like choteo and the broader performance practice of diversión display an investment on behalf of Enrique Santos and Joe Ferrero in performing their cubanía without the constraints of a set political orthodoxy. It is through this enactment of diversión that they were able to articulate and represent a greater range of narratives of cubanía on the air.

In 2010, Univision rebranded 98.3FM by changing its name from "La Kalle" to Mix 98.3. This meant a change from what was primarily a "tropical" format featuring salsa, merengue, and reggaeton to programming that "reflects Miami's diversity by playing a wide range of today's top Spanish and English hits" in an attempt to attract a larger, younger audience composed of bilingual listeners interested in contemporary music in both languages.[72] The station's pronounced aim to "reflect" Miami's diversity has meant rallying programming around a pan-Latina/o marketing strategy that acknowledges ethnic difference in a manner that celebrates the varied aspects of an imagined, singular Latina/o culture. Enrique Santos himself reflected this transformation. He lost a great deal of weight and began dressing in suits—more Ryan Seacrest than Howard Stern. He came out as a gay man and has been active in championing LGBTQ rights. As the face of Univision Radio nationally, he embraced the pan-ethnic label of Latina/o in keeping with the company's marketing strategy.[73]

Santos's once steady engagement with news on Cuba-related issues on and off the island declined because of its limited appeal to a broader Latina/o audience.[74] With syndication in major cities across the United States, the show became more topical. It also focused on integrating content with Univision's other media platforms, namely television and Internet programming.[75] Humor was still incorporated but rarely recognizable as Cuban diversión—no doubt in response to its potential illegibility to listeners outside of Miami. In addition to Univision-owned broadcasts, other stations once committed exclusively to Cuba-related talk have had to tweak formats and juggle talent in order to remain relevant and profitable in the face of changing audience demographics. While there are still some holdouts like La Poderosa 670AM, which continue to align programming with the exile ideology of old, most stations are moving toward a pan-Latina/o programming strategy in which the topic of Cuba is far less prominent. Even stations like Radio Mambí have toned down their rhetoric with the hiring of "more moderate pan-Hispanic voices" consistent with Univision's broader marketing strategy.[76] Narratives of cubanía on the air are moving away from the rhetoric of the exile ideology because of more moderate attitudes among the majority of the Cuban diaspora, and also because it simply does not make good business sense to stay with it in an increasingly diverse Miami.

But change is rarely as cut and dry as the wholesale implementation of a new marketing strategy by a multinational corporate conglomerate. In the next chapter, I examine an annual festival promoted as a celebration of pre-Castro Cuba called "Cuba Nostalgia." At this event, different segments of the diaspora intersect, in varying degrees, to reveal a variety of relationships to the concept of nostalgia—a feeling deeply embedded in academic and popular discourse on Cuban America. I seek to recalibrate how we think about the work of nostalgia while detailing what a spectacle dedicated to celebrating prerevolutionary Cuba can tell us about the present and future of Miami.

3

Nostalgic Pleasures

As you walk into Cuba Nostalgia, any number of things might catch your attention. The smell of roast pork in the air might make your stomach rumble. People dancing to upbeat, Beny Moré standards could catch your eye. Or perhaps you'll want to take a more panoramic approach to the spectacle before you. If so, you'd quickly notice the various "set" pieces meant to transport you to pre-Castro Cuba in both a pastoral and urban sense: massive plastic palm trees alongside a *bohío* (hut) sit under the bright fluorescent lights while a bodega (brought to you by Goya Foods) features ads and images of Havana before the Revolution. But don't get too lost in your thoughts as you take it all in or you could be swept up into one of the scheduled carnival parades that snake around the sprawling event space, featuring drums, dancing, and of course, someone playing *una corneta china* (Chinese suona). Welcome to Cuba Nostalgia, an event "for those who remember the island's glamorous times—and for those who never experienced them"—enjoy.

Cuba Nostalgia takes place over three days at the Tamiami Fair Grounds Expo Center, which boasts 100,000 square feet of usable space.[1] Held annually since 1999, the event draws around 30,000 visitors and features booths selling items like guayaberas, jewelry, music, and domino tables. Other vendors sell more specialized Cuban memorabilia like yearbooks, old Cuban currency, social registries, magazines popular before 1959, and other pre-revolutionary knick-knacks. Music constantly plays, echoing throughout the cavernous space. People run into each other and exchange hugs and kisses. Alcohol flows freely from bars sponsored by Bacardí. Comedy sketches are performed every couple of hours by a hired troupe.

Visually, Cuba Nostalgia is like a Hollywood set of the Cuban exile imagination. Attendees can take pictures "along the Malecón" with the Morro Castle behind them and in the comfort of central air-conditioning.

Visitors can even stop at an exhibit memorializing the grand El Encanto department store of Havana complete with mannequins dressed in styles popular in the 1950s and display cases featuring photos and other historical documents that chronicle the store's glamorous past. Staff include elderly men and women who actually worked at the store (complete with name tags) and who eagerly share their encyclopedic knowledge of its history and departments.[2] Framing all these attractions and events are the many corporate sponsors eager to promote their goods and services with eye-catching advertisements and giveaways framed by the symbolic visual economy of nostalgia. Far from submitting to a passive experience, attendees are encouraged to take part in a number of planned activities: hourly parades that thread around the fairgrounds, dance contests, domino tournaments, bingo, and interactions with performers and local celebrities contracted to entertain them. The signs and activities deployed to conjure up the shared narrative of nostalgia facilitate a ludic sociability that one can sense as people converse, laugh, dance, sing, and eat with one another.

Figure 3.1. Cuba Nostalgia 2014, photo-op near the "Malecón." Author's photo.

As the last chapter indicated, popular culture in Cuban Miami has been shifting away from the exile community to target later generations of US-born Cuban Americans and perhaps most dramatically, a consistent stream of new arrivals from the island since 1994. Yet Cuba Nostalgia continues year after year drawing tens of thousands of people. What can the large-scale staging of an event that celebrates a prerevolutionary Cuba that fewer and fewer can actively remember tell us about the present and future of Cuban Miami? What can it tell us about nostalgia as a public feeling in the history of the Cuban diaspora? I will argue that Cuba Nostalgia represents a *nostalgia for nostalgia*—a longing for a feeling that could once be used to rally a fractured exile community. The significant demographic shifts combined with the fading away of the original exile community make Cuba Nostalgia a kind of memorial in motion, dedicated to that nostalgia and framed within a logic of diversión meant to encourage reproduction, circulation, and consumption in ways deeply connected to the US-born and arrivals since the 1990s.

This chapter also seeks to recalibrate the concept of nostalgia, which enjoys a kind of keyword status in Cuban American studies. Raúl Rubio describes nostalgia as a "community trait, a shared experience, a national form, a common theme, or a patriotic emotion" while Ricardo Ortíz refers to the exile community's relationship to nostalgia as an "addiction."[3] Dalia Kandiyoti calls nostalgia a "corollary of the exile identity that much of Cuban America has claimed" and observes that it is "ubiquitous in Cuban American literature."[4] While these authors and others have examined nostalgia within the realm of the literary, significantly less attention has been paid to how Cuban nostalgia is enacted publicly in the sphere of popular culture.[5] To shift into the public life of nostalgia is to move away from the psychological, subjective experience of nostalgia as exile lament, or as an ambivalent sentiment, bittersweet, a sigh with a smile. While I am sympathetic to these readings, I am more interested in how thinking about nostalgia as a form of diversión illuminates its political, economic, and even generational work through the production of a ludic sociability within the diaspora. Contextualizing and reading nostalgia not just as a look backward at an idealized past but as a product of the needs of the present and future illuminates its role in negotiating understandings of the Cuban diaspora through time. To do this work, I begin by examining nostalgia historically and most importantly, by tracing how events in the tumultuous 1990s set the stage for understanding its work in twenty-first-century Cuban Miami.

Nostalgia, 1990s Style

Nostalgia served as a kind of affective glue to bind the Cuban community as it established itself in Miami in the early years of exile. But nostalgia for what, exactly? The openness of this question and the abstractness of nostalgia offer the key to understanding its adhesive potential. A community of nostalgics, composed of people all nostalgic in their own ways, created a broad notion of belonging that could soften internal differences along political and socioeconomic lines. Themes like lost childhoods as well as memories of a sensory experience of Cuba in sights, smells, and sounds could be easily invoked to appeal broadly. In the first two waves of flight, 1959–1962 and 1965–1973, there was a great uniformity across race, but pronounced differences along the lines of class and politics. Through nostalgia, the man who was a laborer in Cuba suddenly had something in common with the man who was once a corporate executive. The capaciousness of pre-Castro nostalgia was ideal for creating "a common past, symbolically linking them to the land they left behind, while defining their new Exile identity."[6] It did not matter that this common past did not exist. The generous boundaries of nostalgia assured room for everyone.

Though there have always been profound political differences, nostalgia was a way to find common ground. If the communal fantasy of belonging is founded upon an idealized narrative of Cuba before the Revolution betrayed by Castro, then the baseline for a platform is established. The clean, uncomplicated narrative lines that arose from such a sturdy, unquestionable claim intersected to inform the affective and political logic of exile cubanía. This narrative of nostalgia became an accepted way to think and *feel* about Cuba and exile politics. Nostalgia as feeling and as a basis for politics also made for a dangerous, highly charged combination. As Svetlana Boym observes, "Unreflected nostalgia breeds monsters."[7] Those who espoused a more moderate line on Castro or US-Cuba relations became targets for scorn in the local media. Physical violence was also used to silence those who deviated from the conservative politics of certain factions of the exile community. All perpetrated in the name of that lofty, lost Cuba. If you believed in this idealized narrative of pre-Castro Cuba, there was no room for nuanced dialogue. Cuba under Castro could never compare with the nostalgic fantasy.

Interest in this nostalgic fantasy of pre-Castro Cuba exploded in the 1990s when the island came rushing back into the foreground of public consciousness with the fall of the Berlin Wall in 1989.[8] The consensus was that the government would surely fall without the backing of the Soviet Union, its richest and most powerful ally. But with every year that passed, excitement ebbed as the likelihood of regime change decreased. What did not change in those years as people went from jubilation to frustration about the prospects of Castro's fall was diversión as a dependable constant in the form of nostalgia. Though certainly present in popular culture before the 1990s, nostalgia for la Cuba de ayer became an obsession, permeating a massive variety of cultural forms and popular discourses inside and outside Cuban Miami during the 1990s.

Artists and business people capitalized on this heightened interest in the nostalgia narrative. Musicians like Gloria Estefan, Willy Chirino, Albita Rodríguez, and Marisela Verena recorded albums that captured that feeling of "old Cuba" stylistically, lyrically, and aesthetically.[9] Pepe Horta's Café Nostalgia, which opened in 1994, quickly became the most popular club for Cuban music in Miami. While people danced to music popular before the Revolution, black and white film clips of famous artists from the island's "golden age" played on screens in the venue.[10] Others clubs in Miami soon jumped on the bandwagon with variations on a theme called "Havana Nights," which promised patrons a journey back to Cuba before the Revolution.[11] Shops selling prerevolutionary memorabilia in the form of yearbooks, cigar boxes, and other ephemera began to pop up.[12] Flags hung from necks and rearview mirrors. T-shirts with phrases like "100% Cuban" could be purchased at shops with names like Sentir Cubano (Feel Cuban).[13] In 1998, this nostalgia was transformed into a family-friendly board game called "¡Ay mi Cuba!," which featured trivia questions about the island before 1959.[14] There was even demand on the black market for songbirds smuggled from Cuba called *tomeguines*.[15]

Unsurprisingly, these forms of nostalgia were attractive to the older generation of Cuban exiles who had long viewed their past through a

Figure 3.2. Advertisement for "¡Ay mi Cuba!" boardgame in *Generation ñ* magazine, October 1998. Courtesy of the Cuban Heritage Collection, University of Miami.

nostalgic lens. But the nostalgia obsession of the 1990s went beyond the expected demographic of exiles who arrived in the United States as adults or even as representatives of the "1.5 generation."[16] The children of exiles reared in the United States also found this nostalgia narrative alluring, even as they grew up with the broader influences of US popular culture.[17] Bill Teck branded these Cubans "Generation ñ." His magazine of the same name had a circulation of 13,000 in 1997 and featured content that combined a celebration of la Cuba de ayer of their parents' genera-tion and the bilingual popular culture of Miami.[18] An excerpt from the inaugural issue of the magazine captures its target audience perfectly: "If you grew up with Santa Barbara and Captain Kirk, Alvarez Guedes and K.C. and the Sunshine Band. If you know all the words to 'Abusadora' and 'Stairway to Heaven' . . . then you're us. . . . You're Generation ñ."[19]

Nostalgia for this increasingly idealized Cuba also gained traction outside of Miami. The 1990s were a time when mainstream America was succumbing, once again, to what Gustavo Pérez Firmat has called "the Havana habit"—a phrase he uses to describe Cuba's long history in the cultural imagination of the United States.[20] The nostalgia for

Figure 3.3. *Generation ñ* magazine cover, May 1998. Courtesy of Cuban Heritage Collection, University of Miami.

prerevolutionary Cuba in the mainstream is stitched together with sensory signifiers meant to conjure up the island: the smell of cigar smoke, the taste of rum, lively nightclubs, Desi Arnaz's accent, and the beat of a conga drum. This is a Cuba in the service of the United States, a Cuba that once catered to every libidinal need of the American consumer. Though that Cuba is long gone, it is memorialized in cities big and small across the United States. Think of the overpriced plantains at the chic Cuban restaurant in your town, the neatly pressed guayaberas, sepia prints of cigars, conga drums retrofitted to act as seats at the bar, and other "tropicalizing" signifiers meant to transport the customer to the Cuba portrayed in popular posters and scenes from *Godfather II*.[21] These restaurants catering to non-Cubans took off in the 1990s. [22] Cuban American literature also received a great deal of national attention. Oscar Hijuelos's *Mambo Kings Play Songs of Love* won the Pulitzer Prize for fiction in 1990. Cristina García's novel *Dreaming in Cuban* (1992) was a finalist for the National Book Award. And of course, who could forget the worldwide Buena Vista Social Club phenomenon? Composed of mostly elderly Afro-Cuban musicians based in Cuba and covering pre-revolutionary classics, their album was a huge international success, winning a Grammy in 1998. If you stepped into a Starbucks in the late 1990s, you likely had your coffee with a side of the Cuba nostalgia craze served up in the vocal stylings of Buena Vista's Compay Segundo and Ibrahim Ferrer.[23]

How does one make sense of this 1990s nostalgia boom? It is impossible to narrow it down to any one cause. Instead, a number of factors arose simultaneously to produce this celebratory and highly visible nostalgia for pre-Castro Cuba. After the fall of the Berlin Wall, Cubans turned their attention to the island and fantasized about the possibilities of a Castro-free Cuba. Perhaps Cuba could be restored to its former, nostalgically construed condition? While many had given up on the idea of return and any hope of "restoring" Cuba, circumstances certainly injected hope and put nostalgia front and center. At the very least, the possible fall of Castro brought about a reflective period as exiles ruminated on their relationship to the island and their own sense of cubanía at a moment when change seemed inevitable. There is also a generational argument to be made. The original exiles were advancing in age during the 1990s. Looking back at the past through the rosy lens of nostalgia, already a common practice in Cuban Miami, would have intensified. For members of "Generation ñ" who were in their twenties and thirties, the desire to make sense of their ethnic identities would have had been heightened by the possibility of change in the air. Adding to that familiar meditation on one's origins was the rise of multiculturalism, diversity, and the "celebration" of ethnic identity in the 1990s in broader public conversations. Finally, as Marilyn Halter explains, "marketing ethnicity escalated in the 1990s."[24] Immigrants and their descendants were encouraged to engage their ethnicity through the workings of the market.

But there is another development in the 1990s that certainly affected the perception of Cuba's past and present within the exile community. Instead of regime change in Cuba, the island experienced what Castro euphemistically called "The Special Period in Peacetime." The severe economic crisis caused by the loss of Soviet support was exacerbated further by the passage of the Cuban Democracy Act (1992) and Helms-Burton Act (1996), which tightened sanctions on Cuba. The logic of adding pressure instead of engaging the Cuban government in dialogue, championed by the Cuban American National Foundation, won the day. Scarcity of food and the government's growing inability to meet the basic needs of the population heightened feelings of desperation on the island and set the stage for another mass exodus. In August of 1994, Cubans in Havana took to the streets to voice their discontent in what would be called *el maleconazo* after the setting of the uprising near Havana's seafront promenade, El Malecón. With such mass protests virtually unheard of in revolutionary Cuba, Castro once again used migration as an escape valve to release the pressure building on the island. In the summer of 1994 alone, over 30,000 Cubans left the island in improvised rafts for the United States.[25]

The stories these new arrivals brought with them combined with news about the deterioration of life on the island likely added to nostalgia's appeal. The contrast between Cuba's present and the fantasy of its past articulated in the nostalgia narrative was too great. Most knew this was the case for years but the new arrivals helped to put that truth front and center. With this reality becoming increasingly clear and Castro's hold on power remaining stable despite the trials of the Special Period, nostalgia became even more attractive. The Cuba of the exile community would be confined to memory and Miami. In addition to the contrast provided by stories of material scarcity and crumbling infrastructure on the island, these new arrivals were living examples of a cultural shift on the island. They spoke differently, using words that had never made it to Miami. They were more interested in Los Van Van than Beny Moré. Though exiles portrayed these balseros as heroes in order to to condemn Castro yet again, there was also suspicion. What had taken them so long to leave? Born and raised under communism, was there "hope" for them in the United States? Similar questions came up during Mariel but the 1980 boatlift was different; it was a large-scale migration contained within a span of months.[26] The new migration agreements between the United States and Cuba meant that those who arrived in 1994 were just the beginning of a wave of migration that continues today and has completely changed the demographics of the Cuban diaspora. This meant that the "Cuba" created in Miami was changing as well. Cuba Nostalgia, then, is as much about Miami as it is about Cuba.

Cuba Nostalgia, for Whom?

In her book on nostalgia, Svetlana Boym points out that "the stronger the loss, the more it is overcompensated with commemorations, the starker the distance from the past, and the more it is prone to idealizations."[27] Cuba Nostalgia is a response to the loss of Cuba, but also more pressingly, to the loss of a Miami shifting demographically as Cubans continue to arrive and the mortality of the exile generation becomes more apparent with each passing year. Cuba Nostalgia, then, reflects a nostalgia *for* nostalgia—a place where a unified narrative of exile cubanía, though it never truly existed, could be imagined through the revisionist logic of nostalgia. It is a celebration memorializing a feeling that could once be counted upon to mobilize Cuban Miami. It is no coincidence, then, that momentum for Cuba Nostalgia began to increase in the mid-1990s when Cuban Miami was going through its largest demographic transition. Mireya Navarro captures the feeling in Miami in an article she penned for the *New York Times* in 1999, the year Cuba Nostalgia began: "With each batch of immigrants who win the annual visa lottery, each of the smuggled boatloads of Cubans that land almost daily in South Florida, Cuban Miami becomes less cohesive, encompassing a people who differ in social class, race, generation and politics, who increasingly come from different worlds."[28] The dramatic rise in emigration since the 1994 balsero crisis has changed the Cuban character of Miami. The presence of new arrivals is a constant reminder that both Cuba *and* Miami have changed. Cuba Nostalgia is a kind of retreat from these changes, and from the reality of an exile community facing a mortality that becomes more insistent year after year.

The drive to enjoy and disseminate a narrative of unified exile cubanía helps to explain the explicit attempt to remove politics from the yearly stagings of Cuba Nostalgia. No arguments, no tendentious exchanges, just diversión. Political discussion is discouraged while participation in the event's ludic elements—dancing, drinking, making purchases—is encouraged. In this way, attendees are "active rather than passive," with the event "encouraging involvement rather than contemplation."[29] In my interview with co-founder of Cuba Nostalgia, Leslie Pantín, he explained that he has ground rules for those with booths or exhibits: "No Che, No Fidel, and No Raúl."[30] Instead, the pleasures of group identification and the roominess of nostalgia as a concept are retained in a manner that allows for a seemingly endless number of projections yet remains constant as an all unifying, amorphous feeling. Cristina Beltrán's reading of Rousseau on the festival highlights the importance of "feeling" at an event like Cuba Nostalgia: "The festival, or public spectacle, represents an ideal context for citizens to identify passionately with one another and experience themselves as a *moi commun* (a common self). A form of civic engagement capable of transcending self-interest, the Rousserian festival represents a merging of the body politic that feels both mystical and intimate."[31] This intimacy is strengthened by the communal pleasures Cuba Nostalgia cultivates in tandem with the glaring lack of explicit political speech. The "consecratory" function of the event standardizes the general outlines of the story of pre-Castro Cuba by mobilizing nostalgia to produce consensus.[32]

Among whom is intimacy being fostered? It is difficult to discern the precise demographic makeup of the attendees. Tickets are sold with the simple distinction of adult and child. But conversations I have had with organizers along with my own observations as an attendee of five iterations of Cuba Nostalgia seem to confirm certain demographic trends. Every year, the event is held over three days to coincide with Cuban independence on May 20. The attendees on Friday are mostly from the older generation of exiles who are now retired.[33] Saturday brings a crowd composed of older people and US-born Cuban Americans. On Sunday, the event turns into a family affair, with three to four generations walking together around the convention center anchored by the labored pace of the oldest family member. Children and grandchildren shepherd wheelchair-bound grandparents to the assorted attractions and vendors.

Those who are *not* in attendance say as much about Cuba Nostalgia, contemporary Cuban Miami and this narrative of nostalgia, as those who are present. Two groups notably in the minority are post-1994 arrivals and Afro-Cubans. For post-1994 arrivals, the event presents a narrative of Cuba with which they have little acquaintance. Growing up in Cuba, they learned a history of the pre-Castro years that is the direct antithesis of what is staged at the event. While members of this generation are certainly nostalgic for Cuba in their own way, they lack an investment in this particular narrative and the nostalgia-informed politics of the exile community.[34] But as I will show later in my discussion of the consumption of nostalgia, these more recent arrivals play a vital role in the nostalgia industry in South Florida.

The small number of Afro-Cubans in attendance is a product of the reality of Cuban migration and the question of relevance as outlined above. Afro-Cubans did not begin coming to the United States in significant numbers until the Mariel boatlift of 1980.[35] More have arrived since the balsero crisis of the 1990s but they are still a minority in the diaspora. In addition to the generational tensions these Afro-Cubans might feel, they must also contend with the potential discomfort of being the only black faces in a sea of nostalgic white. This would be further compounded by the ways in which Afro-Cuban culture is generally represented at Cuba Nostalgia. For the most part, Afro-Cubans are present in the form of contracted music and dance acts. Exhibitions and vendors sell and disseminate images of Afro-Cubans as pleasure-producing bodies in the service of the white gaze. Cartoonish depictions of voluptuous Afro-Cuban women and the celebration of musicians like Celia Cruz and Beny Moré constitute the symbolic economy of Afro-Cubanness at the event. This is consistent with Alejandro de la Fuente's description of how blackness has been represented historically in Cuba: "It was only in the area of 'culture' that Afro-Cubans' contribution to national life was acknowledged, researched, and publicized in mainstream intellectual circles as part of national folklore."[36]

Cuba Nostalgia commemorates pre-Castro Cuba but it is more urgently a response to the quickening pace of generational turnover in

Miami—those *not* in attendance. This does not mean, though, that this older generation and organizers will stand idly by as these changes take hold. Part of celebrating memory is keeping it alive, passing it along, reproducing it. Cuba Nostalgia carries on a long tradition of reproducing nostalgia in younger generations through the logic of diversión so that this feeling, this mode of being Cuban diasporically, will live on after the exile generation is gone.

Reproducing Nostalgia

Cuba Nostalgia's stated intention to be an event "for those who remember the island's glamorous times—and for those who never experienced them" suggests that it is in large part geared toward those without any memories of the island, particularly US-born or US-reared Cuban Americans.[37] For this segment of the diaspora, the imperative is to enjoy this narrative of nostalgia but also to internalize it as their own history. Pantín speaks directly to the importance of education and the constructed nature of the nostalgia narrative in comments to the *New York Times*: "'For every year you live in Miami you hear 20,000 stories about Cuba. . . . Fifty years later, you get confused,' he admitted. 'Sometimes when I'm talking about Havana, I can't remember if it's my own memory, if somebody told me about it, or if I looked it up in a book of photos . . . The history we show no longer exists in Cuba . . . How else will younger people learn about this era?'"[38] Pantín is indirectly addressing the pleasures and problems of collective memory. Nostalgia is fine, but how to make sense of all the stories one hears? The answer lies in providing a roadmap of historical monuments, facts, and images that facilitate a major goal of the event: teaching the "younger people," the US-born, to feel Cuban through nostalgia. If the event is a reflection of literally thousands of narratives of pre-Castro Cuba, it is given structure and coherence by nostalgia even as it becomes more abstracted from the complicated historical reality. Paradoxically, this "codified nostalgia" becomes more *real* because of the staging of the narrative—the Hollywood set of the Cuban exile imagination—and also a willingness to believe.[39] This narrative of history helps produce the very nostalgia the event celebrates. If you believe in this narrative of Cuba before Castro, how can you not be nostalgic? This configuration of Cuba produces a tautology: pre-Castro Cuba was a "glamorous" utopic space; here is a staging of this utopia so you can see that the narrative presented is *true*. In a Butlerian sense, Cuba Nostalgia and its performative logic illustrate "the power of discourse to produce effects through reiteration."[40] It is a power exercised not through punishment but through diversión and the seductive pleasures it promises.

The cultivation of nostalgia among the 1.5 generation and US-born Cuban Americans has a long history in the exile context. María Cristina García traces organizations dedicated to disseminating the history and heritage of Cuba to the 1960s and 1970s. She explains that the US-born were of particular concern to parents who still had intentions of returning to Cuba. Lessons offered by *escuelitas cubanas* (little Cuban schools) and other forms of cultural programming were meant to serve as a buffer to Americanization and the loss of Cuban culture.[41] While exiles disagreed along contentious political lines, concern for the cubanía of children reared in exile was something parents could agree on.[42]

Educational initiatives were born out of what Ricardo Ortíz has theorized as an anxiety about "'disappearance' as diasporic communities confront both the demands of assimilation and accommodation into surrounding host cultures, as well as the irresistible demands of a future that increasingly diminishes hope for the kind of redemptive return to the homeland that in part constitutes such communities as 'diasporic' in the first place."[43] But when Cuba Nostalgia began in 1999, the vast majority had abandoned the notion of return. Instead, the disappearance that Cuba Nostalgia addresses is generational, most urgently in the form of death. Who will keep this Cuba alive? Or perhaps implicitly, who will keep the memory of the exile generation alive as each year accelerates their passing? Following Ortíz, the response to the anxiety about disappearance "compels an almost obsessive insistence on reproduction, always simultaneously social, cultural, and sexual, as the most effective means for self-perpetuation, and therefore nondisappearance, into that future."[44] Like the event itself, the desire to reproduce nostalgic memories goes beyond pre-Castro Cuba. If the relationship between nostalgia and education in the 1960s and 1970s was primarily inspired by the hope of return and resistance to the "melting pot," today it is largely a means of navigating not only the loss of Cuba, but the loss of the generation of people for whom that nostalgic narrative of pre-Castro Cuba was foundational.

Rebecca Schneider's comments regarding the role of education in the heritage industry are instructive here: "Without YOU in a starring role history might not take place—might not have taken place. . . . Here the historical investment is not as much about preservation as it is about regeneration."[45] While Schneider's use of the word *regeneration* has the sense of "creating again," the word can also suggest a way to think about the desire to produce a generation in the image and likeness of the exile community via a nostalgic education. This regeneration has historically occurred through formal and informal means. In both cases, diversión has been on the front lines playing a key role in the reproduction of nostalgia and exile cubanía.

The intersections of reproduction and education have often occured through cultural programming that has privileged having fun—enjoying your cubanía. This strategy of diversión as a means to educate comes from a playbook created in the 1960s. In 1964, an event called Añorada Cuba debuted in Miami and featured musical performances, dances, and dramatic works. It was immensely popular and was staged at least eight times that year. Tellingly, a majority of the performers in the shows were the children of exiles. These performances of cubanía were meant to pass along cultural memory with the explicitly stated goal of preparing the next generation to lead in a future Cuba liberated from the Castro government: "Today they [children of adult exiles] are united singing and dancing, to attenuate our collective pain. Tomorrow the Fatherland will require their presence on the difficult paths of sacrifice to realize liberty. We trust in them."[46] Younger children could enjoy magazines like *Revista Cabalgata Infantil* (1972), which billed itself as "The Magazine of Cuban Childhood" and offered Cuban history in digestible tidbits alongside pictures of children exhibiting their artistic talents.

An organization called Cruzada Educativa Cubana, founded in 1962, launched radio programming for children, which included "exciting and morally resonant stories about the island's history, republican political traditions, and customs," along with "a weekly patriotic coloring contest" and "sports and games of an educational character."[47] Like Añorada Cuba, the group insisted on the role of the children in the future of the island: "To save the fatherland where we were born, we need the warmth of your hands, the tenderness of your gaze, and the fire of your heart."[48] Older children and teenagers got involved with social clubs and leisure activities that framed the experiences offered through a dose of exile cubanía.[49]

Encoded within the language of groups like Cruzada Educativa Cubana and events like Añorada Cuba was a highly gendered discourse about the roles of men, women, and the family. These traditional roles were the foundation necessary for restoring a Cuba without Castro. With changes in the status of women under the Cuban Revolution and the threat of American youth culture knocking on the door in the 1960s and 1970s, the leaders of Cruzada clung even tighter to these traditional gender roles, and their nostalgia for them, as the way forward.[50] The results could be seen in the cultural production of children, ushering what Ortíz theorizes as the "social, cultural, and sexual dimensions" of reproduction. The image reproduced in Figure 3.4 is from a children's political cartooning contest held in 1962 and sponsored by *Zig-Zag Libre*, a popular *periodiquito* (tabloid newspaper) that circulated for decades in Cuban exile communities. The cartoon, drawn by a twelve-year-old boy from Miami, won first prize.[51] In it, he copies a style of representing the Cuban government in the 1960s, which was popular among cartoonists in *Zig-Zag Libre*. Cuban leadership is reduced to the level of animals, with the Soviet pig ordering "Forward March" in a parody of Russian (*marchuski*) as Che Guevara, Fidel, and Raúl Castro obediently follow. Of particular interest is the drawing of Raúl Castro, whose effeminate, upturned nose is consistent with the animal he represents—*un pato*, a duck in English. In Cuban vernacular expression, *pato* translates idiomatically to "faggot," which alludes to a rumor about Raúl Castro's sexuality that has served as fodder for humorists hostile to the Revolution since its earliest days. This drawing highlights the way that reproducing exile cubanía is not just through an education based upon history and fun facts but also through the pleasure of an ideologically charged *diversión* that condemns the Revolution while asserting the normative boundaries of that cubanía, the "traditional" family unit and heteronormativity. To be Cuban *outside* of Cuba is to fulfill the traditional narratives of gender and sexuality that have been compromised by a Revolution seen as a political and moral failure.

From the beginning, Cuba Nostalgia has been committed to this long tradition of inculcating nostalgia as a form of *diversión* founded upon

Figure 3.4. Kid's drawing contest, *Zig-Zag Libre*, February 16, 1963. Courtesy of Cuban Heritage Collection, University of Miami.

the family unit as its organizing logic. The poster by US-born Cuban American artist David "Lebo" Le Batard, which helped promote the first Cuba Nostalgia in 1999 (Figure 3.5),[52] shows how the event has been imagined and marketed as an experience for the entire family. The event's educational function, symbolized by the old Cuban man, the repository of memory and physical link to the "real" Cuba, happily recounts the nostalgic narrative forever on his mind to a young, smiling grandson.[53] The grounds are filled with signs filled with trivia about pre-Castro Cuba. Older exiles staffing educational exhibits are eager to share their knowledge.

In addition to its marketing logic, formal institutions present at the event continue the work of education through nostalgia. Herencia Cultural Cubana, founded in 1994, is a prime example of an organization

Figure 3.5. Promotional poster for the first Cuban Nostalgia in 1999, by David "Lebo" Le Batard. Courtesy of Cuban Heritage Collection, University of Miami.

deeply committed to inculcating pride and nostalgia for la Cuba de ayer in the younger generations. Their flagship publication, *Herencia*, published three times a year, features articles filled with declarations about the need to recuperate "our history" and to pass it on to future generations, which are consistent with the group's broader mission statement: "Cuban Cultural Heritage is a nonprofit organization committed to educate as well as preserve and promote the cultural values and accomplishments of the Cuban nation for present and future generations."[54] Unsurprisingly, the "accomplishments of the Cuban nation" ceased in 1959. Throughout the pages of their magazine, articles eulogize important figures who died in exile, offer short biographies of Cuban cultural heroes, and include in-depth stories on topics as specific as the uniforms and medals worn in the war of independence fought against Spain. The only time Cuba's present is mentioned is in relation to the topic of regime change and the island's future. Articles like "Reconstructing Post-Castro Cuba" provide, in detail, specific economic and political policies that could restore Cuba to the organization's vision of its ideal past.

While at Cuba Nostalgia in 2011, I engaged some of its members in a discussion about their mission. When I told them that I was a professor, one man's eyes immediately lit up. He recommended a book published by Manuel Márquez-Sterling, a member of the organization, called *Cuba 1952–1959: The True Story of Castro's Rise to Power* (2009), emphasizing its utility as a teaching tool. Sure enough, the promotional material for the book explains, "Written in English, this volume is addressed to those Cuban-Americans who have difficulties in handling the Spanish language." In another article written specifically for the organization's dominant Spanish-language membership, the author asks readers to give a subscription to *Herencia* as a gift to their children and grandchildren, "our Cuban Americans."[55]

The multiple meanings of *herencia* combined with the organization's urging that the magazine be given as a gift perfectly encapsulate the relationship between reproduction and nostalgia. *Herencia* can be translated as either "heritage" or "inheritance." The staging of Cuba Nostalgia, its emphasis on education and on sharing this "glorious Cuban past," involves a kind of "passing on" of an inheritance, of a Cuba younger generations never knew. Explicit in the act of "passing down" a narrative of origins and cultural tradition is the sense of pride one should feel. This is *your* inheritance, a way to feel Cuban that feeds the fantasy and pleasure of belonging, which in turn encourages further dissemination. If in the early years of exile, inculcating "feeling" into younger generations was in large part a project about encouraging identification with the "beauty of noble suffering" for a free Cuba, the project of Herencia Cultural Cubana is to place the source of pride in pre-Castro Cuba so that it may be preserved when the exile generation is gone.[56]

Alongside the more formal institutions charged with passing down a nostalgic inheritance, the event also encourages those more informal, widely practiced moments of the transmission of nostalgia that occur on a quotidian basis. One of the most popular attractions at Cuba Nostalgia is a 1953 street map of Havana blown up to a size that makes walking around the city possible (Figure 3.6). For the nostalgic, this reencounter with the city is almost preferable to the real thing, given the discrepancy between the Havana of their memories and the city as it stands today. The map serves as a schematic, usefully bereft of details beyond street names and intersections. The nostalgic attendee crafts the map's legend to produce a topography of memory that is never self-explanatory. It is in these moments when a nostalgic visitor explains the meaning of places on the map to the uninitiated that the informal "transmission of affect" can be most powerful.[57] In my many visits to Cuba Nostalgia, people-watching at this map and listening in on conversations have been my favorite parts. The map always generates the desired generational diversity imagined in the posters and included in the event's appeal to those "who never experienced" the island's "glamorous times." Its size and central location in the convention center make it an intersection and a meeting place. For those who grew up in Havana, charting old homes, routes, and haunts is a must. Children attracted to the change of scenery beneath their feet run across Havana at full speed. Those with few or no memories of the city search for geographic markers of a cultural identity.

Older people point out the location of family homes and trace routes to schools with the end of their canes. Those confined to wheelchairs yell directions to younger family members pushing them across the map. This is a moment when nostalgia and the *right* to feel Cuban can be most poignantly passed down. Here, affect is transmitted not only through

Figure 3.6. Crowd gathered on the 1953 street map of Havana at Cuba Nostalgia 2014. Author's photo.

stories but by traversing the partial Havana underfoot and translating the map into meaning through simple gestures like looking down together at an old street and holding on to elderly family members as they steady themselves. The pleasure produced in that generational cohesion is what the event hopes to cultivate in order to sustain itself as a business venture *and* as a space for mediating the twilight of the exile generation.

While Cuba Nostalgia certainly mobilizes formal and informal modes to present an at times didactic narrative of prerevolutionary Cuba as lost ideal, I do not mean to suggest that it functions as some kind of sci-fi brainwashing experience creating an army of hardline US-born Cuban Americans taking part in paramilitary training exercises in the Everglades. It is important to note the different ways these Cuban Americans relate to this narrative—or not. Over the years I have seen many teens with their iPhone earbuds on, lagging behind their parents. I have come across a number of men and women on an outing with their elderly relatives, their facial expressions seeming to say "estoy cumpliendo" (I'm doing my duty). And then there are all those who have no idea Cuba Nostalgia even exists. Finally, the earnestness of this nostalgia also makes it ripe for parody—as illustrated in the previous chapter on the *Enrique y Joe* radio show.

Yet this event is a quintessential example of how generations of the Cuban diaspora born or reared in the United States have been socialized to think and talk about Cuba. This socialization, in turn, affects interpersonal relations in a more heterogeneous Cuban Miami. The term *balsero*, once used to refer to those who came during the 1994 rafter crisis, has come to mean any recent arrival from Cuba, whatever the means of transport. Like *marielito* before that, *balsero* functions as a derogatory term meant to characterize newer arrivals as being lower class, *chusma*—lacking education and manners. For those who speak English predominantly, *ref* or *refee*, short for *refugee*, is a synonym for *balsero*, which enjoys popular usage among US-born Cuban Americans as a discriminatory shorthand.[58] These terms are used to describe a person lacking the "refinement" of "civilized" life in Miami, whose Cubanness cannot be placed within the idealized narrative present at events like Cuba Nostalgia. For generations of children born or reared by exiles in South Florida, cubanía is couched in the narrative celebrated at Cuba Nostalgia. The Cuba these newer arrivals represent through their language, style of dress, and cultural interests does not and cannot match up with the fantasy narrative that the children of exiles have been raised on. This, in turn, feeds the condescension and strengthens the obstacles to dialogue that have marked Cuban Miami at different stages throughout its history. Finally, the nostalgic framing of pre-Castro Cuba has been the narrative of power, of authority in the Miami in which the US-born generation has been reared. Aligning with this nostalgia can be a means to identify with the larger narrative of Cuban power in South Florida. In sum, the way in which one enjoys Cuba speaks directly to politics and necessarily affects how different segments of the diaspora relate to one another.

Consuming Nostalgia

Cuba Nostalgia also continues the tradition of aligning the pleasures of nostalgia with consumption. Connecting the strong feelings of nostalgia and cubanía with products and services has a long history in the exile community. Local businesses would often choose names that connected their products with that idealized Cuba of yesterday. Owners of restaurants, theaters, and radio stations named their holdings after their island equivalent no doubt as a reflection of their own nostalgia but also because of its effectiveness in attracting customers looking for a familiar point of reference. Public performances and displays of nostalgia helped to make the unfamiliar space of exile legible. Diasporic communities were filled with commercial and public displays of cue after Cuban cue, covering the landscape with what Patricia Price calls an "affective patina" charged with memory, politics, and feeling.[59] Consumption became a way to form community attachments and perform cubanía, yes, but increasingly an exile cubanía marked by accepted cultural characteristics and the political act of performing one's Cubanness *outside* of Cuba.

A 1973 advertisement for Café Bustelo represents a common marketing strategy framed by nostalgia and aimed at exiles (Figure 3.7). The unpictured speaker uses the word *añoro* (yearn) to describe his or her feelings for Cuba and the pleasures of its carnival seasons. The advertisement conveys nostalgia as a sensory experience: the call of the peanut vendor, the look of a curvy, fair-skinned woman leading the parade, and of course, the taste of coffee. With a simple "buchito de café" (sip of coffee), the consumer will experience "inspiración" (inspiration) through a kind of sensory recall that promises the joy of carnival that is unsurprisingly devoid of Afro-Cuban participation, as the drawing suggests. With Café Bustelo, you can enjoy an experience of nostalgia as sweet as Cuban coffee.

Complementing this marketing strategy is a fascinating defense of nostalgia as a kind of right, a brash assertion of exile cubanía. The very end of the stanza, in a bold font and lettering larger than the rest of the words above it, states: "Y así, digan lo que digan, en mi casa toman Bustelo!" (And so, whatever they say, in my house we drink Bustelo!). The advertisement's speaking voice, meant to function as the communal voice of the exile community, is likely not suffering from persecution for choosing one caffeinated beverage over the other. But in linking Café Bustelo with nostalgia and Cuban identity in 1973, the advertisement implicitly references tensions in Miami between Cubans and other groups concerned with the dramatic influx from the island and their perceived lack of interest in assimilating. This advertisement represents

Figure 3.7. Advertisement for Café Bustelo in the satirical newspaper *Chispa*, 1973. Courtesy of Cuban Heritage Collection, University of Miami.

a trend in the public performance of nostalgia particularly emphasized through consumption. Yes, consuming nostalgia is a means to commune with the sweetness of an idealized, lost homeland. But like the reproductive project encoded within education, consumption also speaks directly to the needs of the present. In the 1960s and 1970s, it indexed the ways in which nostalgia could articulate a political identity resistant to calls for assimilation.

Nostalgia as a means to assert a Cuban identity in the face of a suspicious white majority is no longer necessary in Miami, but Cuba Nostalgia makes it clear that it is still a profitable business strategy. Part of the event's organizing logic is that nostalgia is for sale, and the transaction begins with the price of admission. Exhibitors and sponsors eager to associate their products and services with the nostalgia theme pay for the cost of running the event—renting the space, staff, and other operational costs. Pantín and his associates make their money at the door. With an average of 30,000 visitors a year and an admission fee of $12 for adults and $6 for children, there is certainly money to be made. But not everyone has been happy with this business model.

In a scathing editorial published in the *Miami Herald* in 2006, Cuban American writer Ana Menéndez railed against the commodification of nostalgia, calling it "shameless shilling" and declaring, "Out of the sorrow of leaving family and lives behind, they rebuilt what they could in a new place, struggled through the bad and lean years only to arrive near the end of their story and find it written as a farce."[60] Her critique of the event focused primarily on those sponsors looking to make a buck off of the older attendees. Health plans and clinics target the elderly population at Cuba Nostalgia by using advertising that connects their businesses with the symbolic economy of la Cuba de ayer.[61] Big-name sponsors like Bacardí, Chevrolet, Goya, and Coca-Cola can be seen everywhere attracting attendees with colorful displays, samples, raffles, and product giveaways. It is easy to understand Menéndez's indignation. The presence of sponsors is overwhelming—yet unsurprising given Pantín's extensive business connections. Every exhibit dedicated to showcasing Cuba's "glamorous" past features a conspicuous marker of sponsorship. Employees for the various businesses canvas the grounds with clipboards and cards, exchanging cheap shopping bags for names and phone numbers to be used to target new customers later. While nostalgia as a means to sell products is not new, the intense concentration of sponsorship partnerships can make the event feel predatory.

The dearth of public criticism, aside from the Menéndez piece, steady attendance figures, and favorable coverage from the local press suggest that the public has little problem with this business model. Sponsors returning year after year are clearly getting a return on their investment. How to explain this? For starters, the presence of sponsors at Cuba-themed festivals, pageants, and fairs can be traced to the 1960s. More significantly, the marketing and capitalist flavor is right in line with the narrative of nostalgia being disseminated. The nostalgic fantasy of Cuba before Castro is without question permeated by a capitalist ethos. Consumerism and consumption affirm the classic narrative of a pre-Castro Cuba that was "open for business." But most critically, the Cuba presented at the event is meant to serve as a stark contrast to the Cuba of today, to show what the island could have been if the Revolution did not succeed. At Cuba Nostalgia, Cuba before Castro was a time of plenty, not scarcity, of consumption not *resolviendo*, more "golden age" than Special Period. Consumption in all its forms goes hand in hand with the narrative of nostalgia presented.

The event's promotional materials reveal that this is certainly not a hidden agenda; the connection between consumption and cubanía is made explicit. The May 16, 2013, edition of Spanish-language daily *El Nuevo Herald* included a twenty-page circular paid for by event organizers complete with full-page advertisements, a map of the convention center, details about scheduled activities, and a list of vendors. On the very first page is a numbered list titled "Cómo 'aplantarse' en 15 minutos" (How to Become Cuban in 15 Minutes). Unsurprisingly, each one of the fifteen attributes listed is connected to a sponsor or booth at the fair. To learn about Cuban coffee, visit Café Pilón's exhibit. If food is your preferred route to cubanization, see the exhibit brought to you by Goya Foods. Cubanía as mode of being and belonging is only a transaction away.[62]

Cuba Nostalgia also makes it possible to purchase and own a piece of that "glorious" past constantly emphasized in its pedagogy and visual aesthetic. Cuba Nostalgia was born, in large part, out of what Pantín recognized as a business opportunity in Cuba-themed items and memorabilia. As he explains, in the late 1990s and early 2000s, Cuba Nostalgia had a large share of the market for Cuba-related merchandise: t-shirts with phrases like "Made in America from Cuban Parts," flags, and perhaps most striking, prerevolutionary memorabilia. At the same time that Cuba Nostalgia was taking shape, Gerardo Chávez was busy launching cubacollectibles.com, the most comprehensive online marketplace for

Cuban memorabilia. Like Cuba Nostalgia, Chávez started his business in 1999. But competition quickly picked up to meet demand, as storefronts and websites sprouted up in hopes of gaining a foothold in the nostalgia industry.[63] Pantín and Chávez explained to me that competition has increased substantially over the last decade and has affected profit margins as a result. Over the years, I have noticed this change manifest itself in the reduced number of vendors selling memorabilia. Chávez, who makes his living by selling memorabilia through his website, averaged 300–400 orders a month before the economic downturn in the late 2000s. When I interviewed him in 2013, increased competition and the economic slowdown had brought that number down to 150–200 orders a month from what he estimates is his 95 percent Cuban client base.[64]

At Cuba Nostalgia and online, these businesses sell all kinds of prerevolutionary memorabilia: money, yearbooks, casino chips, old magazines, movies, original photographs of celebrities, cinema lobby cards, posters, postcards, high society social registries, maps, tobacco labels—the list goes on and on. Here, the narrative of nostalgia is curated carefully, rendered three dimensional as one feels the smoothness of an old coin in hand and smells prerevolutionary newspapers in various states of deterioration. The picture in Figure 3.8 captures the kind of feeling an encounter with the memorabilia can offer. A couple holding hands examines the school pins and old Cuban currency for sale on the table. Like so many other people I have seen interact with memorabilia, they would go on to point out familiar objects and place them in the context of their personal histories, often registering astonishment at the items available. People exclaim, "¡Mira lo que encontré!" (Look what I found!) as they make their way through the varied inventory and come to terms with the juxtaposition of their present moment in the cavernous space of the convention center with the historical intimacy that the object offers. The number of businesses in Miami and online are a testament to the market for objects that inspire nostalgic feeling despite the uptick in competition—a feeling that is not cheap.[65] Brushed with the patina of history, yearbooks from old high schools sell for around $200, high society registries for $150, old issues of *Bohemia* magazine for $75, school pins for around $100, and casino chips ranging from $50 to $2,500. Arjun Appadurai's understanding of consumption clarifies the work of the nostalgia market: "The fact is that consumption is now the social practice

Figure 3.8. Couple at memorabilia booth, Cuba Nostalgia 2014. Author's photo.

through which persons are drawn into the work of fantasy. It is the daily practice through which nostalgia and fantasy are drawn together in a world of commodified objects." [66] By purchasing memorabilia and experiencing the pleasures of object possession, consumers can construct and reinforce their own narrative about Cuba and its place in their lives.

The popularity of these objects and the high prices paid for them can be attributed to the way they represent the story of exile in a powerful and necessarily partial manner. As Susan Stewart theorizes in her work on the souvenir, the object "must remain impoverished and partial so that it can be supplemented by a narrative discourse that articulates the play of desire."[67] Like the map covering the convention floor, these objects function as points of departure for the pleasures of narrative construction and the fantasy of Cuba before Castro articulated at Cuba Nostalgia and in quotidian life. Through the supplementary narrative, the object becomes a symbol of what was, what could have been. The high prices for these objects then, are not very surprising. How much for an "authentic" representation of that life? The object represents then the worth of that life, the worth of the narrative created. This connection is furthered by the status of the object as being in a sense, misplaced. That is, these objects have what Igor Kopytoff calls a "cultural biography" representing a specific time and place.[68] Memorabilia can represent the same out-of-placeness exiles may have felt upon arrival in the United States and perhaps continue to feel. In essence then, these objects are survivors. In the narrative of exiles, these objects are not so different from them. Like them, these surviving objects are here in Miami. The pleasures of consumption and narrative reconstruction felt upon purchasing this kind of memorabilia is equaled, if not surpassed, by the pleasure of saving the object that represents not only the Cuba of the past but survival under Castro and the passage to Miami. In this sense, the object becomes a reflection of the exile subject: "Removed from its context, the exotic souvenir is a sign of survival—not its own survival, but the survival of the possessor outside his or her own context of familiarity."[69] It is the object's power not only to supplement and stand in metonymically for the narrative of the nostalgic, but also to reflect a life in exile, outside of its "original" context, that fuels the market for the memorabilia businesses at the event, in the virtual marketplace online, and in storefronts across Little Havana. The ability to exercise purchasing power, in turn, says something about "making it" in America.

This narrative of survival is particularly strong for those objects that represent childhood such as school yearbooks and pins—some of the most expensive and highly trafficked items. Within the exile community, there is a strong belief that in addition to liberty and property, childhood was also "stolen" along with the innocence that comes with it. The connection between the welfare of children and cubanía seen in the mission of organizations such as Herencia Cultural Cubana certainly resonates here. At Cuba Nostalgia, that youth can be recuperated not only by experiencing the spectacle of Cuba as it is staged, but also by acquiring objects that give a piece of that childhood back. How much would you pay to take back your childhood? The business model seems to be that if Castro's brand of socialism "stole" that childhood, US capitalism gives you the opportunity to buy it back, partially, in the form of a supplement.

The appeal of memorabilia goes beyond those with memories of life in Cuba before Castro. Younger generations, those who have spent most if not all of their lives in the United States, make up a large market for the nostalgia industry. The industry and the event itself offer opportunities for performances of "symbolic ethnicity" where nostalgia can be asserted with little or no commitment to, in the Cuban case, political organizations or participation in organized events like anti-Castro rallies.[70] But it would be misleading to simply liken US-born Cuban Americans to those who might identify with, say, European heritages many generations removed. Cuba is often present in the lives of US-born Cuban Americans in a way that it is not for those who might identify, for example, with an Irish heritage that extends back to the nineteenth century. What I want to stress is that for this US-born generation, Cuban identity can often manifest itself through cultural traditions, language, and as the event demonstrates, consuming cubanía as a "leisure activity," as a form of diversión.[71]

How better to supplement this symbolic cubanía than by owning a piece of that past? Jean Baudrillard's theorization of the fascination with antiques provides a model for thinking about the attraction to memorabilia for this generation: "It is our fraught curiosity about our origins that prompts us to place such mythological objects, the signs of a previous order of things, alongside the functional objects which, for their part, are the signs of our current mastery. For we want to be entirely self-made and descended from someone: to succeed the Father yet simultaneously to proceed from the Father."[72] Cuba Nostalgia suggests that these origins are available through an education in the symbolic economy of pre-Castro Cuba and the consumption of memorabilia. With older members of the exile community disappearing, affection for these objects also represents a means to connect with the generation responsible for disseminating a nostalgia narrative that was foundational in the construction of Cuban Miami—ageing parents and grandparents.

I can certainly speak to the allure of these objects. I remember walking around Cuba Nostalgia during my first visit and being completely absorbed in the business side of it all—advertisements everywhere, people selling their art and knickknacks, the constant reminder to buy, buy, buy. But then I came upon an object that productively distorted the clear "argument" I had been constructing in my mind about consumerism and Cuba Nostalgia. It was a 1943 map of Alacranes, Cuba, the small town from which my mother and maternal grandparents hail. Yellowed and creased, the map provided a new way for me to imagine all the stories I had heard growing up about the town. True, I couldn't make much sense of the names of all the neighborhoods or land parcels. But in that moment, Alacranes became tactile, immediate, in a way that it had never been before. I was deeply moved and frankly, delighted. This moment allowed me to see not beyond the endless advertisements, but alongside them, the circle of people cheering an old couple dancing with joyous abandon. It allowed me to hear, more clearly, the pleasure in the trash talking occurring at the domino tables provided by a local health plan business. I bought the map.

But where did that map come from? The question looming in the background of this discussion of the nostalgia industry is *where* does the supply of memorabilia come from to meet demand? Cuba, obviously, but when and from whom? Answering these questions gets at the future-oriented stakes of nostalgia. The flow of capital and goods to Cuba is often thought of as a one-way affair, in a manner that is consistent with narratives of first- and third-world development. Remittances and increasingly larger goods make their way to the island to help family and friends and to assist in the development of small businesses under Raúl Castro's economic reforms.[73] This logic privileges the United States as the site from which capital flows and Cuba as the receiver. The nostalgia industry complicates this narrative by revealing the transnational contours of this business.

Business owners and collectors active in the trade of prerevolutionary memorabilia explained to me that most of the items they secure today come from Cubans who leave the island with the intent of making money in the nostalgia market. When Chávez started cubacollectibles.com, 90 percent of the memorabilia he bought came from dealings with inheritors—people living in the United States looking to sell objects left behind by deceased family members. During our conversation in 2013, he told me he was fielding about ten calls a week from people interested in selling to him under these circumstances. But despite this volume of calls, Chávez estimates that in recent years over half of the objects he acquires have come to him from recent arrivals from Cuba looking to profit in the memorabilia market—a significant shift that reflects the increased movement and fluidity between the island and the diaspora.[74]

Chávez's favorite anecdote about his business captures the visibility of cubacollectibles.com on the island. The story concerns a man who recently arrived from Cuba and said that he knew him. Not having returned to Cuba since he left in the 1960s, Chávez asked the man how that could possibly be true. This man explained that he knew Chávez through his website. Much to Chávez's delight, Cubans on the island interested in cashing in on the nostalgia industry will research cubacollectibles.com before leaving in order to determine which objects are most valuable. When they arrive in the United States with these objects in tow, they contact Chávez to gauge his interest and negotiate a price.

This transnational nostalgia market highlights both the increasing fluidity of US-Cuba migration and exchange and, most interestingly in the context of this chapter, how the pleasures of nostalgia serve as a site for understanding a changing Cuban diaspora. If Cuban memorabilia can provide a means for communing with an imagined past and asserting a cultural identity in the rapidly changing present, the act of selling these objects by newer arrivals constitutes a desire to invest in a Cuban future. Selling Cuba's past to invest in a present and future in Miami *and* on the island is a reality that is often lost in the fetishistic desire for these objects. This fetishism occludes the means by which the objects arrived here or perhaps more directly, *why they are here*. The reality is that the supply of Cuba-related objects is increasingly coming from the island *today*. They are here because of the need to generate funds to sustain the transition to life in the diaspora, to send back to people still living on the island, or both. Furthermore, many of the people working the event are more recent arrivals from Cuba: representatives from insurance companies, women handing out samples of Cuban coffee, the food servers and maintenance crew. For these more recent arrivals, nostalgia is a business and very much a future-oriented project.

Nostalgia, Diversión, Mortality

Without question, the business with the largest presence at Cuba Nostalgia is health and end-of-life care. Companies offering Medicare supplement plans, elderly day care, clinical services, and even cemetery plots are everywhere represented by a *guayabera*-clad army, many of them recent arrivals from Cuba, outfitted with clipboards and smiles used to reel in new customers. These businesses understand that they have a captive, target audience, and they do their best to appeal to them.

Many attendees are elderly and at a point in their lives when health is a central issue.[75] But these businesses also actively court younger generations as well—the children of elderly attendees who help family members navigate the complex world of for-profit health and end-of-life care.

Consistent with the event's greater marketing logic, these businesses are the most likely to align their services with warm, depoliticized symbols meant to produce the pleasure of nostalgic feeling. Preferred Plan Partners sponsors the Malecón sea wall exhibit, while León Medical Centers advertises its services from a *bohío* (hut) with a sign that reads "mantengamos nuestras tradiciones" (we maintain our traditions). Other healthcare companies advertise services with exhibitions on famous Cuban patriots and celebrated sports figures. The effectiveness of this strategy lies in the evolution of the work of nostalgia. For Cubans arriving in major diasporic centers in the 1960s and 1970s, the nostalgia that shaped the landscape of Miami—in names of businesses, radio shows, performance venues—helped make the unfamiliar exilic space legible. It makes sense then, that in the face of mortality, where meaning can so often fail, a Cuba so perfectly "remembered" through the alchemy of nostalgia can once again be called upon to orient the disoriented. Nostalgia, then, assists in negotiating mortality, the more symbolic "passing" of the exile community, and the reality of a Cuban Miami dominated by US-born Cuban Americans and more recent arrivals with little investment in the political elements of the exile narrative. This partly explains the emphasis on education at Cuba Nostalgia and among groups like Herencia Cultural Cubana with their campaign to reach US-born Cuban Americans. If nostalgia was once a component taught to prepare children for their eventual *return* to the island, it is now equally important to teach them as one prepares for *departure*.

Perhaps it is unsurprising, then, to see Memorial Plan Cemeteries at Cuba Nostalgia year after year. In an exhibition space with cheap carpeting and cardboard columns meant to lend an air of gravitas to the presentation, Memorial Plan Cemeteries provides free consultations to people looking to make their "final arrangements." In keeping with the theme of Cuba Nostalgia, Memorial Plan offers a number of options for those looking to "cubanize" their final memorial and resting place: a wreath of flowers in the colors and shape of the Cuban flag, headstones emblazoned with the Cuban national seal, a flag draped over the coffin, and so on. Watching people line up to speak to representatives struck me as terribly morbid. And of course, the marketing tactic is rather unsettling mostly because it is so clearly effective. But if Cuba Nostalgia is anything, it is a controlled narrative of Cuba and exile mediated through consumption. Arranging to pay for the final line of your life story so that it is filled with adjectives that capture your cubanía perfectly complements the event's organizing logic. In the same way that the exile community has historically attempted to control the narrative of Cuba's past in a way that justifies their politics in Miami in the present, the tailored services provided by Memorial Plan Cemeteries offer that same kind of narrative control up to the final memorial and into perpetuity. Cuba Nostalgia itself is a kind of monument to a segment of Cuban Miami nearing its passing—a public memorial to a communal imagining of pre-Castro Cuba *and* exile cubanía complete with souvenirs and diversión.

I have argued in this chapter that the birth of Cuba Nostalgia was in part due to radical changes in Miami, where the exile community is no longer the majority or culturally dominant. Cuban Miami is now, in large part, defined by those who have a less visible role at Cuba Nostalgia— the people "behind the scenes" helping to supply the memorabilia that is a major draw for attendees and working the event itself, making sure it runs smoothly. In the next chapter, the post-1994 arrivals become the focus as the discussion moves to consider how forms of diversión have brought the diaspora and the island closer together while transforming life in both spaces—all of this years before President Obama and Castro announced the warming of relations between the United States and Cuba on December 17, 2014.

4

The Transnational Life of Diversión

On a hot night in Havana in October of 2014, I attended an evening of comedy in honor of the seventy-fifth birthday of Cuban classical composer Leo Brouwer at the El Sauce Cultural Center. Some of the most respected names in Cuban humor were there: Alejandro "Virulo" García, Telo González, Carlos Ruíz de la Tejera, and Omar Franco. The audience applauded early and often as the artists mined their "best of" repertoires. The honor of closing the performance went to Omar Franco, who ended his set with a routine that was different from everything else I had heard that night. He closed with a joke about a Cuban who had moved to rural Pennsylvania to get away from the suffocating heat and overwhelming Cubanness of Miami. Told as a series of diary entries, the joke reveals how the Cuban slowly begins to hate life in Pennsylvania with its unrelenting cold, despite his best attempts to rationalize its virtues. It is not long before he begins to curse the state, the snow, and the plow that is barricading him in his own home. After breaking his leg slipping on a patch of ice and destroying his car in an accident involving a deer, *el cubano en Pennsylvania* decides that he has had enough of the state's "beauty" and moves back to Miami for the heat, hurricanes, and Cuban coffee.

From beginning to end, the crowd was in stitches as Franco expertly shifted his tone over the course of his performance to match the character's joyful discovery of Pennsylvania, his angry disillusionment brought on by winter, and the renewed joy of living among Cubans in Miami. If audience reaction is any indication, he had indeed left the best for last. But the success of the material was never in doubt. What Franco had managed to do was give a fantastic performance of one of Cuban exile comedian Guillermo Alvarez Guedes's most popular routines, "Diario de un cubano."[1] Franco certainly put his unique stamp on it but he never acknowledged the source for his almost verbatim telling of the story. He didn't have to. Alvarez Guedes and his repertoire are known and highly regarded by Cubans on the island.

When Alvarez Guedes died in 2013, an online news magazine with offices in Miami and Havana called *OnCuba* produced a video featuring interviews with the island's top comedians reflecting on the importance of his comedy to their art and lives.[2] Every comedian who participated acknowledged Alvarez Guedes as one of the greatest in the history of Cuban humor.[3] Despite never returning to the island and having had his material banned as counterrevolutionary, Alvarez Guedes's many albums, joke books, and videos have circulated clandestinely in Cuba for decades—and not only among a small circle of humorists and their friends. People I met and talked to on the streets of Havana and small towns alike were well aware of Alvarez Guedes and could even repeat their favorite jokes. On trips to Cuba, people often asked me to share albums on my computer so they could enjoy them with family and friends.

As popular as Alvarez Guedes is on the island, Cuban humor does not simply flow in one direction. Alvarez Guedes performed many jokes sent to him from Cubans on the island.[4] Modesto "Kiko" Arocha has collected political jokes from Cuba and published them in two separate volumes.[5] These examples, of course, do not include the incalculable number of jokes that pass from person to person in diasporic communities as people come and go from the island and share the latest *chiste*.

The circulation of Alvarez Guedes and humor more broadly between the island and the diaspora encapsulates the central focus of this chapter—the transnational life of diversión. While the flow of popular culture in both directions is not new in the era after the Revolution, it has intensified dramatically since the 1990s. Popular culture in the form of comedy, music, film, and television are examples of diversión that play a highly visible role in how Cubans and their diasporic counterparts imagine and relate to each other.[6] Examining these flows will allow me to elaborate the principal contention of this chapter: the movement of popular culture is indicative of the intensification of transnational contact born out of political and demographic changes on both sides *and* is a means by which this intensification occurs. Policy changes before and after the reestablishment of diplomatic relations between the United States and Cuba have made it easier for Cubans to communicate, visit each other, and exchange cultural production. This chapter aims to understand how that intensifying transnationalism is being lived in quotidian life through analysis of highly circulated forms of diversión.

It will thus necessarily engage the relationship between state politics and the politics of culture. Close readings of ludic popular culture attentive to race and gender dynamics will be placed alongside analyses of broader political and economic shifts in the United States and Cuba in the twenty-first century in order to articulate the role of diversión in the production and mediation of this relationship.

Up to this point, I have focused primarily on the exile community and US-born generations through readings of stand-up comedy, radio in Miami, and festivals like Cuba Nostalgia. In this chapter, I privilege the Miami experienced by those hundreds of thousands of Cubans who have arrived since 1994, as well as their connections to the island. To do this work, I have assembled an archive that captures the transnational flow of popular culture: comedians from Cuba who frequently travel to Miami to perform publicly and the consumption of media produced in South Florida and the United States more broadly on the island through a distribution phenomenon called *el paquete semanal* (the weekly package). This heightened transnational exchange is now the norm:[7] parents sending their children to Cuba for the summer to spend time with extended family; the increasing visibility of Cubans whose names begin with the letter "y" in Miami;[8] and people on a bus in Havana discussing the latest episodes of shows like *Caso Cerrado* filmed in South Florida. This is the stuff of quotidian, lived contact, and it is also a point of departure, the fodder for diversión. It is the ephemeral archive of this intensifying transnationalism. Examining the form, consumption, and circulation of diversión reveals the growing continuities and transnational imaginaries that are defining what it means to be Cuban in the twenty-first century.

Miami

Cubans are dying to get to the United States and then when
they get there, they want Cuban entertainment and humor.
—Baudilio Espinosa, interview with author, October, 2014

December 17, 2014, when it was announced that diplomatic relations between the United States and Cuba would be restored, will be the date that people remember in this new chapter in the relations between the two countries. But the reality is that the United States and Cuba had been building bridges facilitating greater exchange and contact years before the now famous announcement. Travel restrictions to the island were relaxed substantially in the early years of the Obama administration, with its policy of encouraging "people-to-people" travel.[9] In 2013, the United States began granting five-year visas with multiple entries to Cuban nationals cleared for family visits and other forms of medical and personal travel. On the Cuban side, the government changed its much-maligned travel policy in January 2013 to make it easier from a bureaucratic standpoint for most Cubans to travel.[10]

The most important policy change for understanding the explosion of Cuban popular culture in Miami came in 2009, when the Obama administration placed a renewed emphasis on cultural exchange as a means of engaging Cuba. The result was nothing short of a transformation in the Cuban popular culture landscape of South Florida, which continues today. Acclaimed actor and comedian Osvaldo Doimeadiós arrived in 2010 and performed at a popular club called The Place in Miami and perhaps most surprisingly, filled in for a couple of nights hosting a late-night talk show called *Esta Noche Tu Night*. This marked the first time that an artist residing in Cuba hosted a local television program. Although there was some criticism in the media, there were no crowds protesting and hurling insults the way they did when Cuban timba group Los Van Van played a concert in Miami in 1999. No steamrollers were used and no fires were set as they had been only months earlier, when Juanes announced plans to perform a concert in Cuba. After Doimeadiós's performances, artists of all kinds began streaming into South Florida to perform in shows and appear on television.

The comedians arrived buoyed by support from a public composed of hundreds of thousands of Cubans familiar with them from their lives on the island. These are the Cubans patronizing clubs in Miami and watching Spanish-language television. Networks and entrepreneurs began to realize that there was money in transnational diversión and began planning accordingly. The presence of these artists soon became normalized in Cuban Miami. When news broke regarding the reestablishment of diplomatic relations on December 17, 2014, national media seemed surprised that Miami was not engulfed in flames in protest. Part of the reason for that, in addition to the obvious generational turnover, is that people had been experiencing the reestablishment of relations more informally through popular culture years before the announcement. Artists, especially visiting comedians who could create a feeling of intimacy with their audiences on a nightly basis, contributed to the wearing down of conservative resistance to engagement with Cuba.

I experienced this new flood of talent from Cuba when I went to see Angel García, better known as Antolín el pichón, at the Miami Dade County Auditorium in May 2014. García is well known for his role on *Sabadazo*, a comedy-variety show that aired on the island during the mid-1990s and is easily one of the most beloved programs in the history of Cuban television. Naively, I expected to walk into the performance and immediately understand the jokes, the contexts, and the crowd's relationship to the performer. I had seen humorists from the island perform on South Florida television without missing a beat. But in the more intimate space of the auditorium, where García was addressing people who had come to see the "Antolín" they remembered from Cuba, I was lost. During a wardrobe change, I asked Sonia Nuñez, my mother-in-law who left Cuba as a teenager in 1966, what she thought of his performance. She summed up her experience rather succinctly, "No le entendí nada" (I didn't understand a thing he said). After a particularly successful rattling off of jokes that had the man on my left in tears, García paused and asked a simple question: "Antolín te recuerda a Cuba, eh?" (Antolín reminds you of Cuba, right?). The crowd confirmed his "suspicion" with raucous applause, urging him along in his routine.

Our inability to understand most of the material was because our answer to that question would be "no." We simply did not share the same "Cuba" as the rest of the people in the audience. I grew up listening to the stories of my family who had left Cuba in the late 1960s and 1970s. Although some aspects of the performance were familiar to me—the Cuban accent, the mannerisms, and even the cadence of clapping from the audience—it became clear to me that in order to understand the appeal of his humor, I would have to learn more about how he was calibrating his performances for this particular segment of the diaspora. I learned that García and other humorists from the island were employing three primary strategies to entertain their audiences: invoking nostalgia; addressing the culture clash between Cuba and the United States; and commenting on life in contemporary Cuba through a comic lens.

In interviews I conducted with García and other island-based comedians who have performed in Miami, all echoed the importance of cultivating nostalgia and memory as ways to connect and entertain the audience.[11] For García, it begins with the embodiment of his character, Antolín, a country bumpkin from a small town in Cuba called Manacas.[12] He walks on stage with his signature cigar in his mouth, cowboy hat, and boots. Even the way he moves his body is meant to invoke the Antolín the audience knew from Cuba. The catalog of gestures, which includes the way he moves the cigar from his mouth to his hand, the position of his hand on his hip as he lets the joke settle, and the way his chest quakes as he tries to suppress his amusement at his own material, are meant to take the audience back to the 1990s when they first encountered Antolín on the Cuban television show *Sabadazo*.

The utilization of old material and period-specific popular culture references across the many comedy acts I have studied is critical to invoking the nostalgia-charged memories of the Cuba the audience members left behind. García will often mention brands of perfume, clothing, and hairstyles from 1980s and 1990s Cuba to the delight of his audience. In an interview with Carlos Otero, he reminisced about his old, weathered boots in Cuba to uproarious laughter from the studio audience. Antolín responded to this laughter by chiding them playfully: "¡No se hagan los gringis!" (Don't act like you're Americans!).[13] This playful commentary is part of a larger strategy constantly mobilized by these humorists to connect their audiences to their past on the island while simultaneously pointing to the pleasures and benefits of being *outside* of Cuba.

The deeper and more obscure the popular culture reference, the more pleasure it produces for the audience. The best example of this is the comedy of Roberto "Robertico" Riverón, who may well be the most popular Cuban humorist among diasporic audiences in the 2010s. In the excerpt below from a 2011 show in Miami, he dives deep into the Cuban popular culture unconscious:

> Technology has affected all of us because if Cubans are anything, wherever they live, they go against *desarrollo* (development). I got here the other day and asked "Hey, where can I buy a double cassette player?" [*Audience laughter; he pauses for effect.*] You see, that's what's wrong; you live in Miami and to hell with the little cassette player!

Everyone seated here knows what I'm talking about. First, the double cassette player of the brand "Crown" that they brought over from Angola, Ethiopia, whatever the hell. Little cassettes made by Maxell, TDK! Everyone here took that cassette when they lived over there [in Cuba] to Varadero with your girl next to you with a pencil going: raka, raka, raka [*mimics the sound and the twirling motion involved in winding the cassette tape*]. The yellow pencil, that one that would stick, the HB [brand of pencil] YOU REMEMBER [*said in English*]?!? [*Crowd expresses approval with applause, yeses.*]

Because if you didn't use the HB [pencil] and you made a mistake and used the grey pencil brand Batabanó, it would break open like a papaya. You remember the Batabanó pencil! When you would try to sharpen the point the lead would fall out![14]

Robertico's strategy is to start with a broad statement about Cubans and technology and then to slowly walk his audience through an increasingly obscure, more detailed set of observations to produce the shared pleasure of recognition among them. As the observations move to the minutiae of experience in Cuba, the pleasure is amplified by such a small, yet widely shared memory. In this way, the audience's engagement with Robertico's pencil is not unlike the exile's encounter with memorabilia at Cuba Nostalgia. In both cases, an unexpected, maybe even forgotten encounter with a past self occurs, creating a moment of recognition, perhaps even self-discovery. Robertico succeeds in producing intimacy with his audiences by excavating memories that are so singularly Cuban, yet so foreign to the Miami context.

What is striking about the act is the invocation not just of objects, but of one's interaction with them. Robertico mimics the sound the cassette would make and the exaggerated elliptical motion of the arm needed to effectively wind the tape. In doing so, he brings out the physicality of memory, a kind of kinesthetic cubanía deeply tied to a place, time, and a shared experience of lack in Cuba. The "raka raka" of the winding sound transports the audience to Varadero, the most celebrated of Cuban beaches. It is the ideal place to go with your romantic partner, to be young and have fun despite material difficulties. This is the Cuba Robertico wishes to conjure for his audience at the beginning of the show to enhance their identification with him and each other. After the "raka

Figure 4.1. Advertisement for Robertico comedy show in Miami, 2014.

raka" of the winding cassette tape, he basks in eighteen seconds of uninterrupted laughter and applause.

He brings the bit home by detailing the pencil brands and explaining the quality of each. Unsurprisingly, the pencils made in Cuba, brand Batabanó, are not suitable for a day at the beach. Robertico confirms what so many Cubans know about the poor quality of material goods produced on the island. And that's just it: the fact that it is not a surprise, that people are intimately aware of both the object and have the inside knowledge of its reputation, the way it must be treated gingerly because of its poor quality, is what strikes such a deep chord among those in the audience. The more "inside" the inside joke in its use of obscure, entirely forgettable details, the more intense the response from the audience. The humorist's ability to capture and dramatize the minutiae of quotidian life in Cuba works to surprise and delight through a connection with a distinctly Cuban way of being and feeling that no longer occurs even in South Florida with its massive Cuban population. The "first world" and its attendant problems erode those highly specific memories of a past that was essential to Cubans' personal formation and their *present* as diasporic subjects.[15]

Context is the vital ingredient of standup comedy that allows the performer to establish a rapport with his audience and to ensure that his jokes will make sense and be well received. Analyzing this particular bit of observational humor in another setting says something about the nature of the audience. This wasn't the first time Robertico performed this material. Weeks before his arrival in Miami in October 2011, he took the stage in Havana at Teatro América to perform his standup show titled *Robertico en 3D: Divertido, Dinámico, Diferente*.[16] He began with the same guiding premise: Cubans and technology don't mix. But he quickly found himself reaching for laughs. When the crowd did not respond to his reference to the Crown double cassette player, he said, "Look at all these Cuban faces acting as if they don't know what I am talking about." As he powered through the bit, the audience offered only the kind of light laughter that acknowledges that the joke landed but did not impress. At one point, perhaps surprised that the bit was not more successful, he posited, "You see, this is what's wrong with Cubans, the CD arrived and to hell with the cassette, the DVD arrived and to hell with the CD."[17] Of course, it is difficult to extrapolate any definite conclusions from this episode. Some bits simply do not work with certain audiences; it is always a question of chemistry between the performer and the crowd on any given night. But these markedly different receptions in Miami and Havana crystalize larger trends I have noticed in my utilization of a transnational, comparative framework to examine humor on the island and in the diaspora. The diaspora is eager to look back at the past, while Cubans on the island are more interested in jokes about contemporary life.

In a place where access to the Internet is severely limited and the newest gadgets are difficult to acquire, there is perhaps less of an interest in looking back pleasurably at memories of the cassette player. It is the new technology that is more engaging.[18] Seemingly every comedian in Cuba has a joke or two about cell phones and how people closely monitor their accounts and ration minutes. But in Miami, surrounded by all the latest gadgets, Cubans are open to nostalgia for their lives in Cuba in a way that does not resonate as strongly in contemporary Havana. Robertico sums it up best when he poses a rhetorical question (in English, no less) toward the end of cassette player bit in Miami: "YOU REMEMBER?!" The answer is a resounding "yes." Like the memorabilia sold to the exile community at Cuba Nostalgia, the popular culture references and meticulous details that comedians like Robertico and Antolín immerse their audiences in act as bridges to pleasurable narratives of the past. The laughter across the audience serves as a connective tissue among subjects to produce a ludic sociability that is not new in South Florida. But in a Miami whose symbolic economy has long been dominated by the exile community and celebrations of life pre-1959, public performances like this validate another relationship to Cuba's past through post-revolutionary popular culture.

While nostalgia and memory connect the audience back to the island, comedians also work hard to dramatize the diasporic condition by joking at length about the cultural and economic disorientation experienced when one arrives in the United States. These jokes function through a comparative framework where Cuba's lack is put into conversation with excess in the United States. Interviewers in Miami love to ask visiting comedians about how they are enjoying the food. Comedians like Angel García (Antolín) oblige them with plenty of material about beef dishes like *churrasco*: "This country is a drug. Not because of any drugs, but because of churrasco. I spent a month in Havana bellowing [like a cow] and I wondered why. I started seeing cows in the yard. Because you take the churrasco here [points to the top of his head]."[19]

These jokes are variations on perhaps the most dependable theme in Cuban comedy on the island: the failure of the state to consistently provide for its citizens. The availability of goods in the United States offers an easy contrast for this theme, and humorists exploit it. But the pleasures of this humor concerning lack acquire new meaning in the diasporic context. Certainly, there is a pleasure the audience experiences in the incongruity between the island and the United States drawn by the comedian. I would also argue that jokes about lack can be viewed through the lens of nostalgia and memory—they express a familiar *kind* of humor. These jokes, which are a recognizable part of the island's comic economy, have the power to return the audience to the quotidian conversational dynamic that for the most part was left behind on the island and thereby produces the desired transnational continuity.

The comedians rehearse this clash of worlds by candidly and comically dramatizing the mind-numbing differences that a fifty-minute flight can produce. This point is perhaps best made by going back to the character of Antolín el pichón. In my interview with García in Havana, he explained to me: "Antolín went from Manacas to Havana and clashed, and now he clashes with Miami. . . . Antolín arrived in Havana ten years behind, in Miami it's thirty."[20] The origin story of Antolín, a self-defined guajiro, is that he travels from the interior of the country and tries to make his way in the big city of Havana. The humor arises out of his inability to adapt to the modernity of the capital. Although he tries and is constantly thwarted, his self-confidence is hardly dented. In Miami, Antolín utilizes the same comic strategy, further emphasizing the incongruity produced when the man from the Cuban interior finds himself in the United States. Perhaps his Cuban audience in Miami can identify with that experience of feeling "out of place," like a guajiro gone to live in the big city. Even those Cubans coming from Havana, a major city, would have experienced a period of adjustment when they felt a bit like Antolín. Through this character, García draws not only on the audience's attachment to the Antolín they knew from Cuba but also on the disorientation that accompanied the move from the island to Miami.

Comedians will often joke about not wanting to return to Cuba, much to the delight of the audience. Throughout their sets, a tacit message is being conveyed: you made the right decision.[21] For all the nostalgia and the memories, there is the very real narrative of *no es fácil* (it's not easy) that serves as the backdrop to so much of the humor. These comedians allow their audiences in the diaspora to enjoy the banter, the familiar joke economy of quotidian life on the island, without having to stand in a long line for a crowded bus home or for powdered milk at a state-operated store. Luis Silva, playing his famous character Pánfilo, likes to say that "the worst part of visiting Miami is going back [to Cuba]."[22] The choice to leave Cuba is always validated by the humorists as the correct one. The nostalgia is balanced by the unflinching characterizations of the difficulty of daily life on the island. Life in Miami can be hard, no doubt, but these comedians provide a not-so-subtle reminder of the circumstances that led people to leave in the first place.

So far, I have discussed two popular strategies that comedians from the island use to engage and entertain their audiences in the diaspora: the mobilization of nostalgia and memory and the articulation of the differences between life in Cuba and the United States. But it would be misleading to suggest that comedians from the island all appeal to the same Cubans living in South Florida. Significant generational differences exist within the post-1994 segment of the Cuban diaspora. Those born in the late 1980s or 1990s, for example, may not have any memory of Antolín or the context of the Special Period that grounds much of his humor.

This leads me to the aforementioned character of Pánfilo played by Luis Silva. Silva is without question the most popular humorist in Cuba today courtesy of a sitcom he stars in called *Vivir del cuento*—the most watched program on Cuban television. The character of Pánfilo is a cranky old man trying to get by in a Cuba that has changed under his feet. A great deal of the show's humor comes from Pánfilo's living in a Cuba where Raúl Castro's economic reforms have taken hold and the social safety net he has grown accustomed to has eroded. Though Silva began gaining national visibility for his humor in 2001, it was not until 2008 that his popularity skyrocketed with the premiere of *Vivir del cuento*. For Cubans coming of age in the twenty-first century, Silva is one of the top comedians of their generation.

The relative youth of Silva's audience was apparent when I attended one of his performances in December 2014.[23] When compared with the audience at the show featuring Antolín, the one at Silva's show was significantly younger. Another major difference was the size of the venue. Unlike other comedians such as Robertico and Angel García, Silva probably could not sell out an entire auditorium in 2014. The theater I saw him perform in was much smaller. Although he is the most popular comedian in Cuba today, the diasporic population has yet to catch up. The youth of the crowd and fashion choices—more Malecón than Miami— reflected the ongoing migration to South Florida and this population's desire to remain connected to island entertainment. It is also important to note that Silva appeared on the bill with Alexis Valdés, quite possibly the most successful Cuban humorist living in the United States today. While the audience was no doubt excited to see Valdés, they were, as even Valdés noted during the performance, there to see Silva perform Pánfilo in the closing set.

Silva's entire act is directed toward providing an aggressive comic perspective on the *present* in Cuba to his audiences on and off the island. His performances in Miami and Cuba have significant overlaps in terms of bits, punchlines, and commentaries. To fully appreciate them, it helps to be in tune with the latest news from the island. For instance, he spent a great deal of time joking about the sky-high cost of cars after the government loosened restrictions in 2013 to allow Cubans to buy them. He also set his sights on new restrictions at Cuban customs affecting the amount of goods that could be brought into the country. There are certainly moments when he strikes nostalgic notes, performing monologues he is famous for that people clearly want to hear, but the bulk of the humor focuses on quotidian life in Cuba *today*.[24]

The show I attended was "back by popular demand" after a previously successful run, which suggests that his popularity is gaining momentum in the diaspora. *Vivir del cuento* is sold on burned DVDs at video shops like Kimbara Video in Hialeah. Episodes have been watched hundreds of thousands of times on YouTube. People hunger for a character who provides a connection to a Cuba they recently left. In narrating the present through the prism of humor, Silva makes it possible for the audience in the diaspora to revel in how the comic irreverence of choteo is being used to narrate life on the island in real time. In quotidian life in Cuba, national news is often run through the logic of choteo to poke fun at the rhetoric and propaganda of state-run media. There is a pleasure in reconnecting with the narrative economy of daily life that Pánfilo's humor captures so well—that particular *way* of joking on the island. It is not an exaggeration to say that Pánfilo's comic quips and reflections about life in Cuba featured on *Vivir del cuento* influence how people think about and narrate quotidian life. His jokes are repeated the next day on the street, at work, and even at school.[25] His performances in Miami invite the audience to feel a kind of continuity that is less about any one news story and more about *how* the news is narrated and spun to produce a critical diversión in which the implicitness of a joke, what is left unsaid, can be more powerful than a more direct critique of a government official.

Part of the popularity of *Vivir del cuento* on and off the island can be attributed to the fact that it pushes the envelope for Cuban television. Historically, Cuban officials have tightly regulated speech on television, especially in regard to material that is seen as too critical of the government. People are often surprised at what the show is able to get away with. It has not gone unscathed, though. Episodes of *Vivir del cuento* have been censored and pulled from the air. The dance between the show and Cuban censors is a dangerous one, and it is certainly part of the reason why people tune in. At his performance in Miami, Silva played right into the audience's familiarity with his character and the precariousness of the "dance" by setting up the final punchline of the night. He began by arguing for laughter as necessary for health and to help Cubans manage the many problems that face "us." He then shifted to his parting shot:

> [*Whispering*] Although they say, they say . . . [*pauses for effect, then raises voice*] Look at me talking so quietly! It's a habit that gets stuck in one's head! I was going to talk quietly! [*Crowd erupts in laughter.*] They say that the solution to the problems of the Cuban people is just around the corner. It just looks like that we live in a rotunda!

The whispering is an immediate cue to an audience well versed in how criticism of the Cuban government has historically been deployed in public   that is, quietly. I could feel myself and the rest of the audience leaning in as if we were on the street in Cuba, accomplices in a way, to hear the "subversive" remark. For a moment, simply by modulating his voice in that whisper, Silva is able to fold his audience back into quotidian Cuban life. Once we are hooked, he breaks the spell to produce the pleasure that comes from the realization, on both Pánfilo's and our parts, that we are not in Cuba, that he can execute his joke without fear of reprisal in a theater in Little Havana.

The metaphor of the rotunda alludes to the popular sentiment that the island has made little progress, that it is stuck in an unending cycle of disappointment, especially since the Special Period. When it looks like some facet of life is going to turn a corner, another problem arises. Cubans can now buy foreign made cars? The government prices them out of range for a vast majority of Cubans. The government opens up opportunities for small business to operate, which spurs the movement of goods from Miami to the island courtesy of Cuban American visitors. Unhappy that this trade is undercutting the potential for state profits, they impose restrictions on the amount of goods people can bring in from abroad. This is the Cuban rotunda.

Beyond Pánfilo's metaphor of the rotunda, the concept of circularity is helpful for thinking about the increased movement of people, goods, and cultural production between the island and the diaspora. The solution to Cuba's problems might not be around the proverbial corner, but cultural flows and capital are already changing life for Cubans on and off the island. Forms of diversión like standup comedy provide the post-1994 diaspora with a means to make sense of the new normal through an embrace of a post-revolutionary popular culture attentive to their histories and relationships to the island.

Race and Gender on the Margins

Though diversión is a powerful lens for understanding the role of popular culture in how people process and feel their way through a rapidly changing present, the tropes mobilized within these cultural forms are not always forward looking. Humorists visiting Miami draw on long-standing comic motifs and targets in relation to race, gender, and sexuality to entertain their audiences. Given that the most popular Cuban humorists on and off the island are white males,[26] the invocation of racial humor and the lack of representation of women in contemporary Cuban comedy signal yet another transnational continuity—the marginal position of particular subjects on and off the island. In working through these representations, we see how popular culture can function as a means both for softening conservative resistance to strengthening ties with the island *and* for reproducing the marginalization of women, blacks, and queer subjects.

In Miami today, blackface remains popular in theater and frequently appears on television produced by smaller stations like América Tevé and Mega TV, which cater to South Florida's Cuban community.[27] José Carlos Pérez, better known as Carlucho, puts on blackface for a recurring sketch called "Madrina Ondina y su conexión espiritual" (Godmother Ondina and Her Spiritual Connection) on his show called *El Happy Hour.*[28] Carlucho plays the role of Madrina Ondina, an Afro-Cuban *santera* who runs a *botánica*—a shop where one can receive spiritual consultations and buy supplies for religious practices and folk healing. As the character speaks in the stereotypically broken and accented Cuban Spanish so often used in the bufo tradition, the audience laughs at the comedy of errors and hijinks that occur within the botánica. In another twist, Cuban-born Carlos Marrero has had a great deal of success on television and the club scene playing a character of his own creation called Yeyo Vargas who is not Cuban, but Dominican. Donning brownface, Marrero uses a cartoonish Dominican accent to add a new spin on old bufo themes.[29] I cite these performances not as "one-offs" but to highlight a successful comic strategy that has been reproduced again and again in Miami entertainment. This continued use of blackface shows how South Florida's televisual and theatrical entertainment landscape is different from so much of the rest of the country, while also indicating the durability of race-based humor on and off the island.

If this type of entertainment sounds familiar, it is because the invocation of race, sexuality and gender has long been present in Cuban diasporic humor and performance. In the first chapter, I discussed how comedian Guillermo Alvarez Guedes drew from the comic handbook of the Cuban blackface bufo tradition *and* popular racist jokes about African Americans in the US context. In doing so, I argued that Alvarez Guedes entertained his audience with familiar comic stereotypes about blackness from the island while simultaneously situating Cuban American whiteness in contrast to Miami's African American community at a historical moment when both groups faced discrimination from Anglo Miamians. Diversión functioned as a means to differentiate white cubanía from a conceptualization of blackness as criminal. Over thirty years later, despite the massive political, social, and generational divides between the early exiles and more recent arrivals raised under the Revolution, Cubans in South Florida continue to represent blackness in popular culture in similar ways to do similar work—to claim a hegemonic identity in South Florida.

The most popular blackface performance in recent years featured island-based actor and comedian Osvaldo Doimeadiós as a character named Mañeña on Alexis Valdés's late-night talk show *Esta Noche Tu Night*. During his stay in Miami in 2010, Doimeadiós performed as Mañeña no less than ten times in the span of a few weeks.[30] The sketch unfolded the same way each time. Alexis Valdés, the host, pretends to get word from his producer that a connection to Havana has been established and that Mañeña is present via satellite. The audience is given a split-screen image of Valdés at his desk and Doimeadiós as Mañeña in full blackface.

To the sound of Afro-Cuban percussion, Valdés introduces Mañeña to the audience as one of the top scientists and inventors in Cuba. With Mañeña, Doimeadiós plays a classic character from the bufo tradition— *el negro catedrático*[31]—who, as Jill Lane notes, is "a free born black with comic pretension toward erudition."[32] Mañeña's regal-sounding full name, María Leticia Aguila Dragones, and occupation, along with the performance of the character as an uneducated, bumbling black *woman*, create the incongruous comic contrast typical of the negro catedrático character. Although Doimeadiós is in the show's Miami studio, Mañeña is described as coming live to the audience from her "laboratory" in Cuba where she sits at a table with a number of rotary telephones, a flashing siren, and a computer station held together by all manner of tubes (Figure 4.2).

The comic premise of these sketches is simple: Mañeña's confidence in her intelligence and know-how is set against a familiar trope of black femininity as incompatible with modernity. This trope is further augmented by Mañeña's constant plea to Alexis for *una carta de invitación* so that she can migrate to the United States. The notion of a backward, black subject living in a "modern" Miami has the intended comic effect on an audience quite familiar with this kind of routine. To drive this comic point home, Mañeña often mentions her friend Hortencia who

Figure 4.2. Osvaldo Doimeadiós as Mañeña on *Esta Noche Tu Night*, 2010. Still image from YouTube.

lives in Arizona and sends her goods. The joke is that Mañeña constantly misunderstands the uses of what Hortencia sends. Mañeña thinks home air freshener is actually perfume, that spray paint is hair dye, and that a doormat is a beach towel. The largely domestic applications of the items that Hortencia sends and Mañeña's subsequent misinterpretation of their uses highlight the character's incompatibility with modernity not only on the level of race but also in terms of gender. Mañeña as the dim-witted "scientist" convinced of her intellectual acumen fits the description of el negro catedrático and illustrates the staying power of not only this form of comedy but the racial and gendered power dynamics encoded therein.

The sketches also provide an opportunity to use Cuban codes about black inferiority and criminalization in the racial context of Miami. In every single appearance, Mañeña mentions her boyfriend in Liberty City to the delight of the audience. Liberty City, a majority black neighborhood in heavily segregated Miami, is synonymous with crime and poverty in the South Florida public imagination.[33] Mañeña talks lovingly about her boyfriend in Liberty City and sets up a number of punchlines that position the neighborhood and its black residents as the butt of the joke. In one sketch, Mañeña explains that people who visit Liberty City "se quedan muertos con las casas" (say the houses are to die for), to which Valdés quickly replies, "No, se quedan muertos con lo que está adentro de las casas" (No, they die from what's inside the houses), a message in keeping with the association of blackness with criminality on and off the island.[34] In another, Mañeña proudly celebrates the fact that her lover in Liberty City has graduated from "probation," which she thinks is a college. The studio audience cheers with delight as Mañeña gets it wrong. But the heart of these particular jokes lies in their pairing the rhetoric of black inferiority in Miami and in Cuba through the coupling of Mañeña and her boyfriend in Liberty City. This pairing across space and social contexts (Mañeña is Afro-Cuban, her boyfriend in Liberty City presumably African American) represents a transnational continuity across Miami and Cuba—the investment in an empowered Cuban whiteness.

Readers may be wondering how it is possible that blackface can be featured so prominently and routinely on Spanish-language television in a major American city. In 2015, Rodner Figueroa, a popular Univision talk show host, was fired by the network after making comments that Michelle Obama looked like a character out of *Planet of the Apes*. The response from Univision and his condemnation on social media came quickly. Where is the pushback from the community in Miami? From Afro-Cubans in particular? Two intersecting factors make the continued use of blackface not only possible, but also economically expedient. First and foremost, the racial profile of the audiences is critical. Miami's Cuban population is overwhelmingly white. Less than 4 percent of Cubans in South Florida identify as black.[35] Unlike Univision, which has a national audience, networks like América Tevé cater primarily to a white Cuban audience in South Florida. They have little to worry about in terms of backlash because they are performing humor that is popular among their core audience—a reality reflected in the station's market research.[36]

The use of blackface on Miami television differs from representations of blackness featured on television and theater on the island. Enrique "Kike" Quiñones, the Afro-Cuban director of El Centro Promotor del Humor in Havana, told me that although aspects of the bufo tradition remain in the sense of music and stylistics, black characters are no longer "objects but subjects."[37] He conceded that humor utilizing black stereotypes still exists, but it is less *burdo* (vulgar) than in years past. But it is important to emphasize that Quiñones's comments represent his own understanding of television and theater. In nightclub acts for more intimate audiences on the island, racist jokes about blacks are frequently employed. The difference between Miami and Cuba lies in who has a say over what representations circulate in the media. In Cuba, Afro-Cuban comedians like Kike Quiñones are visible figures whose voices are heard and have some measure of influence within the island's cultural institutions. Quiñones himself heads a government-supported center devoted to supporting comedic talent and performances across the entire island. In Miami, that influence simply does not exist. So when mostly white Cubans from the island migrate to South Florida, they can see a comic narrative of blackness that may not have been present on national television but still played a significant role in nightclubs, more local shows, and quotidian exchanges. This material has a more mainstream presence in Miami. It is also crucial to note that the people writing and performing this kind of comedy on a nightly basis all came of age in revolutionary Cuba—a reality that reveals the stubbornness of racism and racist humor within the national imaginary despite over fifty years of "revolutionary" egalitarianism.

Another factor that makes this blackface possible is the belief that there is truly nothing wrong with it. Blackface is seen as a cultural patrimony, deeply and intrinsically Cuban, part of the repertoire of diversión, and not to be compared to the history of minstrelsy in the United States.[38] Those who make charges of racism are simply dismissed for their inability to appreciate the nuances of Cuban cultural history. This sort of relativism quickly short-circuits any attempt at a critical dialogue. Audiences tune in to these shows because they want Cuban comedy, and blackface is utilized as a powerful expression of that cubanía—a selling point for networks like América Tevé and Mega TV. In short, challenging blackface performances is an attack on what is construed as a depoliticized element of Cuban culture *and* the bottom lines of actors, producers, writers, and network executives who make a living off of this kind of humor.

As the drag performances of Doimeadiós and Carlucho may suggest, women play a marginal role in Cuban comedy in Miami. Despite a long tradition of female humorists in Cuban history, including Consuelito Vidal, Mimi Cal, Eloisa Alvarez Guedes, Miriam Alonso, and Carmen

Ruíz, contemporary humor on the stage and on television in Cuba is dominated by men. The lack of island-based female humoritsts performing for diasporic audiences can be traced, in part, to the fact that these artists have very little representation in island performance venues. Aleanys Jáuregui, better known by the name of her character, Cuqui la Mora, is the most notable island-based woman who has come to the United States to perform.[39] On the island, she has been a vocal critic of the sexism that prevents her and other women from having more opportunities to perform their comedy. At a conference in Cuba in 2012 on this very subject, she explained: "We always appear as secondary characters, supporting other roles. They underestimate us a great deal."[40] This sentiment was echoed by Carmen Ruíz, a celebrated comedic actress who was a member of one of the most important comedy troupes of the 1980s on the island, the Conjunto Nacional de Espectáculos. In an interview on Miami television in 2013, she declared, "In Cuba there is a lot of machismo in the humor, they are very machista. . . . And they are all my friends but I'll tell you, they are very machista."[41] Both of these Afro-Cuban women, separated by a generation, have been vocal in their criticism of gender barriers on the island and of the systemic exclusion of women.

But it would be unfair to characterize the lack of women humorists coming to perform from the island as a problem strictly related to gender bias in Cuba. While the history of Cuban comic theater in Miami is filled with names of actresses like Norma Zúñiga, Sandra Haydee, Aleida Leal, Blanquita Amaro, and Maribel González, women are routinely overshadowed by men and have fewer major parts on television.[42] There are also no women writers on the staff of the popular variety programs that cater to Cuban audiences in South Florida. Women are most visible on these comedy shows as backup dancers and singers with few speaking parts and even less clothing. When women do appear in sketches, their bodies are often the comic point of departure as either hypersexualized or as embodiments of a kind of grotesque, desexualized femininity.[43] Women involved in Miami's comedy scene all echoed the sentiments of their island counterparts in interviews with me. Denise Sánchez, who has appeared on local television shows and the internationally syndicated *Sábado Gigante*, pointed to the inability of people to see beyond her body to appreciate her artistic and comedic talents.

To push back and assert some control, she explained, she would often have to work with the male writers of these shows to rewrite sketches that she felt were too raunchy. Maribel González, whose theater career as an actress, writer, and director extends back to 1982, pointed out to me that "machismo continues, among Latinos, it continues to exist—the idea that women are behind the scenes and men are in the front."[44] As Gayatri Gopinath has theorized regarding the production of normative diasporas: "The imbrication of diaspora and diasporic cultural forms with dominant nationalism on the one hand, and corporate globalization on the other, takes place through discourses that are simultaneously gendered and sexualized."[45] A white, heteronormative diasporic cubanía is often reinforced through representations of gender, and as I have shown, race, in diversión.

Zulema Cruz's popularity on the Cuban Miami comedy scene is an interesting counter insofar as her performances push back against the usual roles of women in the context of transnational diversión. Before settling in Miami in 2003, Cruz enjoyed a great deal of success in Cuba as a member of the Conjunto Nacional de Espectáculos during the 1980s and on Mexican television in the 1990s. In Miami, she has appeared in comedy sketches on *Sábado Gigante* and on television catering to Cuban audiences in Miami. Locally, Cruz appears at clubs, restaurants, and at private parties performing her standup material. It is in these more intimate settings that she has grown her following in South Florida and crafted a comic persona that is best encapsulated by the titles of her three standup albums: *Malhablando, Volumes 1–3*. The title, which loosely translates to "Talking Nasty," sums up Cruz's standup—explicit jokes about sex and the body framed with the strongest, most vulgar words in Cuban vernacular speech. But Cruz's comedy did not start that way. In a story she tells on *Malhablando 2*, she explains:

> When I arrived to this country, I wanted to be *fina* (refined) but no one gave me work and they told me I would have to work in a factory. One day at a show I said *pinga* (cock) and the audience laughed and they gave me a steady gig. So I said to myself "pinga o factoria?" (cock or factory work?). I'll stick with *pinga*. I know it sounds very vulgar, especially from a woman, but people, we are Cuban. How difficult is it to speak, to express oneself like a Cuban without saying that word?[46]

Cruz confirmed that this story was in fact true when I interviewed her. Her attempts to perform what she called *un humor blanco* (clean humor) simply did not gain any traction. Although she "apologizes" for her use of vulgar language, she claims to understand that this is what the public wants, a twist on the audience's expectations regarding middle-aged femininity. It would be simple to categorize Cruz as simply performing a version of the bad woman, *una mujer malhablada*, perhaps described best by the word *chusma*. Her performance certainly fits the definition of a chusma—a bold woman who has little interest in gendered understandings of decorum and "refuses standards of bourgeois comportment."[47] The chusma is the woman who provokes people to cover their faces with their hands but perhaps fan the fingers so as to sneak a peek. There is an allure in this unfettered, uncaring enactment of a vulgar cubanía. The chusma says things directly, without filter, in the most explicit and descriptive language possible. This might suggest a lack of self-awareness on the part of the character—that she knows not what she does. But Cruz is different.

While the vulgar language and topics she uses would quickly mark her as chusma, she strategically harnesses chusmería to point to its gendered construction. In the passage quoted above, Cruz explains that her decision to use chusma language was in order to get a foothold in Miami's competitive showbiz economy. She is aware that chusmería is

Figure 4.3. Zulema Cruz, Monologue on *TN3*, June 2016. América Tevé Miami.

what the audience wants. While this certainly invites a reading that suggests that her performance practice is coerced, Cruz has been able to produce a kind of meta-chusmería that not only points to its artifice but provides a space to perform a critical choteo wherein a woman's point of view is privileged.

Many of her jokes place women as the protagonists getting the last laugh over men and flaunting their subversion of the patriarchal order that informs so much of gendered Cuban humor: "A woman gets home and takes off her bra and her tits sag. And her husband says, 'Do you realize that if those tits were perkier we'd spend less money on bras, dammit!' The woman looks at her husband while he takes off his pants and says to him, 'If that thing got hard, we would save a lot of money on the gardener, the butcher, and the plumber, *comemierda*!' "[48] The women of Cruz's jokes are unapologetic about their sexuality and are not afraid to confront and overturn the double standard applied to "proper" women's behavior. Apart from her jokes, Cruz brings in aspects of her personal life to further augment the perspective of the bold, assertive woman, weaving in stories about her younger husband and describing how she "wears out" her "good little boy."[49] In a comedy landscape where women are often silent, smiling parts of set scenery or laughed *at* in their performance of a grotesque femininity, Cruz is unapologetic about privileging her sexuality and proves that she can dish out hard-hitting choteo as well as anyone else.

Though women tend to play a peripheral role in Miami's comedy scene, Cruz has managed to achieve something that no other male humorist has done. Of all the humorists now based in Miami, Cruz is the only one that has returned and performed on television and film in Cuba.[50] She had a prominent role in the 2014 comedy *Boccaccerías Habaneras*, directed by Arturo Sotto Díaz. When questioned by Miami media about her decision to appear in a government-supported film, Cruz repeatedly asserted how happy she was to get the call to act in a Cuban movie.[51] In keeping with her persona, she made it quite clear that she was not going to back down because of criticism from sectors of the diaspora that saw her as cooperating with the Cuban state.

But for all of Cruz's strength of character, she does have a weakness: Cuba. She told me that "Cuba para mi es un pulmón extra que necesito para respirar" (Cuba is an extra lung that I need to breathe).[52]

She frequently travels there to see family and friends and to simply enjoy being back in her homeland. This love of Cuba affects what kind of work she does on Miami television. Despite her strong criticisms of the Cuban government, she refuses to participate in explicitly anti-Castro sketches on América Tevé, explaining that "I'm not going to tell a shitty joke so that they don't let me into Cuba."[53] Cruz has broken important ground in her return performances on the island and her defiance of the gendered status quo in Miami but she has also chosen to censor herself on the topic of Cuban politics. This introduces another wrinkle into the movement of popular culture between the island and Cuba. Historically, Cuban artists living in Miami have been concerned mainly with the opinion of the exile community regarding anything that might be read as "collaborating" with the Cuban government. For Cruz, the opinions of those in Cuba can be more important in shaping her performances because they could limit her access to the island.

Follow the Money

While Zulema Cruz highlighted the political calculations that go into her comedy, the logic of how the Cuban government "blacklists" people is a mystery. Most of the humorists based in Miami I talked to have performed or written anti-Castro humor and travel to the island with no problems, though they rarely perform in public.[54] Fear that performing on the island might be read in Miami as "collaboration" with the government still exists but financial concerns are a major reason why many artists who have settled in South Florida since the 1990s do not perform in Cuba.[55] The amount of money paid to performers on the island simply cannot cover the cost of living for Cubans based in the United States. Moreoever, many Miami-based artists have contracts or steady employment and cannot leave to film a movie or participate in a show's run on the island for fear of losing a foothold in Cuban Miami's highly competitive entertainment business. This reality helps explain why the movement of entertainers is primarily a one-way affair from the island to the United States. Economic considerations also have a strong influence on *which* comedians actually travel to the United States to perform. Up to this point, I have cited the Obama administration's institution of the "intercambio cultural," less resistance from older exiles, and the generational shift since the 1990s as the reasons why more artists have been traveling to the United States. But the cultural exchange is very much linked to economic interests on both sides.

One of the primary reasons for this is that however popular they may be, comedians in Cuba do not make enough money to finance a tour in the United States. The costs associated with applying for a non-immigrant visa, flights, meals, and transportation make it extremely difficult for *anyone*, including artists, to travel without sponsorship. And so begins the business of transnational diversión. A growing number of entrepreneurs in the United States have made a business out of bringing Cuban artists to perform on television, in theaters, and in clubs.[56] On their side, artists see travel to the United States as an opportunity to make money to improve their living conditions in Cuba. By US law, island-based Cubans who are on a non-immigrant visa granted on the basis of a "cultural exchange" request cannot charge for their performances in the United States beyond a per diem for living expenses. In all public interviews, humorists will say that they do not profit, that they are here for a cultural exchange program and nothing else. Unsurpringly, when Jaime Bayly interviewed Robertico in 2011 and asked him who ends up with all the money, Robertico quipped: "Obama."[57] Osvaldo Doimeadiós explained in another interview that he does not charge but is given a per diem in line with US laws.[58]

While I certainly cannot speak for every artist from Cuba who has performed in the United States, my conversations with people on the ground indicate that the vast majority of artists are going back with more than just a per diem allowance. Interviews with comedians and people involved with the businesses that promote them all admitted that visiting humorists were making money outside of the legal per diems.[59] Some comedians, like Angel García, have even appeared in advertisements for companies like Tropicaltel, a phone service for calls to the island.[60] But when I interviewed Octavio "Churrsico" Rodríguez in Havana, he told me that he had not made much money on his trip to the United States and was quick to point out that the entertainment and promotion companies take all the risk booking clubs and fronting the money that goes into traveling from Cuba to the United States.[61] Nonetheless, if comedians are making very little, that certainly has not negatively affected how many of them travel to perform in Miami. Since 2009, the number has only grown, yet they still remain overwhelmingly white and male. Even if they are only paid the per diem, that extra money in foreign currency goes a long way on the island. Most of these performers have family and friends who help them take up the financial slack with meals and lodging so that other funds can be taken back to Cuba. Outside of any money recuperated through the per diem or *por la izquierda* (under the table), Cuban artists can take advantage of their time to procure goods to take back with them.

This economic reality partially answers a question that has been perhaps bubbling under the surface throughout this chapter: Why don't these humorists stay permanently in the United States if they clearly have an audience? Bracketing off emotional connections to one's country of origin and family obligations, the answer is that it simply does not make much financial sense. These artists attract crowds because they live in Cuba. They provide a connection to the island, its past and present. That novelty would be lost upon their moving to Miami, and they would have to reinvent themselves in order to achieve staying power. While some have been successful in doing just that, making it in show business in Cuban Miami is extremely difficult. Interviews with comedians involved in television and the club scene all pointed to the stiff competition, low pay, and constant hustle to succeed.[62] For island-based artists, money brought in from performances abroad goes much farther on the island. With outside income, one can live relatively comfortably.[63]

Robertico is a good example of what is possible with money from abroad. He owns a popular club called 3D Café in the Vedado neighborhood of Havana. The club serves food and offers nightly entertainment featuring other humorists and musical acts. When I visited in October of 2014, I was taken aback at the cover charge, five CUC (Cuban convertible pesos)—a price beyond the means of most Cubans on the island. Upon entering, I felt like I was transported to Miami. New leather furniture, state-of-the-art sound and stage equipment, and a number of LCD televisions filled the space. But it wasn't just the furnishings and the equipment that made me feel like I had left Havana. The audience was composed of many Cubans from abroad with the economic means to pay the cover and drink prices. His performances for Cuban audiences *outside* of Cuba in the United States provide him with the capital to invest in his business on the island—a business that is then patronized in large part by Cubans visiting from abroad, island-based artists, athletes, and a rising class of more affluent Cubans.

Miami-based business ventures also have plenty to gain from transnational diversión. Although it is difficult to determine exact financial figures, the constant arrival of artists year after year suggests that sponsoring acts from the island is a profitable endeavor. The relationships at play to maximize the economic benefits of these visits are highly organized and reflect a reality at odds with the spirit of the intercambio cultural. But all sides are getting something they want out of the arrangement.[64] Comedians have access to goods and foreign currency either in the form of a per diem or money exchanged por la izquierda. The diaspora gets access to artists they want to see, while businesses receive a boost in the form of ticket sales, advertising, and television ratings.

The economic reality of the intercambio cultural has had a profound effect on the kinds of diversión that make their way from the island. When Miami business interests are making the decisions about whom they should sponsor, their calculations are primarily based on profit, not artistic diversity. In Cuba today, the biggest rift within the community of humorists is between those who perform in theater versus those who work the nightclub and cabaret circuits. Those involved in theater are often highly educated, having studied their craft at the university level and through courses offered by El Centro Promotor del Humor. These actors often draw inspiration from the rebirth of comic theater that occurred in Cuba in the 1980s, particularly the work of Cuban writer Hector Zumbado and an Argentinean group called Les Luthiers.[65] Social criticism is often mobilized through wordplay and the absurd—more subtly than many standup comedians, who tend to go directly to observational humor about the difficulties facing Cubans in quotidian life. Generally, proponents of theater-centric humor see their work as more highly wrought, "humor elaborado," as the director of El Centro Promotor del Humor explained to me in an interview.[66]

But for promoters, theater is not the best way to turn a profit in Miami.[67] It requires more resources: actors, visas, paperwork, per diems—in short, there is more overhead. What we have then is a situation in which the most polished, educated comedians whom the state supports are not, by and large, those who travel to Miami. Instead, it is largely the comedians working the club scene in Cuba who will receive sponsorship from Miami promoters. Large-scale theater productions simply do not have the same earning potential as the lone-stand-up artist packing the Miami-Dade County Auditorium. The result is a limited view of what the island has to offer in the way of humor and impressive theatrical talent.[68]

The financial benefits of popular culture flows are reaped not only by Miami businesses capitalizing on the changing demographics of a diaspora hungry for artists who connect them with the island's past and present. US popular culture and specifically media produced in Miami for Cuban audiences have a massive presence *on the island* through a form of media circulation called *el paquete* (the package). As I demonstrate in the next section, the movement of popular culture is not a one-way affair. Artists based in Miami and unable to travel or perform for political and/or economic reasons still manage to make it to Cuba this way. Analyzing the currently steady flow of popular culture from the United States to Cuba illuminates the evolution of the economy under Raúl Castro and captures the conversation happening between the island and diaspora through diversión.

Unpacking El Paquete

The scale, circulation, and consumption of US popular culture and entertainment on the island dwarf what is "exported" to the diaspora. This is made possible by a phenomenon called *el paquete semanal* (the weekly package)—a bundling of mostly foreign popular culture production that Cuban intellectual Victor Fowler has referred to as "if not the most important cultural phenomenon in this country in the last twenty-five years, then one of them."[69] Updated weekly, el paquete features the latest Hollywood blockbusters, serialized television shows like *Game of Thrones*, sitcoms like *Two and a Half Men*, programming from the Discovery Channel, music, sports contests, funny video compilations, cartoons for children such as *Dora the Explorer*, gossip magazines, and soap operas from all over the world. In addition to US-based popular culture broadly conceived, material produced by Cubans in Miami in the form of YouTube videos and variety and talk shows all circulate on el paquete—a fact that I will take up in more detail later. Furthermore, content produced by and for Cubans on the island is also included in the form of classified ads, songs by local musicians, magazines, commercials for businesses, and pictures from Cuban nightlife hotspots.

Foreign media in the form of books, cassettes, CDs, Betamax videos, VHS tapes, and others have circulated on the black market in post-revolutionary Cuba for decades.[70] In all cases, the government has

Su mejor Información (930GB)Neww

Antivirus Actua (Avira, Kavp, Nod 32, Avast, &+)

Revolico (Porlalivre Portable, www.revolico.com Portable, &+)

Deportes (Boxeo, Futbol, MLB, Moto, Nascar, NBA, Noticieros, UFC, WWE, X-Game,&+)

Discovery C (Filmes Documentales, [3D], Variados, Series Documentales x Cap Sueltos y DVD, &+)

Games (! PC, ! PS1, ! PS2, ! PS3, ! PSP, ! Minigames de PC, ! WII, &+)

Humor (Tablazos, Videos Divertidos Show Humorísticos, &+)

Interesantes (Catalogo Excursiones Cubanacan, Lo último de la Red de Redes, Aplicaciones para "AND, MAC, WIND", Enciclopedias, Horóscopos, Libros, Lo último de la Tecnología, Recetas de Cocina, Revistas 2013, Wallpapers 2013, &+)

Música (Discografías en MP3, Música Actualizada [2013], &+)

Mangas (Comics, Mangas DVD, Mangas Tx, Mangas [Cap. Sueltos], &+)

Muñes (Clásicos, Estrenos, Estrenos en DVD, [3D], [HD], Series Clásicas, Series DVD, Variados Chick, &+)

Novelas (Doramas Cap. Sueltos & DVD, Novelas de 1DVD, Finalizadas, &+)

Novelas Tx (Doramas Cap extreno, Cap. Sueltos, DVD, &+)

Películas (! 3D, ! AVI-MKV-MP4, ! Clásicos HD, ! Clásicos AVI, ! Clásicos Latinos, ! Combos, ! De Cuba, ! HD, ! VCD, &+)

Recitales (Coming Soon, Fotos de la Farandula, ©Colecciones en DVD, ©Conciertos, ©[3D], ©Promo, ©Selección Semanal "internacional y Nacional" ©TopTen"internacional y Nacional", &+)

Series (Cap. Sueltos, DVD, Mini series, Clasicas, &+)

Series Tx Extras (Series, Animados, Documentales, TV Shows, Calendarios Semanales, &+)

Show (X Carpetas, DVD Variados)

Tráiler [New] (! Games, ! Novelas, ! Películas, ! Series, &+)

Ventas (&+)

Todo actualizado de la semana
Sábado 09:00AM a 08:00PM * 15 cuc
Domingo 09:00AM a 08:00PM * 10 cuc
Lunes 05:00AM a 08:00AM * 6 cuc
Lunes 10:30AM a 08:00PM * 4 cuc
Martes 08:00AM a 06:00PM * 2 cuc
Miércoles a viernes 09:00PM a 06:00PM * 1 cuc
Tenemos otras + nuevas ofertas cada semana !! llame para + Información !!
MEJORAMOS CUALQUIER OFERTA DE LA COMPETENCIA EN 50% &+

Se le ofrece 1 muestra gratis solo debe pasar a recojerla para ver nuestro contenido
100% GRATIS

TODO A SU GUSTO
Con Seriedad y Profesionalidad +8 años d´ Experiencia...
No espere más, llame ahora
al: 05-361-1081 ó 693-82-54 "EL CHINO"

ArteM@x
Ediciones Manuel®

Figure 4.4. Promotional advertisement for el paquete. Havana, Cuba, October 2014.

cracked down on the trade. So when Elio Héctor López, a key figure in the compilation of the weekly paquete, participated at an academic panel on the topic in Havana in 2014, he expressed concerns about the future: "There are many people who are in favor of el paquete, but I have met many who are against it, and the reality is that today I cannot be certain about the future, of what will be decided."[71] This uncertainty about the future in addition to its own evolution as a form can make pinning down "the facts" about el paquete difficult.[72] Some parts of the story are clear, though. El paquete as a social phenomenon began to pick up steam in 2008. Its content is downloaded by people with illegal satellite feeds or fast internet connections at state-run enterprises, hotels, government offices, and universities. Once compiled, the finished paquete is sold to vendors who spread it across the island through a diffuse network of people who then resell it from Pinar del Río to Guantánamo.[73] The primary technological breakthrough that makes this possible are high capacity external hard drives and thumb drives that place a terabyte of data in the palm of your hand.

Getting a copy is easy. Unlike the bureaucratic inefficiency that characterizes much of Cuban society, el paquete is dependable. Kiosks throughout Havana sell it as a whole or in pieces, depending on customer demand. Because I was interested in securing a copy of the full terabyte in order to examine its contents while in Havana, my cousin called a co-worker who has a side job delivering el paquete to people in their homes. A couple of hours later he came by and allowed me to download the entire terabyte for the going rate of two CUC, the equivalent of about two dollars.[74] For the most part though, this is not how most people experience it. Those who do download all of the content often do so because they resell it to customers, and it benefits them to have the largest selection possible to cater to diverse interests.[75] Most do not have the disk space to download an entire terabyte, nor are they interested in all the content el paquete offers. But that reality is in itself noteworthy. El paquete contains a broad array of entertainment options so that consumers can *choose* what they want to see. Choices when it comes to consumption, including media, have been lacking on the island for years. Regardless of political orientation or cultural tastes, it would be difficult not to find something of interest in that terabyte. Because of these factors, people form their own "paquetes" in collaboration with local vendors. For those who do not have the requisite drives or prefer DVDs, it is possible to purchase a burned disc with a number of movies or series compressed on it. The idea of el paquete in Cuba then, functions as a kind of shorthand for the availability of and market for foreign-produced media and entertainment made possible by high-capacity drives and discs.

El paquete's massive popularity on the island has spilled into official government-sponsored discourse on roundtables, panels, print news coverage, and even television.[76] High-ranking government officials and their supporters have expressed wariness about el paquete, pointing to the "low-brow" content and its potential for corrupting Cuban culture more broadly. Tellingly, when Luis Silva as Pánfilo took up the topic of el paquete on *Vivir del cuento*, the government censored it.[77] Critics like Victor Fowler, Irina Pacheco, Mario Masvidal, Yasmín Portales, and Gustavo Arcos have been more measured, championing approaches that push back against the moralistic, often paternalistic, critiques issued by government officials and their supporters.[78] These figures often highlight the context and reasons behind el paquete's popularity—namely, the declining quality and choices offered by an underfunded Cuban media. Beyond the shortcomings of Cuban programming, there is also the very real desire to consume uncensored popular culture as a means to engage with worlds *outside* of Cuba.

The truth is, el paquete deserves an entire book-length project that more thoroughly chronicles its genesis, circulation, and evolution. That kind of in-depth work is impossible in the context of this book. Instead, I will focus on what the consumption of el paquete as a form of diversión built primarily on US cultural production means for a country undergoing significant social and economic change. Engaging el paquete on these terms reveals the central role diversión is playing in both the economic evolution of Cuba and the intensifying transnational links and continuities between Cubans living on and off the island.

Paquete Economics

While the government openly criticizes the growing role of el paquete in quotidian Cuban life, it is impossible to understand its rise without taking into account the reforms Raúl Castro began to implement when he took his brother's place as head of state in 2006. One of the most important reform efforts has involved taking steps to decentralize the economy and reduce dependency on the state. In the fall of 2010, the government announced that the number of people on the state pay-roll would be cut substantially. To counter this loss, the government released a list of approved jobs that one could hold as a *cuentaprop-ista* (self-employed worker). This list of 178 jobs included categories that made the sale of audiovisual material a legal occupation.[79] It is important to note that el paquete is not a black market phenomenon. Though the government criticizes el paquete, distributing it is techni-cally legal—covered under the legal occupation of selling media in the form of music and audiovisual materials.[80] In fact, I would argue that el paquete is one of the most visible and felt results of Raúl Castro's economic reforms.[81]

But these economic reforms were not enough to spark the creation of el paquete as we know it today. El paquete is also intimately tied to in-tensifying transnational flows. In 2008, the tools needed to circulate and consume large troves of data became accessible when it became legal for Cubans to buy and own home computers, DVD players, and cell phones. Not that the state was providing such electronics at reasonable rates. Remittances in the form of cash and goods from Cubans living abroad made acquiring them possible. It is not an exaggeration to say that although the Cuban government set the stage at the level of the law, el paquete as we know it today would not be possible without the dias-pora. Cubans have taken advantage of relaxed government restrictions on electronics, education in information technology, and the influx of money and hardware from abroad to create el paquete and participate in its circulation and consumption.

Exact statistics documenting the extent to which el paquete is con-sumed are unavailable. Fernando Ravsberg and his team at *OnCuba* have done the most extensive, in-depth reporting on the topic, complete with interviews of people involved with its compilation and distribu-tion. They estimate that 30,000 Cubans participate in the creation and distribution of el paquete and that it reaches more than three million Cubans to the tune of 1.2 million CUC generated a week.[82] This does not take into account the number of people who trade or watch mate-rial for free. Though these are published findings, Ravsberg told me in an interview that he suspects that the numbers are in fact higher. While this statistical picture is flawed, it is clear from interviews, the visual landscape of Havana, and the amount of attention the Cuban government and academics have paid to el paquete that it is a powerful force in Cuban society today.

The economic impact of el paquete cannot be measured solely by its sale and purchase. Cubans are now manipulating its contents to stimulate other areas of the economy opened up by Raúl Castro's reforms. One of the most fascinating aspects of el paquete is the inclusion of commercials advertising goods and services for businesses *in Cuba*. Businesses throughout the island pay to have advertisements made and included in el paquete. In my research, I found the most popular advertisements to be for photographers, restaurants, party entertainment, cell phone repair, and printing services. Cuentapropistas take advantage of its popularity to promote their goods and services in a country where the only advertising visible in public media promotes state-run initiatives and propaganda. Commercials for party clowns can be found in children's cartoons, while photographers advertise their services for events like Sweet 15 parties and weddings in beauty contests like Univision's *Nuestra Belleza Latina*.[83]

In addition to exposure, advertisements boost the Cuban private sector economy in other ways. I was constantly impressed at the level of sophistication of these advertisements. While watching a trailer for a Hollywood adventure drama called *In the Heart of the Sea*, I was quickly greeted by "Pablo el payaso," a clown who danced along the bottom of the screen while the trailer played and promoted his party appearances complete with crisp, fluid animation. Other full-length commercials contained music, voiceover narration, sleek transitions, animation work, and even full-out story lines likely inspired by US marketing practices.[84] Businesses like ETRES bill themselves as publicity companies that produce commercials and circulate advertisements on el paquete and classifieds sites like Revolico. The talent and training to produce this material exist on the island and a growing employment sector is rising to meet the demands of an evolving Cuban economy.[85]

The most memorable commercial I have come across in my research was for a theme park called Abuelo Machungo in San Antonio de los Baños, Cuba. Abuelo Machungo's tag-line and slogan say it all: "Grandpa

Machungo: Children's Paradise. Parties, diversions, and adventures for young and old." A voiceover describes park attractions as the animation slickly transitions between images of children enjoying video games, mini motorbikes, an inflatable playhouse, and a haunted house, among other things. Framing the spectacle of the commercial and the park itself are images and characters straight out of US popular culture. The commercial proudly showcases employees dressed as Mickey and Minnie Mouse and Winnie the Pooh interacting with happy children. In one image, a life-sized replica of cartoon revolutionary hero Elpidio Valdés holds a revolver in his hand and has an angry expression on his face, perhaps because of his inability to beat back the Disney invasion. Duniesqui Jiménez, a middle-aged Cuban man who left Cuba for Peru in 2007 in search of better economic opportunities, returned to the island with his savings to open the park when he heard about the opening for private enterprise.[86]

Unpacking this commercial and the business it promotes helps crystalize the powerful and evolving relationship between popular culture, diversión, and Cuba's shifting economic model in the age of Raúl Castro. Lured by the opportunity offered by economic reforms, Jiménez returned from abroad with his savings to start a business that promotes itself through the visual economy of US popular culture, primarily Disney. The commercial for the park was created by businesspeople in Havana who no doubt took marketing cues from foreign advertisements and used pirated software. The advertisement for Abuelo Machungo is then embedded on el paquete, which circulates principally because of the desire to consume popular culture from the United States. While Cuba has long benefited economically from remittances, the consumption and production of diversión reveal the ways in which the island and the United States are becoming increasingly connected through the relationship between popular culture *and* the economy. Abuelo Machungo is yet another example of how government politics and the politics of culture are intersecting within a transnational framework to produce changes on the island.

In addition to advertisements, Cubans have been able to promote island-based artists and cultural production left out or actively criticized by the government. Although photos and videos from the island's *farandula* (show business) and nightlife worlds are relatively few, they

are included in el paquete. The Cuban government has silenced reg-
gaetoneros in official media because of their "vulgarity," but on el paquete the artists, music, and videos of Cuban reggaeton circulate freely.
El paquete is also the primary means for the circulation of a monthly
digital publication called *Vistar Magazine*, which launched in March of
2014 and features advertisements for Cuban businesses, entertainment,
and interviews with popular artists, all packaged in a sleekly designed
layout.[87] Even artists aligned with the regime, such as Kcho and Omara
Portuondo, have appeared on its cover. Most interestingly, the magazine
regularly features a section called "Cubanos en el exterior" which includes
interviews with artists who have left the island to pursue their careers
outside of Cuba—a marked departure from how such artists have been
treated historically in the island's media culture. Here, diversión serves
as a means to disseminate a narrative of Cuba in a public arena that
stretches beyond the boundaries of the nation.

When I have presented material on el paquete, I am often peppered
with questions about statistics. Is the advertising effective? How many
people is it reaching? If el paquete is most often experienced in piece-
meal form, how does that affect ad exposure? I have little to offer those
interested in quantitative analysis. There are no Arbitron studies or embedded software to track click counts or views.[88] Those on the ground
are experimenting and figuring it out as they go along. But while questions remain about how it will evolve, one thing is indisputable. The
combined factors that make el paquete possible—economic reforms in
Cuba, remittances in the form of cash and computer hardware from the
diaspora, and increasing engagement with popular culture from abroad—
point to the future of Cuba economically and culturally.

Diasporic "Returns"

So far, I have discussed el paquete as composed primarily of US popular
culture broadly conceived. But there is one particular kind of content
that is especially relevant to the question of transnational diversión. Programs produced by three television stations, América Tevé, Mega TV,
and Mira TV, which cater to the Cuban community in South Florida, are
prominently featured in each weekly update.[89] Like the broader reasons
for el paquete's explosion across the island, the circulation of diasporic

cultural production cannot be understood outside the context of reforms that have taken place under Raúl Castro. In this sense, there are interesting parallels between Cuba and Vietnam. In 1986, the approval of the *doi moi* economic reforms transformed Vietnam "from a reclusive Marxist-Leninist state into a market economy ever-increasingly incorporated into the global capitalist system."[90] Ashley Carruthers points out that the adoption of the doi moi policy in Vietnam led to a massive influx of Vietnamese diasporic popular culture in the form of pirated videos, music, and popular variety shows like the *Paris by Night* series.[91] Much like the Vietnamese case, the Cuban government's reaction to a similar influx of content mirrors its ambivalent feelings toward the diaspora. On the one hand, the presence of diasporic cultural production on the island is a result of the government's calculated attempts at facilitating exchange between the diaspora and the island in the form of goods, travel, and money in order to boost the economy. At the same time, the state criticizes diasporic cultural production as suspect and a threat to Cuban "political culture."[92]

The Cuban government's desire for economic remittances has had the unwanted effect of creating an opening for "cultural remittances" that fuel the transnational imaginary on the island.[93] Of course, el paquete is not a remittance in the classic sense of diasporic subjects physically sending these cultural materials to people on the island. But through el paquete, Cubans can download and circulate diasporic cultural production and be almost simultaneously exposed to the cultural forms that mark aspects of quotidian life outside of Cuba. This augments the sense of what Peggy Levitt and Nina Glick Schiller have called a "transnational social field," where individuals "may participate in personal networks or receive ideas and information that connect them to others in a nation-state, across the borders of a nation-state, or globally, without ever having migrated."[94] Watching Americans speaking in English against the backdrop of expensive Hollywood special effects can feel abstract, a "first world" experience disconnected from life in Cuba. But viewing television shows featuring Cubans in Miami who speak with the same accent, who had careers in Cuba, and are achieving success in the United States, can make the consumption of that content feel more immediate—a visual and sonic representation of cubanía outside the borders of the nation that occurs in the *now*. As Brian Larkin succinctly puts it, "Media technologies do not just store time, they represent it."[95] El paquete represents an opportunity to synchronize with trends and conversations outside the island. It is not just news but the ability to watch sports contests, even those featuring Cuban athletes who have defected, days after they have aired, or to read about showbiz gossip from the United States to Europe. Serialized shows like *Homeland* and *American Horror Story*, are offered as they appear on a weekly basis instead of if and when the Cuban government decides to play them on television, years later and in censored forms.[96]

The consumption of Cuban diversión produced in Miami on el paquete provides those on the island with access to a Cuban cultural continuity across space and time. Previously, I discussed this concept of continuity in terms of humorists from the island performing in the diaspora. A similar logic is at work on the island with viewers watching shows produced for Miami television featuring artists and personalities like Alexis Valdés, Carlucho, Zulema Cruz, and El Pible who had successful careers in Cuba. These well-known personalities are joined by the many writers and people behind the scenes that make these shows possible.[97] It is now common to see the hosts and guests of these shows directly addressing their audiences on the island. In a December 2013 interview with *OnCuba*, Valdés reflected on his popularity in Cuba: "One day we were told 'the show is a smash hit in Cuba' and we said, then we must consider that we are also working for people in Cuba, and . . . also think about the public who needs to laugh in Cuba."[98] Laughing with Cubans "over there" can create an affinity, a cubanía that is shared through diversión and feeds a transnational imaginary. When an audience on the island can see how Cuba is enacted *outside* the island, that transnational imaginary is expanded courtesy of the artists featured, content on the shows, and even the commercials for South Florida businesses.

Over the years, with more artists from the island going to Miami to perform thanks to the intercambio cultural, they inevitably appear on these variety shows in South Florida to promote their appearances. Through el paquete, people in Cuba can watch some of the most popular humorists on the island like Luis Silva, Robertico, and Angel García being interviewed on television in the United States for a mostly Cuban audience. In consuming these forms of diversión, the audience can experience simultaneously that Cuba and cubanía is happening elsewhere and that they are part of a cultural conversation that extends beyond the island. That connection is a product not only of familiarity with a given artist or humorist, but also of subsequent performances *on the island*, which often feature material based on their experiences in the United States.

With the relationship between Cuba and the United States being so highly politicized, one might ask where, amidst all the diversión found on el paquete, political content fits in. The answer is that clips from C-SPAN featuring Ileana Ros-Lehtinen and Marco Rubio lambasting the Castros are nowhere to be found. Even local political commentators like Pedro Sevcec and Oscar Haza, who are featured on Miami television stations and take up Cuban issues, frequently are absent from weekly offerings. Dissident blogger Yoani Sánchez's latest posts are not included either. As one of the editors of el paquete explained in an interview, "We include everything that people ask except for political issues so that we do not get into trouble."[99] This self-censorship is a response to the very real fear of a government crackdown. It is a fear that even Zulema Cruz, an established artist and resident of Miami, worries about when she performs in sketches on television in South Florida. There is a sense that el paquete could be banned from one day to the next.

It is not news that Cubans have internalized the government's power. Those who put together and distribute el paquete "know better" than to include explicit political material that could be read as counterrevolutionary. But the absence of explicit politics does not mean that the content and consumption of el paquete are not doing complex political work on a number of implicit, subtler levels under the cover of "harmless" entertainment. Artists from Cuba are treated as guests on Miami television, with all the excitement, fanfare, and applause that accompany the appearance of any other guest. Cubans on the island see that there is respect and joy, not antagonism. This goes a long way toward dispelling the idea of a hostile "Miami mafia"—an old Cuban government refrain—closed to the idea of working with island-based talent. The political barriers between Cubans from *here* hostile to the Cubans from *over there* are fading, and that is nowhere more apparent than in popular culture. Even more striking is that fact that artists excluded from Cuban television make appearances on Miami-based programs. Robertico, easily one of the best known and recognized comedians on the island, is all but banned from Cuban television. He performs often in Havana, but primarily at his upscale club where the costs of entry, food, and drink are out of reach for a majority of Cubans. The most cost-effective way for a Cuban living on the island to watch Robertico's latest material would be to download his performances and interviews *in Miami* from el paquete.

While explicit political commentary from talking heads in Miami and US politicians is not available, there is still plenty of political speech through the irreverent choteo that fuels so much of Cuban Miami's evening television programing. Shows like *El Happy Hour*, *El Arañazo*, and *TN3* use skits, impersonations, and monologues to satirize social life in Cuba and more provocatively, figures like Fidel and Raúl Castro.[100] In Cuba, the Castros cannot even be mentioned by name in public comedy performances, never mind television.[101] Also significant is the fact that a great deal of the humor has nothing to do with politics. When I interviewed writers for these shows, I was consistently told that while they strive to make comedy from a Cuban perspective, it is not always *about* Cuba.[102] That Cuban lens remains in place, creating familiar scenes for audiences on the island, but they are also exposed to content that touches on world events, local life in Miami, and of course, various representations of race, gender, and sexuality. In *not* being explicitly political all the time, these shows demonstrate that, unlike the government's portrayal of the diaspora as obsessed with Cuba, there are many interests beyond the island's politics.

Critics of el paquete such as the former minister of culture Abel Prieto have described television coming from Miami as being of low quality, somehow beneath the island's "revolutionary" culture. In remarks made at the eighth Congreso de la Unión de Escritores y Artistas de Cuba (UNEAC), Prieto singled out shows like *Caso Cerrado* in particular.[103] *Caso Cerrado* is a courtroom show that is best described as a cross between *Judge Judy* and more sensational daytime talk shows like *The Jerry Springer Show*. Presiding over the "court" is Dr. Ana María Polo, a Cuban American lawyer who left the island with her family at the age of two. The show features staged cases with participants paid for their participation. The appeal is in part due to the sensational cases—infidelity, sexual practices, violence, and family squabbles abound. But much of the draw is Dr. Polo, whose tough talk, sharp wit, and life advice have ensured her popularity in the United States, Cuba, and a number of other countries in Latin America. Even here, though, politics are palpable. Many of the participants on the show are Cuban, in large part due to the fact that the show is filmed at studios in Hialeah, Florida, the city most densely populated with Cubans outside the island. Whenever the topic of Cuba or the situation on the island comes up in a case, Dr. Polo takes the opportunity to let her strong feelings about the Castro government be known by blasting the Castro brothers and openly mocking them.[104] Despite dissident Yoani Sánchez's international awards for her blog *Generación Y*, it is more likely that Cubans on the island are hearing critiques of the Cuban government from Dr. Polo, not Sánchez whose work is heavily censored.

I end with a moment that crystalizes so much of what I have discussed in this chapter. In September 2014, Luis Silva and his character Pánfilo appeared on Alexis Valdés's late-night talk show in Miami. Audiences watching in Cuba would have seen a fascinating generational intersection of Cuban popular culture. In the host's chair sat Valdés, an actor and comedian much beloved in Cuba, who left the island to further his career in Spain and eventually Miami. To his right sat Luis Silva, who is without question the most popular comedian on the island today. As they chatted in a brightly lit studio, engaging in the usual talk show banter, they represented, quite vividly, a cultural continuity between Cuba and its diaspora that is by no means new, but has historically been downplayed, if not explicitly criticized, in both Cuba and Miami. Audiences in both places had the opportunity to hear Silva reflect on censorship of his show on the island and how it affected his approach to creating content. But they also heard Silva's commitment to continue doing his show in Cuba, despite the allures of Miami.

Their amiable conversation ended with a powerful symbolic gesture. Silva cited two role models for his development as an entertainer: Consuelito Vidal, who never left Cuba, *and* Alexis Valdés, based in Miami now for many years. I read this moment, along with their playful waving to people watching in Cuba on el paquete, as an affirmation of the present and future of Cuban popular culture as a truly transnational project. Engaging the at times ephemeral archive of diversión and its pleasures provides a glimpse at how people are narrating the new normal and perhaps most crucially, how diversión has created and sustained a form of relation, a ludic sociability, among Cubans on and off the island before and after the December 17, 2014 announcement regarding the reestablishment of diplomatic relations. Of course, diversión is not some utopic solution to the questions and problems that accompany this ever-growing transnational cultural dynamic, including representations of race and gender, prohibitions by the state, and the role of capital in what kind of popular culture gets disseminated. But through analysis of widely consumed forms of cultural production and the ways in which the politics of culture intersect with and diverge from the politics of the state, we can begin to decode how cubanía is being understood and imagined in the twenty-first century.

To better grasp how narratives of cubanía are shifting in the twenty-first century, it is critical that we examine the role of digital spaces in the production of relationships and communal imaginaries. In the final chapter, I consider how diversión manifests itself online—especially in social media—and explain how ludic sociability and narratives of cubanía get produced and circulated digitally.

5

Digital Diversión

Feeling Cuban Online

PATATÚ: Attack of obscure origin that can strike at any time. Could be serious enough to require hospitalization, yet is undetected by medical technology. Victims tend to be males and females over the age of 50 years.

MOÑO VIRADO (TWISTED BONNET): Psychological imbalance of short duration that causes strange mood swings, violent irritating behavior, as well as general unpleasantness. Extremely common. Can strike anyone regardless of age or sex.
—Forwarded email titled "Guide to Cuban Diseases."

My earliest memories of interacting with cubanía digitally extend back to my early teen years in the 1990s—a time when your screen name served not only as a login credential but also as a way to present yourself online in a world where text was king and images still played a secondary role. My world online was populated with variations of screen names like NJCubanito337 and CubanQt201, which reflected not only pride in ethnic identification but also the spatial groundedness of my peers in northern New Jersey during the multicultural 1990s. I don't recall that Cuba or latinidad more broadly was a topic of conversation as I instant messaged and chatted my way through the seemingly endless America Online free trials that I rescued from my family's junk mail pile. But there it was all the same, the performance of an ethnic identity online as a means to engage—directly or indirectly—with a world inside and outside Hudson County, New Jersey.

Screen names were not the only ways to perform an ethnic identity and hail others in those early days of the web. The inbox was also a key site for encounters with cubanía in the form of personal messages and of course, the email forward. Although the epigraph to this chapter is from an email forward I received in 2008, its content was making the rounds in the late 1990s, if not earlier.[1] In this email, words and phrases like *patatú* and *moño virado*, which figure prominently in Cuban vernacular expression, are defined in English in a manner that attempts to capture a certain scientific rigor and tone in the service of comic incongruity. More importantly, this email's popularity over the years suggests that it has accomplished what all forwards and chain messages are meant to do—circulate widely. In this way, the "Guide to Cuban Diseases" is a lot like many other email forwards that attempt to produce a pleasurable encounter with a Cuban cultural identity. Pepito jokes, PowerPoint slide shows featuring low resolution images of Havana before the Revolution, "fun facts" about Cuban history, prayers for La Caridad del Cobre, and lists detailing Cuban linguistic and cultural idiosyncrasies of which the "Guide to Cuban Diseases" is one of many, have all been featured prominently in these forwards. The primary message behind so many of these emails? It feels good to be Cuban. Pass it on.[2]

Over the years as these forwards became a predictable part of my email routine, *diversión* was probably not the word I would have used to describe the arrival of yet another recycled Pepito joke. But as fewer of them trickled in, I began to feel their absence. It was at that moment, around 2010, that I began to ask people to send me their forwards in the hopes of constructing an archive. I was attracted to their organic quality, the "do-it-yourselfness" reflected in the multiple font colors, clumsy formatting, and animated, flapping Cuban flags. My interest in the content and style intensified when I came to appreciate the extent to which these forwards circulated. They carried with them the marks of their travels. Dozens of unfamiliar email addresses in the recipient field and the comments added to them by previous readers captured the degree to which this content made its way across the global Cuban diaspora.

Though I receive few forwards today, it does not mean that the kinds of content and spirit of diversión that characterized them have disappeared. Instead, they have simply evolved along with how we engage with the Internet in the age of Web 2.0—a time when our online and offline lives are deeply intertwined with social media platforms like Facebook, Twitter, Instagram, and YouTube.[3] Throughout the course of this book, I have delved deeply into popular culture to understand how the Cuban diaspora in the United States has narrated itself in the pleasures, big and small, of everyday life: sharing a joke with friends, attending comedy shows, television, listening to morning talk radio, and reveling in nostalgic narratives of pre-Castro Cuba. In this final chapter, I end with what is increasingly becoming a fundamental part of how we are social and construct narratives of ourselves and our communities—our digital lives online. As Lee Rainie and Barry Wellman explain, "Social networking sites have become the dashboards of the Internet," where people search for news and entertainment, as well as to make connections along the lines of commonalities in the form of race, ethnicity, hobbies, and politics, among others.[4] Here, I investigate how narratives of cubanía are being constructed, circulated, and consumed by the diaspora online in order to reveal the rising importance of digital spaces for imagining and performing ethnic identity in the twenty-first century.

Though my focus is digital diversión in the Cuban context, the kind of material I examine is certainly not limited to any one group, ethnic or otherwise. If the Internet is anything, it is a place for amusement. A basic inventory of the most widely spread forms of content would include cute babies, cats, pranks, mashups, memes, and parodies of all kinds. This is not a new phenomenon. Even in the 1990s, when social media as we know it did not exist, scholars like Brenda Danet chronicled the central role of play in online chat rooms and hacker culture.[5] The intersection of play and the digital has only increased with the rise of social media. In the world of networks like Facebook, "ludic self-construction" plays a role in how we want to be perceived by others: likeable, creative, engaging, funny.[6] Studies of virality, memes, spreadability, and email forwards all highlight the importance of the ludic specifically for inspiring the circulation of content.[7] In the United States, this holds up to quantitative analysis. The Pew Internet and American Life Project consistently reports that comedy and humor are powerful drivers behind social media use and online video consumption. A 2014 Pew study states that nearly 40 percent of Facebook users polled report humor as a "major" reason they log on.[8] A separate study of online video habits concluded that for adult Internet users, comedy/humor videos are one of the most viewed genres, with a whopping 82 percent of 18–29 year olds, 75 percent of 30–49 year olds, and 61 percent of those 50 and older regularly watching.[9]

Forms of play online and the ludic sociability they foster on sites like Facebook are directly connected to how we develop relationships and connect with others based on what is shared. According to Nicholas John, "Sharing is the fundamental and constitutive activity of Web 2.0 in general, and social network sites in particular."[10] It is, in fact, a significant part of what makes life online enjoyable. Sharing, on or offline, is a form of expressing and building relationships with others. What we share helps to define relationships, how we imagine others, and, especially, how we create narratives of the self. You are, in many ways, what you share. Sharing communicates one's interests, politics, loves, and hates explicitly or implicitly. It builds connections and intensifies existing ones, but we do not share everything that comes across our social media feeds or inboxes. Instead, content that is shared widely often adheres to the logic of "emotional intensification"—it makes us *feel*, it moves us to act, to try to relate to someone through the "broadly shared feelings" that popular culture can conjure.[11] This is especially the case with the circulation of humor. Ted Cohen explains, "I need reassurance that this something inside me, the something that is tickled by a joke, is indeed something that constitutes an element of my humanity. I discover something of what it is to be a human being by finding this thing in me, and then having it echoed in you, another human being."[12] Social media is the means by which this echo can be "heard." It is in the sharing of content that feelings and narratives of the self can be magnified, "echoed," in Cohen's understanding of the term, online.

In this chapter, I seek to trace how cubanía echoes on social media through close readings of popular, highly circulated forms of diversión. If Web 2.0 is primarily about sharing and we know content that spreads often produces amusement broadly defined, examining widely circulated forms of diversión online is a productive analytical route for understanding how and why certain narratives of cubanía resonate. I will be especially interested in how this resonance develops in relation to representations of race, sexuality, and generations. How do different generational segments of the Cuban diaspora intersect (or not) on social media? Answering such a question will both expose intragroup boundaries and tensions and highlight points of affinity. As I consider content produced by comic personalities with large followings on social media—a puppet named Pepe Billete and Los Pichy Boys—I unravel part of the "affective fabric" of the digital Cuban diaspora, "the lived and deeply felt everyday sociality of connections, ruptures, emotions, words, politics and sensory energies" that fill quotidian life as people produce and consume content on social media.[13]

Cubanía Online

When the topic of Cuba and the Internet arises, the conversation usually goes in one of two predictable ways.[14] The first discusses the Cuban blogosphere on the island and the ways in which it is (or is not) affecting political discourse.[15] Yoani Sánchez, a high-profile dissident blogger on the island who has earned a number of international awards, is often mentioned in this regard. But although the number of bloggers is rising, their work suffers from "limited domestic exposure."[16] In addition to government censorship, the reason for the restricted reach of Cuban bloggers on the island brings us to the second way the Internet is talked about in relation to Cuba—through the language of lack. Cuba has "one of the lowest internet penetration rates in the Western hemisphere" despite recent moves by the government to expand public access with Wi-Fi hotspots.[17] While connecting to the Internet is possible at government-controlled hotspots and hotels, expensive hourly rates for a less than optimal "broadband" connection put access out of reach for most Cubans in a country where the average monthly salary hovers around $20. Some do have access to the Internet for work purposes, and there is also a black market economy that provides dial-up connections to people in their homes. But the crackling and pinging of a 56k modem demonstrate just how far behind Cuba is in providing the necessary infrastructure for its citizens to connect.

For those who have left Cuba since the mid-1990s, a period that lines up nicely with the balsero crisis and the rise of the Internet as a resource increasingly available to the public in the United States, connecting to the Internet has been a means to participate in what scholars have called "digital diasporas." Defined as "the distinct online networks that diasporic people use to re-create identities, share opportunities, spread their culture, influence homeland and host-land policy, or create debate about common-interest issues by means of electronic devices," digital diasporas have grown considerably as access to the Internet has increased worldwide.[18] But communication with the country of origin via the Internet, a significant focus in digital diaspora scholarship, is less pronounced in the Cuban case because of lack of access on the island.[19] This reality has prompted me to focus exclusively on how Cubans in the increasingly diffuse diaspora are cohering and making sense of life *outside* of Cuba through digital networks and the content that circulates on them. Blogs, news websites, affinity groups, message boards, sports coverage, videos of family and friends reuniting on the island, and Twitter hashtags are just some of the ways in which Cubans gather information and interact online.

Much of this content, regardless of platform, is channeled through social media websites. The result can be a kind of ambient cubanía where content appears, ebbs, and flows at varying intensities. The degree to which one encounters this material is a product of a host of variables: the number of groups or pages one "likes" or is a member of; one's friends and the amount of posting they do that reflects an interest in Cuba or a Cuban cultural identity; and Facebook's shifting algorithmic formulas that determine what appears in a user's news feed.[20] Whatever the degree to which one may "feel" Cuban online, what is clear is that social media is particularly adept at providing opportunities for identification—especially in relation to content that is newsworthy, stirring, and most important for this study, entertaining. This is due not only to the kind of content people tend to share but also to the very affective logic that underpins social media. As Richard Grusin explains, social media platforms "work to produce and maintain positive affective relations with their users, to set up affective feedback loops that make one want to proliferate one's media transactions. . . . The fact that Facebook offers its users the option to 'like' or 'unlike' an item but not to 'dislike' it epitomizes its bias towards fostering positive individual and collective affect."[21]

The everydayness of social media paired with the high circulation of ludic content shows how diversión can shape one's engagement with a Cuban cultural identity on a quotidian basis. The relationship between cubanía and the ludic becomes ordinary—a performance that has the potential to be repeated daily. Social media accounts like "We're Not Yelling, We're Cuban, That's How We Talk" count on thousands of followers and cater primarily to US-born Cuban Americans with images and Spanglish memes that feature Cuban food, advice from *abuela*, and affirmations of broadly shared cultural characteristics.[22] Tellingly, these kinds of accounts seek to be in conversation with their audience's daily routine. In the morning, pictures of *pasteles de guayaba* appear alongside videos of hot, sugary espresso being poured into demitasse cups. People return the friendly "buenos días" in the comments section and spread that morning greeting among their friends by tagging one another and adding their own message to the image.

Other sites, like "Periódico Guamá," which ran from 2008 to 2014, spoke to a completely different segment of the diaspora by representing everyday life in Cuba. Started by a Cuban cartoonist named Alen Lauzán residing in Chile, "Periódico Guamá" featured hard-hitting parodies of Cuban state-sponsored discourse.[23] Taking his cue from Cuban news events, Lauzán would translate them into satire through the irreverent logic of choteo. The example shown in Figure 5.1 refers to Fidel Castro's January 2014 visit to Cuban artist Kcho's studio in Havana. Lauzán uses the font and graphic presence of the official government newspaper *Granma* to put out a news bulletin that parodies state-run media, Castro, and Kcho. While Castro is compared to the zombie characters in the comic film *Juan de los muertos* (2011), Kcho is heckled on the left-hand side of the image with rhymes meant to be read in the cadence of chants recited during *actos de repudio* when government supporters and agents shout down dissidents: "KCHO, my friend, the mummy [Fidel] is with you!" To understand Lauzán's parodies one needs to be well acquainted with news in Cuba as it happens—a far cry from the mostly symbolic, apolitical nature of "We're Not Yelling, We're Cuban, That's How We Talk."

Though different in their target audiences and approaches, both examples get at the relationship between diversión, cubanía, and quotidian life on social media. These narratives are available offline, but in the digital space, the *point* in large part is to be visible to others in a particular way through the engagement with, and circulation of, content. The repetition of this content, the cycle of tagging, sharing, and commenting, structures a common way of relating to others through a ludic sociability. Reposting or tweeting a link to the latest Guamá parody communicates a certain literacy with respect to current events in Cuba and a political position, as well as aiding "ludic self construction." Tagging a friend in a post by "We're Not Yelling, We're Cuban, That's How

"EL DIVERSIONISMO IDEOLÓGICO NO HA MUERTO" · ESTE BLOG NO ES DE FIDEL, ESTE BLOG ES DE GRATIS · SEDICIÓN ÚNICA · AÑO 6

Guamá

09.01.14

GUAMÁ, TERRITORIO LIBRE DE MUELA

KUBANA YANA YAGUA COACOA FOTUTO

474

CANDELONES CON CANDELONES

JUAN DE LOS MUERTOS ACTUALIZÓ SU FOTO DE PERFIL

¡KCHO, AMIGO, LA MOMIA ESTÁ CONTIGO!

¡KCHO CUENTISTA NO TE HAGAS EL ARTISTA!

¡KCHO, ENEMIGO, NOS TIENES DE MENDIGOS!

¡KCHO, CHIVA, PERDISTE LA PERSPECTIVA!

OLA K ASE

HERMANO DE RAÚL CAMPOS RUZ ACTUALIZÓ SU ESTADO

"Dando bote"

Figure 5.1. "Periódico Guamá," January 9, 2014. Courtesy of Alen Lauzán.

We Talk" is an attempt to solidify a common bond around a picture of sticky *pastelitos* by invoking a shared cultural sensibility.

Kathleen Stewart's work on "ordinary affects" strikes me as a supple way for thinking about how cubanía can appear in quotidian life online: "A world of shared banalities can be a basis of sociality, or an exhausting undertow, or just something to do. It can pop up as a picture of staged perfection, as a momentary recognition, or as a sense of shock or relief at being 'in' something with others."[24] As these forms of diversión appear in one's social media world, they can mean different things at different times: a way of feeling, a sense of belonging, or exhaustion from yet another joke or image of the Cuban flag. Regardless of one's relationship to this content on any given day, it serves as an invitation to engage. But the broader logic of social media as a sharing economy affects what we do with that encounter. Do we chuckle to ourselves? Scroll through barely noticing? Or do we interpellate others by tagging them in particular comments as an invitation to engage a piece of content? In what follows, I look at content that has been highly successful in getting people to do just that, to share in a process that shapes how one engages with cubanía online.

Pepe Billete

Easily one of the most visible Cuban American social media personalities online, Pepe Billete (Pepe Money) appeared on the scene in 2011 with YouTube videos featuring relationship advice, commentary on the Miami Heat basketball team, song parodies, and collaborations with other South Florida personalities. While this kind of content is certainly not unique, his physical appearance is. Pepe Billete is a puppet.[25] More Calle Ocho than Sesame Street, Pepe draws an audience of primarily US-born Cuban Americans who appreciate his at times off-color humor and celebration of and pride in the city of Miami. Local popularity in Dade County has translated into national opportunities. He now hosts his own talk-radio show, *Pepe Billete Uncensored*, on Sirius XM radio and enjoys sponsorship from local and international brands. His appeal to primarily US-born Cuban Americans and his success, courtesy of his ability to harness social media like Facebook and Instagram, make Pepe's cultural production an ideal site for examining how narratives

Figure 5.2. Pepe Billete cover photo, Facebook.

of cubanía are being consumed and circulated among a less discussed segment of the Cuban diaspora—US-born Cuban Americans of the millennial generation.[26]

As far as first impressions go, it is not difficult to see the potential for amusement that a foul-mouthed puppet can present. But the true key to Pepe Billete's success is in the crafting of his persona. His backstory is that he came to the United States during the Mariel boatlift and made money (hence the name, *billete*, which is slang for money) in the drug trade. Now a reformed *marimbero* (drug dealer), Pepe's content ranges from scatological humor to more deeply developed political critiques penned for news outlets like the *Miami New Times*. The constant across all of Pepe's content is his pitch-perfect performance of a stereotypical, hypermasculine, white cubanía communicated with Cuban slang, idiomatic expression, and anti-communist rhetoric. In my interview with the artist, he explained that "Pepe is a series of stereotypes wrapped up into one caricature. . . . [Pepe is] my uncle, my old boss. . . . Alvarez Guedes, Carlito D'Mant, every fucking Cuban you see at Versailles hablando mierda de la política" (talking shit about politics).[27] This inspiration from an older exile generation is reflected even in how the puppet *looks*. When the idea for Pepe Billete arose, the artist sent a picture of iconic exile comedian Guillermo Alvarez Guedes to the puppet maker as inspiration.[28]

But Pepe's success cannot be attributed solely to his ability to draw on Cuban idiomatic expression and choteo. If that were the case, his

US-born Cuban American audience could get their fill by watching the South Florida television networks geared toward Cuban audiences, which were discussed in Chapter 4. Although choteo is critical to Pepe's legibility and the subsequent pleasure he inspires in his audience, most of his material is in English with Cuban Spanish as the primary vehicle for delivering his most popular punchlines. And unlike the older generation, Pepe is plugged into US popular culture in the form of sports, music, and politics. From comments on Kim Kardashian to interviews with Miami politicians like Ileana Ros-Lehtinen, Pepe's cultural repertoire and interests reflect his creator's US-born Cuban American generational context. The success of Pepe Billete can be attributed, then, to what seems like an incongruous combination: the vocabulary and imagined perspective of an older generation of Cuban exiles applied to contemporary US popular culture. Pepe functions as a bridge that makes the cubanía of the older generation both accessible and relevant to a US-born Cuban American audience that is nostalgic for it while being primarily engaged with the popular culture mainstream.

Pepe Billete has succeeded in filtering popular culture through the lens of cubanía in a number of YouTube performances. In a parody video called "I'm in Love with the Mojo," Pepe and his cast of collaborators borrow from a song called "I'm in Love with the Coco" (2014) by rapper O. T. Genasis.[29] The object of affection in the song shifts from cocaine in the original to a marinade often used on Cuban dishes like roast pork called *mojo*. The parody samples the beat and lyric delivery to produce a song that captures the Cuban love for pork, that other white meat. Released in December 2014, the song speaks to the Christmas season and the traditional practices for celebrating the holiday on Nochebuena, December 24. Santa hats abound in the video, along with shots of backyards in Miami where families gather to celebrate over traditional Cuban fare.

Before expressing his love for the mojo, Pepe sets up the song parody with the following as the beat drops: "La Nochebuena este año se hizo en la casa del primo mío y ese está casado con una gringa, que no sabe cocinar ni pinga!" (Nochebuena this year was at my cousin's house and he's married to a white girl who can't cook for shit!). This quick preface sets the tone generationally for US-born Cuban Americans. As subsequent generations of Cubans are born, the rate of marriage across racial and ethnic lines increases. Cultural clashes can also arise, especially during annual holidays, when the desire to retain traditions can also be accompanied by anxiety about loss of those practices.[30] Not content with the food offered at his cousin's house, Pepe explains that he is "in love with the mojo," a shorthand for Cuban cultural traditions and practices. Despite assimilation and changing family dynamics, Pepe writes a love letter to cubanía during the holiday season when cultural traditions are often most felt.

It is not just any mojo, though. As I have explained throughout the book, the deeper the reference, the more inside the joke, the more pleasure is produced in an audience that recognizes their increasingly exclusive access to the "inside" of the content. The bottles of mojo featured throughout the video are of brands with a strong presence in South Florida like La Lechonera and Badía. These cultural references are then presented through a kind of kitschy appropriation of hip-hop music video conventions. The cast pops bottles of the mojo like champagne while a "video vixen" pours the marinade all over her body in a moment that short-circuits the trope of the hypersexualized female body present in much of music video culture with the stomach-churning image. These visuals set the stage for the parodic lyrics of the song:

> Nochebuena, puerco asado.
> Caja china, soy guajiro.
> Arroz, frijoles, platanitos,
> Esta noche cago rico.
> Chicharrones pa' mi socio.
> You a vegan that's a no-no.
> No tengas pena come mijo,
> Que ya tú eres un gordito.
>
> Nochebuena, roast pork.
> Caja china, I'm a peasant.
> Rice, beans, and plantains,
> Tonight I'll take a nice shit.
> Pork cracklings for my friend,
> You're a vegan that's a no-no.
> Don't be shy eat my boy,
> Because you're already chubby.

The lyrics are a catalog of Cuban cultural signifiers: roast pork; cooking instruments like the *caja china*; the insistence that veganism is incompatible with cubanía; and the Cuban everyman, the *guajiro*. While they are delivered in Spanish, they maintain the cadence and vocal similarities to the original song performed by Genasis in a manner that allows the audience to engage two cultural contexts and vocabularies, to feel Cuban and American simultaneously.[31]

But it is not just the cultural signifiers Pepe chooses that produce the pleasures of recognition. Diversión also encapsulates the manner of joking, what makes the performance feel Cuban. Turns of phrase like "esta noche cago rico" invoke the scatological elements of Cuban humor.[32] The lines "No tengas pena come mijo, / Que ya tú eres un gordito" are even more telling of Pepe's desire to foster affinity since they call to mind the well-worn trope of the *abuela* eager to see her grandchildren eat. Terms of endearment like *mijo* and *gordito*, complete with the more intimate diminutive *ito*, provide more of that familiar Cuban texture. The use of *gordito*, especially, speaks to an important reason why Pepe and this video have been so popular. In US mainstream notions of childrearing, calling a kid fat, chubby, or worse, a nickname along those lines, is frowned upon. Questions of self-esteem and the delicate psyches of children all rise to the fore. But for a generation of older Cubans, weight is a common theme in observational humor and quotidian conversation. Comedians like Alvarez Guedes, for example, frequently commented on how Cubans talk about issues like weight.[33] Nicknames like *gordo* and *flaca* follow people long after they have lost or gained weight. Pepe plays on that understanding in his lyrics and offers his audience a suspension of a certain political correctness around language and the body through a nostalgic detour through cubanía. As I will show in detail later, detours around what is considered acceptable language in the affirmation of a cultural identity can become more fraught around questions of race and sexuality.

Surely, dramatizing the point at which cultures clash and mix for the sake of comedy is nothing new. In the Cuban context, the bilingual sitcom *¿Qué Pasa, USA?* featured three generations of the Peña family as they navigated life in 1970s Miami and was able to touch on the comic potential born out of such cultural encounters. But generally, efforts at producing explicitly bicultural programming have had trouble finding audiences consistently. This is especially the case for mainstream media outlets. Attempts at reaching English-dominant Latina/o audiences with channels like Fusion Network, a joint venture between Disney and Univision, have been largely unsuccessful.[34] What social media networks provide is an opportunity for performers like Pepe Billete to target particular segments with great precision. In July of 2016, Pepe Billete's Facebook page, his primary means of engagement with his audience, registered over 57,000 fans, while his videos attracted views ranging from a couple of thousand to over 400,000. In the case of "I'm in Love with the Mojo," the video has been viewed over 190,000 times on YouTube and Facebook, "liked" over 1,700 times, and shared from his page by around 3,800 users. On the surface, these numbers are not particularly impressive when stacked up against viral videos on YouTube that have attracted hundreds of millions of views. But as Karine Nahon and Jeff Hemsley explain, "Virality is a process of diffusion and so the way it spreads, socially, during many to many communication, is more important than how many people actually end up seeing it. Virality is scalable."[35] In my interview with Pepe's creator, he explained that he is most interested in reaching his core audience, which he calls his "tribe," and making content for them. Such an approach has been profitable. The artist behind Pepe was able to quit his day job once the character began to catch on in South Florida.

He may not have as many followers or "likes" as other social media personalities, but his audience is highly engaged with his content. For example, in a typical active week in November 2014, Pepe's Facebook posts reached a respectable 2.4 million people. But the number of people engaged with his content in that same week is more telling. Those who liked, shared, or commented on his posts numbered over 279,000.[36] This speaks to Pepe's ability to consistently strike a chord among his audience. He remains popular because he is able to dramatize and even comically defamiliarize the lived, bicultural context that informs *how* his audience practices sociality. Or for those outside of large Cuban communities, Pepe's material can be a way into a world you wish for, or perhaps just like to check in with now and again. Using digital tools to produce and disseminate his carefully calibrated content gives Pepe Billete the nimbleness to reach an audience that bigger networks on television or radio would find cost-prohibitive to target.

While Pepe's bicultural fluency gives him a great deal of comic flexibility, it also crystalizes the generational negotiation of how race, gender, and sexuality are represented in a bicultural context. The character of Pepe Billete is a stereotype of brash, white Cuban masculinity. Accordingly, his cultural repertoire of idiomatic expression also includes a particular vocabulary for race and sexuality. In a tweet in April of 2012, Pepe posted the following: "Van Gundy [former coach of the New York Knicks basketball team] lost his virginity to un negro en Harlem when he was 17. That's why he's so biased toward the knicks #HEATLive."[37] Months later, he posted a series of tweets with the hashtag #ItsACuban-Thing in order to capture, in 140 characters or less, cultural elements that would resonate among his audience as "Cuban." One of these was "No sir, negro is not a racial epithet. #ItsACubanThing."[38] The tweet was not directed toward anyone in particular or in response to someone calling him out for his use of *negro* on Twitter. Instead, it was a rhetorical move to highlight a kind of Cuban exceptionalism often featured in Pepe's work.

It may seem like Pepe is invoking a weak cultural relativism to justify using *negro* as a means to celebrate a cultural identity. But such a reading does not go far enough to understand how racial representations might signify in a bicultural context. When these tweets are read against Pepe's broader cultural production, the picture becomes more complicated. Pepe has been active in calling out racist sports mascots and has been extremely critical of how the media has represented black protests in the wake of Ferguson.[39] In my interview with the artist, he spoke at length about black segregation in Miami and the Latina/o brown face performances prevalent in the media—criticism he has often channeled through the puppet. I offer these examples not as a means to balance the moral equation of minoritarian representation but to muddy the waters a bit.

When Pepe uses the hashtag "ItsACubanThing," to forcefully claim that *negro* is not a "racial epithet," he is drawing from a depoliticized, and certainly dehistoricized, understanding of race in a Cuban context, one that is disconnected from the ways racism has manifested itself in and been reinforced by popular constructions of "el negro" throughout the history of Cuban popular culture.[40] Comparing US-based legacies of racism—a history US-born Cuban Americans would be much more familiar with—to the superficially "benign" language around racial difference in a Cuban context might inform the insistence that the use of *negro* is inherently harmless. Adding to this is the way in which invoking "el negro" is consistent with Pepe's persona and his strategy of striking nostalgic chords by reminding the audience of the humor and idiomatic expression of the older exile generation. Pepe is playing his part. But racism is indeed a "Cuban thing" and that is clearly communicated in studies of the relationship between Cubans and African Americans in Miami historically—this book included.[41] While Pepe might be inclined to cite the way *negro* is used as a term of endearment among Cubans, in saying that Van Gundy lost his virginity to "un negro en Harlem," Pepe draws from a long history of hypersexualized blackness in the Cuban context, especially in humor. Specifically, Pepe calls on the figure of the hypersexualized black male as the *bugarrón*, "the active-insertive during anal intercourse" to which Van Gundy submits to as the *maricón* in the receptive role, thus forfeiting any claim to true masculinity.[42] By making such a comment, Pepe once again mobilizes Cuban idioms to remark on US popular culture, in this case basketball, but in doing so captures an element shared by Cuba and the United States, which I have noted throughout this book: representations that hinge on racist constructions of blackness and homosexuality as incompatible with masculinity.

Another example of generational and bicultural dissonance around charged language can be found in the title of an article Pepe wrote for the *Miami New Times*, "Banning Same-Sex Marriage is Tremenda Mariconada." In this article, Pepe positions himself as a strong supporter of same-sex marriage by countering the religious argument against it and announcing his participation at Miami's annual pride parade with his own float.[43] Pepe uses the word *mariconada* in the article title, whose root is *maricón* (faggot), to describe a potential ban on same-sex marriage. He wants to be able to use a word that will resonate strongly among his audience—a word that circulates widely in Cuban popular culture and vulgar expression. But he also wants to represent his social liberalism, a position that increasingly reflects his generation's attitude toward same-sex marriage. Squaring the politics of using the term *maricón* clearly weighs on Pepe. In a 2013 article, he slammed Dwayne Michael Carter, better known as rapper Lil Wayne, for disrespecting the city of Miami by using the word *maricón* to describe the performer. But in the middle of his rant, he inserted an aside, a socially liberal commercial break: "Un maricón has nothing to do with being gay; I wouldn't dare insult the gay community by associating them with the likes of you [Lil Wayne]. No, un maricón is an ostentatious little bitch who has to constantly draw attention to himself because he has no substance or charisma otherwise."[44] In both the tweet discussed above and this article, Pepe attempts to shield himself against accusations of sexual or racial bias. But while he goes out of his way to make sure his comments are not read in a manner contrary to his intent, what remains in both cases is a reliance on normative understandings of masculinity. To deride Van Gundy and Lil Wayne, Pepe attacks their manhood, suggesting that they are less than masculine through a reliance on language that would be instantly recognizable to his audience.

How can we read this use of language? It would be easy to dismiss Pepe as wanting it both ways. A similar parallel can be drawn with people who use the word "gay" as an insult but seek to divorce it from an attack on homosexuality. For me, it is more interesting to consider the justifications, the intellectual and emotional acrobatics, made in order to validate how words like *maricón* and *negro* can be deployed to mobilize feelings of affinity around a Cuban cultural identity while those using them simultaneously demand justice for racial and sexual minorities. I would argue that this is not a unique situation. Bicultural and bilingual subjects of all ethnicities negotiate how language accrues meaning in different contexts. The intimate relationship between language and meaning necessarily carries the historical weight of normative cultural values. Some of Pepe's followers and critics may reject these words outright as representing a form of Latin American prejudice no less destructive than racist practices in the United States. Some may embrace it as an overlap between their racist views in both contexts. For others, these words might be less associated with prejudice and more about an emotional or nostalgic relationship to their ethnic identity. I highlight this not to justify this kind of language but to point to the complexity of negotiating cultural contexts when language is not only about what a particular word means but how words *feel*—the Cuban "thing" Pepe claims as the reason for invoking the word *negro*.[45] This is not meant to be a kind of "nostalgia dispensation" for language loaded with the weight of racist histories. Instead, these examples get to the lived complexity of racial representation in quotidian contexts and the different ways such language can resonate to produce pleasures—fraught or not. It also reveals what kind of language evokes a defensive posture (words about race and sexuality) and what does not, namely, normative notions of masculinity broadly conceived.

Pepe's success is in large part a product of his ability to mobilize his persona and the language that accompanies it to narrate a necessarily evolving popular culture landscape. But while the topics he addresses shift as tastes and trending topics change, the narrative of what it means to be Cuban remains constant. This is partly because the narrative of cubanía Pepe draws from and which his audience recognizes is necessarily built on what they have seen and heard growing up in Miami with Cuban family members. From the latest pop hit on the radio to local and national political races, Pepe's audience is more American than Cuban. They are significantly less invested in or knowledgable about matters related to contemporary Cuba. Cubanía is static, a reservoir of ethnic feeling and attachment that functions as a means for relationality, enjoyment, and engagement within a broader narrative of self that draws primarily from the cultural example of the older generation.

This "static" narrative of cubanía manifests itself in how Pepe imagines life on the island and represents more recent arrivals. As a guest on his SiriusXM radio show, I was asked to discuss my research and experiences in Cuba in the context of the announcement regarding warming US-Cuba relations. Pepe and his callers were consistently surprised at the information I provided. Yes, Willy Chirino and Celia Cruz albums are easy to find for sale on the streets of Havana. Yes, Cubans are allowed to visit hotels. Regardless of their political position on whether the United States and Cuba should develop closer ties, I have found in looking at posts and user comments and in interacting with fans on his radio show that an understanding of Cuba's shifting political, social, and economic landscape is often limited. Because this audience has little knowledge of political and social developments in Cuba, the narrative around the island is often boiled down to the always-dependable anti-Castro sentiment. So when the news broke of warming relations, Pepe did not weigh in with any strong opinion. Instead, he released a video that his entire audience could agree on—a cartoonish assassination of Fidel Castro that ended with that familiar exile refrain: *Cuba sí, Castro no.*

While Pepe declares that he knows little about politics in relation to US-Cuba relations, he certainly has a great deal to say about the "psychology" of Cubans on the island, in large part based on his interactions with more recent arrivals in Miami. In an article called "Memories of My Abuela" published by the *Miami New Times* in January 2015, Pepe reflects on the generation of his *abuela*, the exile generation, on which his performance of cubanía is based. He comes to the conclusion that the deaths of Raúl and Fidel Castro would change very little on the island. His abuela's Cuba is gone. He explains his logic this way:

> To say today's Cuba is a façade of the Cuba she [Pepe's grandmother] was forced to leave is a gross understatement. Through necessity, propaganda, and rationing, the Castros have successfully reprogrammed the psychology of the people into a state of perpetual dependency upon the government and skewed ethics to a point where stealing from the government, or any other giant, faceless entity, is a necessary part of life. When one generation reinforces that survivalist ideal daily upon the next generation, it becomes more and more decriminalized in the mind of the subsequent generation. . . . Cubans on the island are still as willing to work and struggle to make a dollar just as hard as my abuela did, but the taboos that guide the generation of Cubans the Castros engineered are definitely built upon a very different set of ethics. . . . It's the engineers who systematically oppressed the people into submission who are to blame; it's the Castros themselves, because it was their methodical destruction of the Cuban culture.[46]

The argument he makes above is certainly dripping with political claims that are in part based on an idealized narrative of *la Cuba de ayer* passed to him in what I theorized as the education of nostalgia in Chapter 3. This narrative combined with the characterization of more recent arrivals as being tainted by *el comunismo* feed this sentiment. But according to Pepe, there is reason for hope: "The Cuban culture of my abuela's generation strongly lives on in the hearts and minds of the four generations of Cuban-Americans that have prospered in the United States since their displacement."[47] Today's Cuba might be marked by skewed ethics and a culture that suffered "destruction," but the idealized narrative of Cuba Pepe heard from his grandmother lives on in generations of US-born

Cuban Americans for whom Miami is the only "Cuba" they have ever known.

One might ask: If the sentiment that Pepe expresses is widely held, where does that leave more recent arrivals raised under the Revolution? How does Pepe then represent the very Cuban subjects he describes in the passage above who make up a significant portion of the Cuban diaspora today? Answers to these questions can be found in a genre of Pepe's most popular posts on Facebook and Instagram: user-submitted photos of people who are, either real or imagined, recent arrivals from Cuba. Pepe's fans submit pictures from around Miami in hopes that he will post them with his comic captions in the form of social media hashtags. In this way, these extremely popular posts reflect a conversation already in full swing regarding how US-born Cuban Americans see and represent more recent arrivals.

One such post features a slightly out of focus image of a man wearing swim trunks while walking barefoot in a gym. Pepe captioned the photo this way: "Name that gym. . . . #PataSuciaPilates #BalseroCrossfit #AccidentWaitingToHappen #tremendaPinta #TremendoPompiado #SurfingOnABalsa #Air #LAFitness #HialeahStyle #HopeTheyHaveInsurance."[48] In this photo and so many others like it, the key words repeated across many of these captions are *balsero* and *Hialeah*. In this example, the shoeless man at a gym in Hialeah is dubbed a *balsero*—a term that refers to a more recent arrival from the island who has yet to assimilate and can carry a derogatory meaning depending on the context.[49] Whether or not this man is Cuban or a recent arrival is of little importance to producing the intended response from the audience. When the term *balsero* is used in Miami slang, it can signal a lack of refinement, an inability to assimilate, and a kind of tainted cubanía produced under the Revolution as discussed above.[50] The man's appearance fits into the narrative of the unassimilated and uncivilized balsero.[51]

The setting for this photo, imagined or otherwise, is Hialeah, Florida. While Hialeah has long been a haven for working-class Cubans in Miami, in the last twenty years it has become home to a large population of Cubans who have arrived since the rafter crisis. The city's name has long had a metonymic function in Miami as a shorthand for working-class, unassimilable cubanía closer in spirit to the island and marked by the excesses of an unapologetic *chusmería*. José Muñoz's definition of *chusmería* is especially relevant in relation to the place of Hialeah in the popular South Florida imagination: "Chusmería is, to a large degree, linked to stigmatized class identity. Within Cuban culture, for instance, being called chusma might be a technique for the middle class to distance itself from the working class. . . . In the United States, the epithet chusma also connotes recent immigration and a general lack of 'Americanness,' as well as an excessive nationalism—that one is somewhat over the top about her Cubanness."[52] That "excess" of Cubanness in the context of Hialeah inspired a great deal of highly circulated Internet content years before Pepe Billete came on the scene. Enrique Santos and Joe Ferrero created a music video parody of the Lynyrd Skynyrd hit "Sweet Home Alabama" titled "Sweet Home Hialeah," which made much of the chusmería in references to nosey neighbors, *chisme* (gossip), and over-the-top urban legends.[53] Mimi Dávila and Laura Di Lorenzo parodied the "chonga" or what Jillian Hernández calls the "chusma-as-teenager" in their 2007 hit "Chongalicious" which has attracted over 7 million views.[54] The figure of the chonga, deeply connected to Hialeah and notions of ethnic excess, has circulated broadly due to this video.[55] It is not uncommon to hear someone say, "Are you from Hialeah?" or "Did you get that in Hialeah" as a means to characterize a person or thing with all the Hialeah adjectives enumerated above.[56] One of the hashtags for the "balsero" at the gym describes this sentiment with a simple "#Hialeah-Style" to communicate the imagined essence of the city embodied in the mismatched dress, swimming trunks for a gym workout, and bare feet.

The Hialeah balsero is symbolic of the intragroup boundaries within the ethnic sign of "Cuban" in South Florida. These boundaries can be observed in the way that Pepe crafts the "inside" of the joke with his hashtags. Consistent with his style of mixing Cuban Spanish and American popular culture, the hashtags capture a bicultural context written with US-born Cuban Americans in mind. They feature plenty of Spanish, especially when they can produce the desired alliterative effect, but also a number of references to Miami and broader US popular culture. Crossfit, a fitness fad popular across the United States, juxtaposes the perceived backwardness of the balsero and his attire with the hipness of Crossfit to produce comic incongruity. There is even a deeper musical reference with #SurfingOnABalsa #Air, which alludes to the French electronic duo Air's song "Surfing on a Rocket." And as I have explained throughout, the combination of recognition and humor encourages the audience to share.[57] It is the through the recognition of the joke in play, the notion that "comedy flatters us, our competence with the world and our critical understanding," that ludic sociability and the act of sharing occur.[58]

In soliciting these images and captioning them, Pepe provides a ludic framework for a conversation well underway within the Cuban diaspora regarding the "differences" between the more recent arrivals, the older generation, and their children.[59] For the most part, people tag their friends, share on their own Facebook pages, and demonstrate their approval with laughing emoticons and short comments. When people do comment in a substantial way, we see just how layered reception can be. In the example above, a user named Christian showed anger about the "shit" coming from Cuba, while Victor urged him not to "generalize" and to "teikerisi" (take it easy). But the lack of engaged dialogue regarding the image does not mean that it is not doing work. As Sara Ahmed usefully theorizes, "Affect does not reside positively in the sign or commodity, but is produced only as an effect of its circulation."[60] The affect produced through diversión intensifies as this image circulates around one's social network and plays a role in how subjects construct and share their narratives of self. Clicking on the image and seeing its many comments, tags, and shares contributes to the feeling that this is a mutual experience for a significant number of people.

But while those who submit and share this content draw pleasure from these posts, it is not without a cost. When images like these appear on Pepe's accounts, it is impossible to disconnect them from his article in the *Miami New Times*. These are the Cubans Pepe talks about as being psychologically "reprogrammed," as well as ethnically suspect from having been raised on an island where "the destruction of Cuban culture" by the Castros has changed what it means to be Cuban. Regardless of how harmless some of the images might be to the casual observer, it is impossible to extract them from a larger conversation about how the Cuban community in Miami is narrating itself and the fault lines and intragroup boundaries that are currently in play.

While laughing at "balseros" can serve as the outside against which a US-born, Miami-centric Cuban identity can be defined, it would be unfair to characterize them solely in these terms. In the diasporic imaginary, each new arrival is a symbolic condemnation of the Cuban government. Those who take to the sea in makeshift rafts, especially, are celebrated as courageous freedom seekers in an abstract sense that is often in contrast to the way that older generations and US-born Cuban Americans treat and see them as different, as being less authentically Cuban. Nonetheless, the continued infusion of Cubans into South Florida makes it possible to think of Miami as a city where Cuban culture is still relevant. More recent arrivals provide "ethnic raw materials—ethnically linked symbols and practices—that are necessary for the construction of a salient ethnic identity."[61] They are hosting cultural events, fueling media content, opening businesses, and keeping existing ones like Cuban restaurants open by patronizing and working for them. And perhaps most obviously, they are speaking Spanish. In one way or another, US-born Cuban Americans are "replenished" by continued migration regardless of their opinions of more recent arrivals.[62]

Pepe Billete's brand of diversión has succeeded in large part because of his ability to appeal to the bicultural sensibilities of US-born Cuban Americans. But digital diversión broadly conceived does not need to appeal to a particular niche. In the section that follows, I look at a group that aims to be more inclusive and less polarizing in its politics in order to attract a Cuban audience across generational cohorts.

Los Pichy Boys

Los Pichy Boys' comic talent and appeal across various segments of the diaspora have helped to make them the most popular Cubans in online diversión.[63] Composed of Alejandro González and Maikel Rodríguez, Los Pichy Boys is a duo of cousins who arrived in the United States as teenagers in the 2000s.[64] While they have had success on television and radio, their popularity can be traced to content produced for platforms like YouTube and Facebook, which includes parody videos, pranks, and spoofs of all kinds. The numbers of viewers and followers are staggering. In an interview I conducted with them in February 2015, they reported having received well over 85 million views on YouTube alone. They have accrued close to 700,000 likes of their Facebook page, the platform where they have established their web presence most aggressively. Their average "reach" on Facebook is 7 million people weekly, with 40 million being their record for a single week. More impressive is the level of engagement with their content on Facebook. On a weekly basis, they average around 2 million people liking, commenting on, and sharing their content with their own networks. Of course, not all of their fans are Cuban. Part of their success story is how they have been able to appeal to a broader Latina/o and Latin American audience. For the purposes of this chapter, I will focus on their Cuba-related content not only because of its relevance to this book but also because of their avowed investment in cubanía as a means for producing their comic material.

The ability of Los Pichy Boys to appeal across different segments of the Cuban diaspora is due in large part to their own generational positioning. Because they arrived in the 2000s, Los Pichy Boys sit at the intersection of the two largest and fastest growing segments of the Cuban diaspora: the US-born and Cubans raised on the island who have left since the 1990s and the 2000s in particular. Their work reflects this generational intersectionality with content that showcases their intimate knowledge of life in contemporary Cuba, the difficulties in acclimating to life off the island, and a deep understanding of and love for main-stream US popular culture. Though particular examples of the content they produce might be more appealing to certain segments of the diaspora over others, they generally attempt to create material that resonates broadly by performing a recognizable narrative of cubanía through diversión. González described this approach as being "natural," marked with an unmistakable Cuban *sabor*.[65] Interrogating the "flavor" of their diversión will reveal the reasons for their broad appeal online and the social logics that ground their popularity.

Cuban comic *sabor* alone does not make social media superstars. In my interview with them, Los Pichy Boys frequently cited how unfettered, direct communication with their fans has allowed them to get a clear sense of what works and what does not. Unlike the imprecision baked into radio and television ratings, social media metrics and more importantly, actual messages and comments from the audience, constantly provide the feedback necessary for them to tailor their content to their audience's shifting interests. Fan feedback also serves material purposes. While Los Pichy Boys seek to entertain, they are also very much a business. They make money by serving as spokespeople for local and international businesses and embedding ads in their content.[66] The

Figure 5.3. Maikel Rodríguez (left) and Alejandro González (right) of Los Pichy Boys. Photo courtesy of Castellanos Photo Design, Miami, Florida.

pattern of diversión as a strategy for capital accumulation discussed in previous chapters in the context of el paquete, visiting artists from the island, a festival called Cuba Nostalgia, and others continues online. Accordingly, their entire business is premised on ludic sociability, on the notion that people will be moved to interact and share their content based upon the feelings of affinity and amusement it produces. Unpacking their Cuba(n)-related content reveals the diversity of the Cuban diaspora online, *how* it appeals broadly, and perhaps most importantly, what has the capacity to *move* people to share.

Los Pichy Boys rocketed to Internet fame in 2007 when they began producing *doblajes* (dubbings) of Hollywood blockbusters.[67] In these doblajes, Los Pichy Boys piece together scenes from a film and then dub their voices over those of the actors with the intention of transforming them into Cuban comic characters. The visible action of the movie and the facial expressions and body language of the actors over which they dub their voices make their comic narration come alive. In one example, the movie *Captain Phillips* (2013)—which originally chronicled the hijacking of a cargo ship by Somali pirates—becomes a story about Cubans from the El Cerro neighborhood in Havana commandeering a ship to Miami. Disney's *Pirates of the Caribbean* (2003) is transformed into *Los piratas del Caribe*—a tale set in Cuba about how Captain Jack Sparrow stole a Caribe television and lied to his girlfriend about its quality by telling her it was a more expensive plasma television.[68] Through parodic ventriloquism, characters like Harry Potter become "Pototo" from Havana with all the street savvy language and knowledge necessary to navigate that world while simultaneously being framed by all the special effects and visual dynamism of the Hollywood spectacle.[69]

The success of the doblajes can be explained in part through the many openings that they provide for audience engagement across generational cohorts. For US-born, English-dominant, Cuban Americans, references to life on the island today may be difficult to tease out. Despite this, Los Pichy Boys claim that the US-born watch these doblajes in great numbers and as a whole, constitute a significant portion of their audience.[70] In addition to the pleasure of seeing a Hollywood blockbuster "translated" in a manner that reflects the familiar performance of Cuban idiomatic speech and joke motifs, audiences experience a kind of comic defamiliarization. Hollywood and the dominance of whiteness within it are reconfigured by the intimate language and sonic performance of a Cuban cultural identity framed within the visual narrative of the mainstream film industry. For those familiar with life in contemporary Cuba, the doblajes project references to particular streets in Havana, material cultural (like the Caribe televisions), and musical acts in twenty-first century Cuba onto the spectacle of the Hollywood blockbuster. The juxtaposition of highly wrought special effects and modern or even futuristic settings with interpersonal and social situations common to life on the island produces an incongruous effect wherein the audience can see its own cultural context in a completely different register. Doblajes, then, can also function as metaphors for the experience of migration, of squaring the home country with life in the new land and the comedy that encounter can produce.

In doblajes, the remixing of the primary source material allows the audience to enjoy it as *un momento de diversión* that speaks to their particular relationship to cubanía. Under this logic, these doblajes function as instances of what John Fiske has described as the "producerly." Henry Jenkins explains that "Fiske's notion of the 'producerly' introduces guiding principles for transforming commodities into cultural resources: openness, loose ends, and gaps that allow viewers to read material against their own backgrounds and experiences are key."[71] Fiske's idea that "people produce culture when they integrate products and texts into their everyday lives" resonates with the ways in which doblajes are enjoyed and circulated across generational cohorts.[72]

While their doblajes appeal widely, some target particular audiences more than others. This is certainly the case with a doblaje called "Elpidio se fue de Cuba" (Elpidio left Cuba).[73] In this video, we see how the transformational energy of the "producerly" partners with the logic of parody.[74] The video parodies the Revolution's most famous cartoon character, Elpidio Valdés, created in 1970 to assimilate children into the revolutionary project through animated adventure stories. As a colonel in the Cuban independence army fighting against Spanish colonialism, Elpidio was meant to embody the revolutionary ideal, the man who fights for justice against imperialism and, most importantly, for Cuba. Despite the cartoon's setting during the nineteenth century wars for Cuban independence, the writers made it easy for audiences to read

Elpidio Valdés as an allegory for the present, critical of US imperial aggression against Cuba. The actual episode Los Pichy Boys dubbed over is called "Elpidio Valdés against the Gunship" (1980) and features honorable Cuban freedom fighters up against blood-thirsty and bumbling Spaniards who use American-made weapons to attack Elpidio and his heroic collaborators.

Los Pichy Boys transform Elpidio into something else entirely. In the world of this doblaje, Elpidio is trying to escape from Cuba in order to pursue a career with Disney and its most famous character, Mickey Mouse. The Spaniards in the original are now the Cuban military doing everything in their power to stop Elpidio from leaving the island. While this basic plot is amusing in its own right, the emotional and ludic hook derives largely from the way the dubbing *sounds*. Elpidio is no longer the humble, respectable, and courteous Cuban peasant from the countryside. Here, he is the *cubano de la calle*, the man on the street, describing the world with the rapid-fire slang of contemporary Havana: "Dime broder, ya e'to ta cuadrao? Mira que si me cogen me van a dar una desaparecida a mi y al Palmiche del carajo" (Tell me brother, is this all squared away? If they catch me [trying to leave Cuba] they are going to disappear me and Palmiche [his horse]).

The dubbed version of Elpidio reveals the failures of revolutionary discourse in the words he uses, his heavy accent, keen awareness of the state's surveillance apparatus, and the consequences of capture. This Elpidio is not the model "New Man" that Che Guevara envisioned when he wrote "Socialism and Man in Cuba" in 1965. Individual ambition and needs trump loyalty to the Revolution. Consequently, this Elpidio sees his future not in Cuba but in the United States.[75] The Elpidio created to be a model to Cuban youth would be horrified at the idea of leaving the island and abandoning the revolutionary cause. But in the dubbing, this Elpidio, like the Cuban baseball stars also mentioned in the video as defectors and the Cuban diasporic audience watching, has decided to leave the island. Laughing at the parody is a way to "acknowledge having moved with the joke to other territory, and having been treated to an alternative view of that territory."[76] Engaging with the content on social media is a means to connect with others in that "movement" that occurs metaphorically and physically both for Cubans who "get" the joke and for those who have made the literal journey from the island to the United States. Through this doblaje, the character of Elpidio beloved by generations of Cuban children but tethered to a particular political project speaks, once again, for those who left courtesy of Los Pichy Boys and their parodic ventriloquism.

This parody also furnishes a political critique of the Cuban government on the level of form. Well aware of how state-sponsored art and media can be charged with a pro-Revolution message, Los Pichy Boys exhibit a keen understanding of this framework by providing their own for the dubbing—a movie trailer. This move further distances Elpidio from revolutionary rhetoric and places him squarely within a US capitalist entertainment package. The language and timing of the narrator's voice perfectly mimic the narrative arc for commercial film releases in the United States: "This is the story of a man who everyone thought was a patriot. . . . Don't miss it this summer. . . . Elpidio se fue."[77] Through this manipulation of the way in which Elpidio is presented to audiences, the parody "provoke[s] reflection and re-evaluation of how the targeted texts or genre works."[78] The original operated under the rhetorical umbrella of the Revolution and its messaging but through parody, the ideological spirit of the original can be subverted in a manner that allows for the nostalgia felt for Elpidio and the critique of revolutionary propaganda to coexist.

The doblajes of Cuban cartoons like Elpidio Valdés have endeared Los Pichy Boys to an audience eager to connect nostalgically to the Cuba of their youth while simultaneously being critical of the government's ideological project. But most of their content builds a much bigger tent by focusing on quotidian life in the United States, Miami in particular, and on the complications that arise when newly arrived Cubans try to make sense of their unfamiliar surroundings. Many of these videos dramatize answers to the following question: What do particular examples of American cultural phenomena look like from a Cuban point of view?[79] One answer took the form of a video called "iPhone Cubano: Asiri," a parody video posted on their YouTube account in December 2011.[80]

The comic kernel of this video is in the clever wordplay of its title. Siri is the name Apple gave to its voice-controled personal assistant application on the iPhone. By changing the name to Asiri, Los Pichy Boys are punning on the popular Cuban slang term *asere* (friend). The video takes the form of a commercial featuring Los Pichy Boys selling their

Cuban audience the Asiri application, a "personal assistant made for Cubans." Viewed over 700,000 times on YouTube, it is one of their most popular uploads.

The guiding premise of the video is that of a late-night infomercial. Los Pichy Boys are "selling" a new app for iPhone users who have trouble using the English-dominant Siri. The voice-over narration, performed by González in Spanish, frames the video: "Frustrated by those moments when Siri doesn't understand you because your English isn't perfect? Asiri has arrived! The personal assistant made for Cubans." The comic moments are then produced by Rodríguez's inability to communicate with Siri because of his heavy accent:

> RODRÍGUEZ [*in heavily-accented English*]: Siri, can I walk to the dollar store?
> SIRI: Tractor, Homestead, 2 miles.

Siri, dubbed by one of Los Pichy Boys in English, misunderstands Rodríguez's accent and responds with "tractor," a word that loosely rhymes with "store" and where it can be found, in Homestead, a less developed area south of Miami. Following the classic trope of late-night infomercials, the narrator explains that this unpleasantness could be remedied with the advertised product, Asiri:

> RODRÍGUEZ [*heavily accented Cuban Spanish*]: Puedo ir caminando hasta el dólar store?
> ASIRI [*heavy Cuban accent*]: Claro asere, si en Cuba tu caminaba como un caballo!

Asiri's response, which translates to "Of course [you can walk to the dollar store], asere, in Cuba you walked like a horse!" and is articulated in a husky voice and Cuban accent, aligns the technology of Apple with the metaphorical economy of Cuban Spanish. Beyond the obvious incongruity produced by replacing Apple's personal assistant with a rapid, Cuban-accented Spanish, there is an idiomatic richness at work throughout this video that defies translation. A phrase like "caminaba como un caballo" can be easily translated to "you walked like a horse" or more nearly, "walked as much as a horse." But that translation cannot capture the richness of the phrase and its relationship to diversión, what makes it "feel" Cuban. The pleasure produced by the incongruous pairing is again enriched by a performance practice that evades description. The way in which Asiri says "caminaba como un caballo" can be best communicated with another phrase used to describe people whose Cuban accents are too heavy: "habla con una papa en la boca" (he or she speaks with a potato in his or her mouth). Invoking the horse gets at the prominent role of animals more broadly in Cuban sayings and comedy. These are the moments that spark the ludic sociability and intimacy that encourage audiences to share their content so widely. In so doing, they help produce cultural touchstones and narratives by which people imagine themselves as Cuban and relate to one another.

As in the doblaje of Elpidio Valdés, Los Pichy Boys have reimagined a pop culture icon not meant for their audience. Elpidio was created with the intention of instilling revolutionary feeling among Cuba's youth, not for those who would leave the island and criticize the Revolution. The narrative of middle- and upper-class whiteness that dominates both the popular and marketing discourse of the iPhone also excludes these newer arrivals from Cuba who have yet to master English in a manner decipherable by the software.[81] The hypercubanization of the iPhone aims to reconfigure mainstream popular culture in a way that works for that imagined "us" of Cubans living in the United States who, if they have access to this technology, find that it does not fully interface with their cultural contexts and experiences. In transforming the utilitarian, rather robotic Siri into a resource articulated through recognizable forms of Cuban expression, the video allows the audience to indulge in a fantasy wherein the new country can be navigated with the codes of the old. For US-born Cuban Americans, the opposite is often true. Pleasure is drawn from seeing the iPhone reimagined in a manner that allows them to engage a Cuban cultural identity learned in the United States. Like Pepe Billete, who serves as a bridge between exile cubanía and mainstream US popular culture, "Asiri" juxtaposes two worlds that do not often meet.

In this chapter and throughout the book, I have actively stressed the sonic dimension of content, the way it *sounds* Cuban, and how that articulation helps to communicate a particular political and diasporic subjectivity. But sound is not the only way in which cubanía is communicated. Unlike the doblajes, the Asiri video features Cuban bodies.

The catalog of gestures featured in the Asiri video—Rodríguez puffs his cheeks, shakes his head, and registers anger with a number of demonstrative flourishes with his arm and wrists—speaks to what Joseph Roach calls the kinesthetic imagination.[82] This repertoire of bodily movements and manipulations shared by a community produces a recognizable kind of kinesthetic cubanía. It is difficult to convey just what is "Cuban" about these gestures except that they are easily recognizable as such. One need only watch video footage of Fidel Castro's speeches to understand the relationship of gesture, performance, and meaning in Cuban culture. In the comments to the video on Facebook and YouTube, the bodily enactment of a recognizable narrative of cubanía is rarely if ever mentioned. People instead cite quotable lines and register their enjoyment with different versions of "lol" and by sharing and tagging friends. But the kinesthetic vocabulary Rodríguez draws on in this performance is key for enriching the spoken dimension of the video. Rodríguez's embodiment of cubanía through the literal manipulation of his body contributes to what makes this video a prime candidate for sharing and the ludic sociability that follows. Working in tandem, the sonic and physical enactment of cubanía help enhance its spreadability.

The physical dimension of cubanía also has a corollary in the representation of race in many of the videos by Los Pichy Boys. Rodríguez's body signifies in a particular way not only because of his movements, but also because of his whiteness. This fact, along with the demographic reality of a majority-white Cuban diaspora, further contributes to the video's success and appeal. When blackness does factor into their videos, Los Pichy Boys often graft stereotypical understandings of Afro-Cubans onto African Americans. They do this by using an "uneducated" Spanish that would be recognized as needing refinement and by relying on stereotypical representations of Afro-Cuban religious practices, as in a doblaje featuring LeBron James as a practitioner of *santería*.[83] As I have noted throughout the book, this is consistent with how white Cuban comedians have used a strategy of melding US and Cuban racial codes in order to reproduce racialized comic tropes that would be recognizable to their audiences.[84] A similar strategy is at work in the way that they represent homosexuality. Much like Alvarez Guedes, whose jokes concern *locas*, Los Pichy Boys represent homosexuality as a kind of failed masculinity.

Representational strategies related to blackness and sexuality came together when news about warming relations between the United States and Cuba broke on December 17, 2014. Now known simply as 17D, the event immediately triggered a flurry of responses from Cuban communities online in the form of diversión.[85] Polished political cartoons circulated alongside crudely edited images of McDonald's restaurants in Old Havana and Barack Obama and Raúl Castro in various states of embrace—from coquettish handholding to deep kissing. Los Pichy Boys, ever quick to capitalize on trending topics in order to draw audience interest, quickly pounced on the opportunity to create a doblaje with their own comic take on the historic announcement.

For this doblaje, Los Pichy Boys took clips of Obama addressing the media and of Raúl Castro in the company of aides in Havana to craft a story about how the agreement to establish diplomatic relations came to be. According to Obama, the reason he reached out to Raúl Castro was that First Lady Michelle Obama wanted to vacation in Cuba. When he reached his Cuban counterpart to smooth over tensions, Castro suggested that they exchange "un viejito sin diente" (a toothless old man, a reference to jailed US government contractor Alan Gross) for "los tres chivatones" (the three snitches)—the remaining imprisoned members of the Cuban 5.[86] When Obama presses him on the fact that he is demanding three for the price of one, Castro responds, "Oye estamos al fin del año, mi chino, recarga doble lo que toca" (It's the end of the year, my love, give me two for the price of one).[87]

The video utilizes the leveling tendency of choteo to mock the powerful. A diplomatic breakthrough of historic proportions is reduced, "leveled," to domestic drama. Michelle Obama wants to travel to the island, and Castro wants to haggle with Obama like a street vendor in Havana. Through the lens of diversión, the serious can be reduced, evacuated of gravity, allowing people to contend with the psychic stress this breakthrough entails. And there is plenty of stress to account for. With this announcement, a fifty-year entrenched political status quo was shaken to its core. Cubans on and off the island, regardless of whether or not they disagreed with the announcement, wondered how it would affect travel, the Cuban Adjustment Act, and families and friends on both sides. After they had spent decades adapting to the complicated reality of US-Cuba relations and its effects, two powerful men were able to disrupt all that in short, televised announcements.

Sound is once again crucial for understanding this doblaje. While the person's actions animate the words spoken, it is the articulation of language and recognizable speech patterns of the dubbed voice that communicate the subjectivity of Castro and Obama. And much like the sonic blackface utilized in representations of LeBron James and the blackface character of Mañeña discussed in Chapter 4, the ventriloquism at work in this video draws upon the audience's deep-seated understanding of Cuban comic tropes and the relationship between sound and subjectivity. In the video, the "Cubanization" of Obama begins by dubbing over his voice in a manner that aligns him with the language of the street. He greets the press with the phrase "¿Qué bolón?" a variation of the slang phrase "¿Que bolá?" meaning "What's up?" At first blush, this is not particularly problematic. Obama is no longer the statesman, the president, but "leveled" in the irreverent logic of choteo through a street vernacular unbecoming of his office—hence the comic incongruity. But the sonic representation of Obama's blackness also contributes to this leveling. Obama's dubbed voice pronounces the word *ayer*, meaning yesterday, as *ayel* in a nod to mispronunciations attributed to blacks in Cuba who fail to "master" the Spanish language and replace the "r" at the end of words with the "l" sound. This legacy of representing blackness comically through particular speech patterns in Cuba can be traced to the nineteenth-century blackface tradition of teatro bufo.[88]

Playing opposite Obama's caricatured blackness is Raúl Castro, whose high, nasal voice and speech patterns are meant to convey effeminacy and most crucially, homosexuality. The notion that Raúl Castro is a closeted homosexual has circulated since the 1960s. Exile *periodiquitos* like *Zig-Zag Libre* frequently featured cartoons of him as "limp-wristed" and dressed in an "unmanly" fashion. These representations continue today with a seemingly endless number of digitally altered memes and other images of him in full make-up and referred to in comments with feminine articles. In the doblaje, this effeminacy gets communicated in tone and pitch through his voice and choice of words. His speech is interspersed with comically bad English and the use of words ending with the diminutive *-ito*, which signify that Castro is to be understood as *una loca*. His dubbed voice even goes as far as to address Obama as *mi chino*—my love.[89] Raúl Castro has been called La China since the 1960s because of his perceived Asian features and rumored homosexuality. In their exchange on the doblaje, Obama becomes the *chino*, the object of affection, to Castro's *china*, thus closing the symbolic circle that equates warming relations with an Obama-Castro "romance" and the racial and sexual economy that makes that coupling familiar and comic to the audience.

Part of the success of this video lies in its subtlety in relation to politics. While Los Pichy Boys are aggressive in their jabs, especially when it comes to Raúl Castro, they do not come out in favor or against the reestablishment of diplomatic relations. This allows the video to be palatable across a broad audience and thus more likely to be shared. In all their posts regarding 17D on Facebook, Los Pichy Boys asked their audience what they thought of the news, thereby allowing followers to project their politics onto their video and make themselves heard in the comments section. Surely, Los Pichy Boys are not simply doing this as a means to open a space for civil discourse. More comments lead to more engagement, which is then quantified and sold to potential sponsors. This does not change the fact that people for and against the warming of relations are having a conversation under the broad appeal of diversión. I do not mean to suggest that simply laughing our way across ideological poles will bring about substantive dialogue. There is plenty of uncivil discourse, including racist and anti-gay sentiments, relayed in the comments section. But there are also moments of pushback and dialogue about the politics of the situation and the representational choices made in the video. In this video, the audience does their own kind of dubbing of the doblaje, layering their political, generational, and affective sensibilities over a text that asks them to laugh, to feel Cuban, yet simultaneously provides flexibility for the audience to use their own particular lens and share the content accordingly.

17D

As I stood in front of my television on December 17, 2014 (17D), dumbstruck by the news of the impending reestablishment of diplomatic relations, I tried to process what it all meant. What would this news mean for my family on and off the island? For the exile generation, the desire to bring about the fall of the Castro government has been met by decades of frustration and anti-Castro fervor. More recent arrivals have had to deal with regulations on both sides inhibiting their ability to move freely and engage with family and friends. The lives of Cubans on the island have been framed by *el enemigo* to the north and constant propaganda blaming the United States for a myriad of social ills. For US-born Cuban Americans, a hostile foreign policy to Cuba is all they have ever known. But now, in one televised announcement, the framework for thinking about the United States and Cuba had changed forever. There was no military coup. No large-scale uprisings on the island demanding change. No invasion. None of the bombast that has characterized over fifty years of tense relations. Just two men reading some prepared statements. It felt almost absurd. I shook my head and laughed.

Feeling pulled in a number of different intellectual and emotional directions simultaneously, I logged onto Facebook more as a reflex than as a calculated decision. I was eager to read what people were saying, but I also wanted to experience this moment—to *feel* it—in the company of the people (at least virtually) whose lives had been profoundly shaped by a political stalemate that had lasted for over half a century. I quickly found that I was not alone in my laughter. Ludic popular culture was once again being deployed as a means to filter an unfamiliar present and future through the familiar performative logic of diversión. It was serving, as it often has, as a means to engage one another as the news unfolded through a shared narrative economy in the service of a broader ludic sociability. Memes, parody videos, political cartoons, and comic commentary broadly defined spread quickly across social media platforms and feeds. The aforementioned Pichy Boys doblaje accrued over 2.5 million views between Facebook and YouTube in just a matter of days. More revealing is the fact that the video was shared over 28,000 times in less than a day. With all the uncertainty surrounding what this announcement meant, people wanted to laugh, to frame the uncertain world that this event would usher in with something familiar: *relajo, jodedera, choteo*. 17D did not become a truly Cuban event until the diversión began.

That experience online made me think of the audiences in small theaters in Little Havana laughing at the latest show satirizing the Cuban government in the 1970s and 1980s. It reminded me of the longest laughs on Alvarez Guedes albums and how they were so often related to the politics of their present. It encouraged me to make a note to look into the many comedians based in Cuba who visit Miami to perform standup; this is the kind of big news that comedians dream of. It also pointed, yet again, to the durability of comic motifs related to race and sexuality and the broader multivalences of popular culture. It revealed how choteo inflected with stereotypical notions of blackness and queer sexualities can also be a means to critique those on both sides who may not have the interests of the Cuban people in mind—from corporate America to Cuban politicians eager to maintain the political status quo. It is in this complex popular culture grammar, where multiple narratives are articulated simultaneously, that I have tried to situate this study in hopes of capturing the textured complexity of quotidian life.

Throughout this book, I have also tried to merge academic research—archival work, historical contextualization, theoretical interventions—with an attunement to the performative and affective elements of diversión that so often frame social relations. Doing so has meant paying attention to those moments and practices that can get lost in our cultural histories. They are the ephemeral moments, the performances, that shape the present but fall outside the usual archival logics of the academy. They are the moments that stay with people but not necessarily as physical records in a box or on a shelf: inside jokes, pronunciation of a word, the wave of a hand, the daily practice of tuning into your favorite radio show or "liking" an image of a *croqueta* on Facebook. Yet as I have shown throughout this book, diversión has been critical for narrating the world, producing a shared context for relationality, and providing a means for the intensification of transnational relations. All this is often accompanied by laughter—an eruption, an interruption even, that insists on a "time-out." Diversión has been my way of interrupting the way we think about the Cuban diaspora by highlighting the central role of ludic sociability and all its messiness in the context of profound demographic shifts in Cuban Miami in the last twenty-five years. With the 17D announcement and aging leadership in Cuba, there is a great deal of uncertainty about what will happen next. Is the end of the Cuban Adjustment Act near? Are political changes on the horizon in a Cuba where the original revolutionary leaders are succumbing to old age? Whatever comes, a sense of humor will be indispensable, as it always has been.

Perhaps then, it is fitting to end with song lyrics that opened up Alvarez Guedes's eighth stand-up album, words that I repeated to myself throughout the writing of this book to produce a mindset that privileged diversión in a world where humor can sometimes be difficult to find:

> ¡Ñó qué rico!
> ¡Ñó qué loco!
> Si quieres reírte un poco, espérate un momentico
> Porque es mejor el relajo, que la seriedad.[90]

NOTES

INTRODUCTION

1 Enrico Mario Santí, "Cabrera Infante: El estilo de la nación," 22.

2 There were important exceptions that made me hopeful about the potential of this ludic line of inquiry. I am thinking of Roberto Fernández's novel *Raining Backwards* and José Esteban Muñoz's *Disidentifications: Queers of Color and the Performance of Politics*, in particular.

3 Guillermo Alvarez Guedes, *Alvarez Guedes 11*.

4 The racial tension I speak of was a product of the acquittal of four white police officers (one of whom was Cuban American) in the killing of an African American man named Arthur McDuffie. For a fantastic reading of the Miami uprising in relation to Mariel and Cuban American whiteness, see Antonio López, "Around 1979: Mariel, McDuffie, and the Afterlives of Antonio," in his *Unbecoming Blackness*.

5 See Alejandro Portes and Alex Stepick, *City on the Edge*, 21. Although this description applied only to a small percentage of the 125,000 incoming Cubans, the image of the criminal, maladjusted, belligerent marielito served to stigmatize the entire population. Figuring out the exact number of hardened criminals that came during Mariel is a difficult proposition due in part to definitions of criminality in Cuba. One could be considered a criminal for dissent against the state or even for "dangerousness"—a condition that describes the likelihood that one many commit a crime in the future. Portes and Stepick *City*, 22, estimate the figure at "perhaps 10%," while Jorge Duany has more recently put the number of "common criminals" who arrived under 2%. See "El éxodo del Mariel, 35 años después," *El Nuevo Herald*, Oct 26, 2015, www.elnuevoherald.com.

6 Portes and Stepick, *City*, 27.

7 When I asked Alvarez Guedes's family about this particular moment, none of them could remember the exact circumstances around it. They were convinced that he had planned to have the man in the audience ask about Mariel. If so, such a strategy was never repeated again on any of his stand-up albums of which there are thirty-two—hence my doubts. If it was planned, it speaks to the delicacy of the Mariel crisis and the need to address it indirectly.

8 Alvarez Guedes, *Alvarez Guedes 11*. All translations from Spanish to English are mine.

9 Ibid.

10 The 2016 Republican primaries featured two candidates of Cuban descent, Marco Rubio and Ted Cruz, both of whom cling to a hardline stance on Cuba that most in the diaspora now reject.

11 The phrase is Anca Parvulescu's in conversation with Henri Bergson's theory of the comic. See *Laughter*, 5.

12 Tara McPherson, *Reconstructing Dixie*, 125.

13 See Ricardo L. Ortíz, *Cultural Erotics in Cuban America*. The Cuban population of the greater Miami area is over 1 million, by far the largest concentration in the United States. In recent decades, Miami's non-Cuban Latina/o population has grown significantly. See Anna Brown and Mark Hugo López, "Mapping the Latino Population, by State, County and City."

14 Though this book focuses exclusively on the diaspora post-1959, there has been significant research published on Cuban communities in the United States during the nineteenth and early twentieth centuries. See Rodrigo Lazo, *Writing to Cuba*, and Nancy Raquel Mirabal, *Suspect Freedoms*.

15 Jorge Duany, *Blurred Borders*, 41.

16 Taking the work of Cuban anthropologist Fernando Ortíz as his starting point, Gustavo Pérez Firmat defines *cubanía* as a "self-conscious, willed *cubanidad*, a feeling of deep and pervasive identification with things Cuban. . . . Unlike *cubanidad* which is essentially a civil status, *cubanía* is a spiritual condition, but a spiritual condition identified by an act of the will, one that is fundamentally a desire, a wanting." Gustavo Pérez Firmat, *The Cuban Condition*, 30.

17 Antoni Kapcia, *Cuba*, 7.

18 José Esteban Muñoz, "Onus of Seeing Cuba," 455.

19 Readers versed in the work of Martinican theorist Edouard Glissant will likely wonder if there is a connection between his concept of *détour* (translated in English as "diversion") and how I am using *diversión* here. Scholars like Emily A. Maguire and Román de la Campa have examined the relationship between Cuban forms of play like *choteo* and Glissantian diversion. Maguire explains that "practices of diversion subvert the sociopolitical status quo, often through trickery or humor, as is the case with Signifyin(g) and the *choteo*" (*Racial Experiments*, 105). Juan Flores, writing in a Puerto Rican cultural context, affirms that "Glissant's 'diversion' bears obvious traces of the [Bakhtinian] carnivalesque" (*From Bomba to Hip Hop*, 39–40). While there are certainly parallels between my theorization of diversión and how the concept has been mobilized in a Glissantian sense, the social, political, and historical context that I engage in this book is not wholly consistent with Glissant's theorization. Glissant's context for thinking about diversion is "a colonized population (or one emerging from the experience of colonization)" and how it "attempts to deal with the experience of domination when that power structure is not present in a way that allows it to be openly contested" (Maguire, *Racial Experiments*, 105). Glissant writes, "There is no diversion when the community confronts an enemy recognized as such. Diversion is the ultimate resort of a population whose domination by an Other is concealed" (*Caribbean Discourse*, 19–21). The colonial or recently postcolonial context does not apply to the Cuban diasporic sociopolitical context, as will be apparent throughout this book. See also Román de la Campa, "Resistance and Globalization in Caribbean Discourse."

20 For a book-length study of choteo, see Narciso J. Hidalgo, *Choteo*. The most thorough investigation of *choteo* as a concept written in English is Gustavo Pérez Firmat's in *Literature and Liminality*.

21 Jorge Mañach, "Indagación del choteo," 54.

22 Efraín Barradas, "Cursi, choteo, guachafita"; Israel Reyes, *Humor and the Eccentric Text in Puerto Rican Literature*.

23 Félix Valdés García, "El Caribe."

24 Reyes, *Humor*, 13.

25 See José Antonio Ramos, *El manual del perfecto fulanista*; Mañach, "Indagación del choteo"; Fernando Ortíz, *Entre cubanos: Psicología tropical* and *Nuevo catauro de cubanismos*. These intellectuals can be tied to what Jorge Duany refers to as "the quest for national identity . . . a major concern for Latin American intellectuals during the 1920s and 1930s, as witnessed by the cases of Antonio Pedreira in Puerto Rico, José Carlos Mariátegui in Peru and Samuel Ramos in Mexico. . . . *Indagación del choteo* inaugurates an entire generation's soul searching for the essences of Cuba's national character" ("Reconstructing Cubanness," 21–22).

26 Juan Antonio García Borrero, "Invitación al choteo," 84.

27 See Jill Lane, *Blackface Cuba*. Many of the tropes in race-related humor in Cuban popular culture can be traced back to the bufo tradition.

28 See Arístides Esteban Hernández and Jorge Alberto Piñero, *Historia del humor gráfico en Cuba*; Jorge L. Catalá Carrasco, "From Suspicion to Recognition?."

29 For choteo in the work of Gutiérrez Alea, see Aída Beaupied, "Libertad con minúscula y el choteo de los jueces en el cine de Gutiérrez Alea"; Raquel Aguiliú de Murphy, *Los textos dramáticos de Virgilio Piñera y el teatro del absurdo*, provides an analysis of choteo in the work of writer Virgilio Piñera. Gerard Aching examines choteo in the context of Guillermo Cabrera Infante's writing in *Masking and Power*. See also Sara E. Cooper, "Irreverent Humor in Postrevolutionary Cuban Fiction"; Lázaro Lima, "The King's Toilet."

30 According to Yeidy Rivero, *Los cuatro grandes* was the first program to air on Cuban television in November 1950. The show began as a radio program. Variety shows and comedies were extremely popular on Cuban television during the 1950s. See Rivero, *Broadcasting Modernity*, 54, 80. Comedies were a mainstay on radio years before the advent of television.

31 Roberto González Echevarría mobilized the term "fiesta" "to signify a celebration of some kind" and included "the humor, the antiauthoritarianism" of choteo as a feature of the fiesta (*Cuban Fiestas*, 138). Damián Fernández has connected choteo to what he calls the world of *lo informal* (the informal) as a social mode; see *Cuba and the Politics of Passion*.

32 Many scholars have commented on the difficulty of defining the comic. I have found Alenka Zupančič's explanation to be most compelling: "It may come as little surprise to say that comedy is an extremely difficulty subject of investigation—not only because of the multiplicity of various techniques and procedures involved in its process, but also because this process is in constant

motion. Indeed, this irresistible motion is one of the key features of comedy, which is why it seems so difficult to pin it down with concepts and definitions" (*The Odd One In*, 3).

33 Ann Cvetkovich, *An Archive of Feelings*, 7.

34 This phrase literally translates to "it heaves the mango." Depending on how it's used, it can signify incredulity and/or being upset with a situation. In the final chapter, I will look at how US-born Cuban Americans deploy this kind of code-switching with Cuban idiomatic expressions to produce viral content online.

35 Gustavo Pérez Firmat, "A Willingness of the Heart," 3.

36 The phrase "listening in detail" is from Alexandra T. Vazquez, *Listening in Detail*, in which Vazquez proposes a mode of engagement with the "details" of Cuban music as sound and performance in order to capture the ways in which Cuban music "resist[s] coherent narrative structures" (21).

37 For a history of political cartooning in Cuba with some notes on nineteenth-century work by exiles in New York, see Hernández and Piñero, *Historia del humor*.

38 "But life among the tabaqueros was not all serious and sober. There was a lot of fun too, especially on the part of the Cuban comrades. Many were the times that, after a stormy discussion, someone would take his turn by telling a hilarious joke. Right away tempers would cool down and the whole shop would burst out laughing" (Bernardo Vega, *Memoirs of Bernardo Vega*, 24). Many thanks to Antonio López for pointing me to this passage.

39 Antonio López discusses the career of Afro-Cuban stage performer, editor, and cartoonist Alberto O'Farrill, specifically as a bufo performer and satirist for a newspaper called *Gráfico* in his *Unbecoming Blackness*, chap. 1. Christina D. Abreu explores the history of Cuban musicians and entertainers from 1940 to 1960 and their role in the production of "Cuban, Afro-Cuban, Latino and Afro-Latino identities and communities" in her *Rhythms of Race*.

40 Those key players were the director, José Roseñada, and two of the island's most popular cartoonists: Silvio Fontanillas and Antonio Prohías. Fontanillas and Roseñada would work together on *Zig-Zag Libre* in exile but Prohías would go on to draw the well-known *Spy vs. Spy* comic strip for *Mad Magazine*. José Quiroga provides an excellent reading of Prohías's work in his chapter titled "Espionage and Identity" in *Cuban Palimpsests*.

41 These satirical comic newspapers were part of a much larger print culture within the exile community, which addressed life in the United States and the political situation in Cuba. The largest collection of Cuban diasporic print culture can be found in "Cuban Heritage Collection Exile Newspapers" at the Cuban Heritage Collection at the University of Miami.

42 For more on the "politics of childhood" in Miami, see Anita Casavantes Bradford, *The Revolution Is for the Children*.

43 Pablo Gómez, "Su artista favorite puede ser un comunista." Gómez later affirms in his article that "the best communist is a dead communist" and names actors

like Sammy Davis, Jr. and Frank Sinatra as suspect. Over the years, other nightlife guides and celebrity magazines would be published with the Cuban exile community as the intended audience: *Aquí Miami: Guía nocturna del espectáculo*, *Bambalinas*, *Enjoy/Disfrute*, and *Cubamena*, among others. All the periodicals mentioned can be found in "Cuban Heritage Collection Exile Newspapers" in the Cuban Heritage Collection at the University of Miami.

44 Theater among Cuban communities in the United States was not a new development either. As Antonio López and Nicolás Kanellos show, theater played an important role in artistic life of these communities. See the first chapter of López's *Unbecoming Blackness* and Kanellos's *A History of Hispanic Theatre*. The high visibility of comic theater in post-1959 Miami caught the eye of the national media, as this article attests: Kerry Gruson, "Cuban Theater Is Thriving—In Miami," *New York Times*, November 15, 1981, www.nytimes.com.

45 There was also a significant amount of dramatic theater. Teatro Prometeo, founded in 1973 and still active, has long been a vital part of Miami's dramatic theater scene. For an introduction to Cuban theater in Miami, see "Cuban Theater in Miami: 1960–1980," Cuban Heritage Collection, University of Miami Libraries, online exhibit, scholar.library.miami.edu. Cuban theater expert Lillian Manzor has led a project to digitize materials related to theater on and off the island; see www.cubantheater.org.

46 Teatro Las Mascaras, Teatro La Comedia, and Teatro Blanquita Amaro are good examples of theaters that staged comedies principally. Others that often featured comedies include Teatro Trail, Teatro Manuel Artime, Teatro Miami, Teatro Martí, and Teatro de Bellas Artes.

47 For scholarship on this important sitcom, see Yeidy Rivero, "Interpreting Cubanness, Americanness, and the Sitcom," and Michael Bustamante, "*¿Qué Pasa, U.S.A.?*"

48 Though this is not the focus of this book, scholars working on questions of Latina/o performance and its consumption by white audiences have helped me to think about how I theorize popular culture more broadly. See Frances Negrón-Muntaner, *Boricua Pop*; Myra Mendible, ed., *From Bananas to Buttocks*; Mary Beltrán, *Latina Stars in US Eyes*.

49 It is important to note here Joe Cardona's 2001 documentary *Nuestra Risa* (Our Laughter), which chronicles the role of humor in the exile community through interviews with Cuban artists active in theater, stand-up comedy, and radio.

50 More recently, some Cuban American politicians have proposed tighter restrictions on the Cuban Adjustment Act. Others have suggested doing away with it completely. I address this controversy in more detail in Chapter 2.

51 This insight is indebted to the work of José Esteban Muñoz in "Feeling Brown" and his assessment of how affective performances are instrumental in the way subjects become legible ethnically, racially, and politically.

52 Henry Jenkins, Tara McPherson, and Jane Shattuc, "The Cultural That Sticks to Your Skin," 10.

53 Ana M. López coined the term "Greater Cuba" to describe a Cuba "that exceeds national boundaries and that includes the many individuals and communities outside the national territory that identify as Cuban and contribute to the production of a 'Cuban' cultural discourse" ("Memorias of a Home," 15, fn. 3). See also López, "Greater Cuba."

54 López, "*Cosa de Blancos*: Cuban American Whiteness and the Afro-Cuban Occupied House," in *Unbecoming Blackness*.

55 Ibid., 187; emphasis in original.

56 As Portes and Stepick write, "For their part, Cubans always disclaimed any intentional racism, and to a certain extent they were sincere. Cuban discrimination operated more by neglect than by deliberate action. Preoccupied with their own economic progress and with the political struggle with Castro, Cubans had little time for the complaints of Blacks" (*City*, 199). Contrary to this, I will show how blackness in Miami has played a major role in diasporic popular culture throughout this book.

57 This is by no means an unexamined area of inquiry, but more is necessary given the role of anti-blackness in political and social formations. For work that has taken this up, see Tanya Katerí Hernández, "'Too Black to be Latino/a'"; Miriam Jiménez Román and Juan Flores, eds., *The Afro-Latin@ Reader*; Tomás Almaguer, "Race, Racialization, and Latino Populations in the United States"; Silvio Torres-Saillant, "Inventing the Race."

58 Stuart Hall, "Notes on Deconstructing the Popular," 233.

59 Richard Iton, *In Search of the Black Fantastic*, 24.

60 Muñoz, *Disidentifications*, 136. Muñoz's description of disidentification in this context is in relation to his theorization of choteo and queer performance artist Carmelita Tropicana.

61 Sara Warner, *Acts of Gaiety*, xiii. For an example of work on Native humor, see Kenneth Lincoln, *Indi'n Humor*.

62 Glenda Carpio, *Laughing Fit to Kill*, 27. African American Studies has seen the greatest amount of scholarship on humor and play when compared to Latina/o, Asian American, and Native American Studies. See also Daryl Cumber Dance, *Honey, Hush!*; Mel Watkins, *On The Real Side*; Bambi Haggins, *Laughing Mad*; Darryl Dickson-Carr, *African American Satire*.

63 Frances R. Aparicio connects the language of seriousness to institutional racism: "One of the forms institutional racism takes is the dominant perspective that Latino studies lacks seriousness, intellectual complexity, and important theorization" ("Latino Cultural Studies," 12).

64 For scholarship that foregrounds humor and the ludic more broadly in Latina/o Studies, see Carl Scott Gutiérrez-Jones, "Humor, Literacy and Chicano Culture"; Michelle Habell-Pallán, *Loca Motion*; Reyes, *Humor*; Tanya González and Eliza Rodriguez y Gibson, *Humor and Latina/o Camp in Ugly Betty*; Guillermo Hernández, *Chicano Satire*; José R. Reyna and María Herrera-Sobek, "Jokelore, Cultural Differences, and Linguistic Dexterity." Other scholars who engage

humor as part of a broader analytical project include Frances Negron-Muntaner, *Boricua Pop*; Frances R. Aparicio, *Listening to Salsa*; Urayoán Noel, *In Visible Movement*. In *Disidentifications*, Muñoz takes up queer Cuban American performance artist Carmelita Tropicana's use of choteo. This study is more engaged in analyzing popular culture forms that circulated among majority Cuban audiences in South Florida. Performance artists like Carmelita Tropicana get little exposure among the segments of the Cuban diaspora I want to shed light on in this project.

65 Flores, *Bomba*, 29.
66 The "Special Period in Peacetime" is the phrase Fidel Castro used to describe the difficult times that the island would face as a result of the loss of Soviet subsidies in the 1990s. See Silvia Pedraza, *Political Disaffection in Cuba's Revolution and Exodus*, 7–8.
67 Jorge Duany, "¿Nueva crisis de balseros?," *El Nuevo Día*, November 12, 2014, www.elnuevodia.com.
68 Duany, *Blurred Borders*, 41.
69 According to Susan Eckstein, approximately 225,300 Cubans left Cuba for the United States between 1959 and 1962. She puts the number for the Freedom Flights (1965–1973) at over 260,000 entrants. See *The Immigrant Divide*, 12.
70 These numbers are current as of October 2015. As I write this, Cubans are continuing to find ways to the United States by land, sea, and air. See Jens Manuel Krogstad, "Cuban Immigration to U.S. Surges as Relations Warm."
71 Chris Girard, Guillermo Grenier, and Hugh Gladwin, "The Declining Symbolic Significance of the Embargo for South Florida's Cuban Americans," 17.
72 According to the *New York Times*, "an estimated 400,000 Cubans and Cuban-Americans visited [Cuba] from the United States last year [2014]." Victoria Burnett, "Explaining the Flight News and Rules on Travel to Cuba," *New York Times*, September 21, 2015, www.nytimes.com.
73 Bureau of Western Hemisphere Affairs, "US Relations with Cuba Fact Sheet."
74 Eckstein, *The Immigrant Divide*, 4.
75 Girard, Grenier, and Gladwin, "Declining Symbolic Significance."
76 Guillermo J. Grenier, Lisandro Pérez, Sung Chang Chun, and Hugh Gladwin, "There Are Cubans," 94. Recent elections have shown that support for conservative politics is eroding in Cuban Miami. In the 2012 election, Barack Obama won a significantly higher percentage of the Cuban American vote than in 2008, and Joe García defeated the incumbent Republican Representative David Rivera to become the first Cuban American Democratic elected to Congress from Florida. See Juan O. Tamayo, "Did Obama or Romney Win the Cuban-American Vote?," *Miami Herald*, November 12, 2012, www.miamiherald.com. Since the announcement of warming relations on December 7, 2014, support for the move has grown steadily among the diaspora in the United States. See Mimi Whitefield, "Polls of Cuban-Americans Shows Support for New Cuba Policies Growing," *Miami Herald*, April 1, 2015, www.miamiherald.com.

77 Alejandro Portes explains, "Second-generation politicians born and bred in Miami and who have never been to Cuba, repeat without hesitating the same fervent anti-communist mantras and the same calls to arms learned from their elders. They do this, in part, because of political expediency, but there is also an element of genuine conviction" ("La máquina política cubano-estadounidense," 617). Andrew Lynch uses linguistic analysis to come to a similar conclusion in a discussion about second-generation Cubans more broadly; see "Expression of Cultural Standing in Miami." William Haller and Patricia Landolt found in their analysis of the Children of Immigrants Longitudinal Study (CILS) that "Cubans (and especially the children of earlier exile waves) are the group least involved with their parents' country of origin" ("The Transnational Dimensions of Identity Formation," 1192). My analysis in later chapters will lend evidence to support and complicate these findings.

78 There are, of course, younger generations of Cuban Americans that continue to hold the hardline. Republican Senator Marco Rubio is one example of the next generation taking up the banner of hardline exile politics.

79 Girard, Grenier, and Gladwin, "Declining Symbolic Significance": "Table 2 reveals relatively low support for the exile ideology among Cubans not born in Cuba" (16).

CHAPTER 1. UN TIPO TÍPICO

1 Guillermo Alvarez Guedes, *Alvarez Guedes 2*. The gist of the joke is that a man's car breaks down on the side of the road and he is in need of a jack (*un gato*) to change his tire. He sets off to a house in the distance and begins to think of all the things that could go wrong when he gets there. When he finally knocks on the door, the homeowner opens the door and says, "Good evening," to which the stranded motorist replies, "¡Métete el gato por el culo!" (Shove the jack up your ass!). A person described as being "el tipo del gato" then, is a self-defeating pessimist.

2 Cristina Saralegui, "Guillermo Alvarez Guedes no necesita una presentación formal," *El Miami Herald*, May 28, 1976, capitalization in the original.

3 Lisandro Pérez, "Cuban Miami."

4 Alejandro Portes, "The Cuban-American Political Machine," 129.

5 Pictures of his performance along with handwritten set lists can be found in the Guillermo Alvarez Guedes Collection of the Cuban Heritage Collection at the University of Miami.

6 María Cristina García calls the 1970s in Miami a "transitional period" with the exile community "developing along parallel courses, one of adjustment and acceptance, the other of increasing militancy and desperation" (*Havana USA*, 137). For more background on this historical moment, see also María de los Angeles Torres, *In the Land of Mirrors*.

7 In addition to stand-up recordings, he released an album of songs called *Alvarez Guedes Canta* and an at times comic spoken-word album that imagined the fall of Fidel Castro called *El día que cayó Fidel Castro*. He published joke books, including *De la vida, de la muerte—y otras mierdas más* (1984) and *Malas palabras*,

buenas palabras y otras palabras (1981). In 2001, he released a novel from the point of view of a 1959 Cadillac detailing what it sees as the failures of the Revolution called *Cadillac 59*. Movie credits include starring roles in *A mi que me importa que explote Miami* (1976) and *Dios te salve, psiquiatra* (1966?) among others. He was also a mainstay on local radio with shows like *Aquí Está Alvarez Guedes*.

8 Many of the top comedians in Cuba appeared in a video titled "Los humoristas cubanos hablan de Alvarez Guedes" in tribute to his memory and career. They cited him as a vital influence in their own careers despite the comedian never returning to the island. I will discuss this example and others regarding the transnational circulation of Cuban humor in chapter 4.

9 Not *all* of Alvarez Guedes's material deals with Cuba, though his cubanía certainly colors all of his performances. He also toured frequently throughout Latin America and Spain and was popular among non-Cuban audiences.

10 José Antonio Evora, "Guillermo Alvarez Guedes, El Natural," 172.

11 Guillermo Alvarez Guedes, *Alvarez Guedes 4*.

12 Emilio Ichikawa, "Prólogo."

13 Wilfredo Cancio Isla, "Fallece en Miami el célebre humorista cubano Guillermo Alvarez Guedes," www.cafefuerte.com.

14 I explain the long intellectual history of choteo on the island in the introduction. Mañach, "Indagación," 54.

15 In *Unbecoming Blackness*, Antonio López cites the work of Portes and Stepick in *City on the Edge* to explain that early Cubans exiles "generally ignored or, at worst, went on to benefit from and exacerbate" racism experienced by African Americans in South Florida (191). Black Miami makes its way into diasporic popular culture from the 1960s to the present as I will show here and in the chapters to come.

16 For a discussion of the discrimination early arrivals from Cuba faced, see Torres, *In the Land of Mirrors*, especially 76–77. Of particular note is an organization founded by "a group of Hispanic and Cuban American residents" called SALAD (Spanish American League against Discrimination) in 1974. See also García, *Havana USA*, 28–30.

17 Cheris Brewer Current, "Normalizing Cuban Refugees," 45.

18 According to Torres, Cuban exiles were also wary about discussing discrimination they faced because it could potentially fuel Fidel Castro's criticism of the United States and his propaganda war against the exile community. See *In the Land of Mirrors*, 85.

19 See Lane, *Blackface Cuba*, 15. Other scholars have tracked choteo and the ways in which it has functioned to narrate racial conflict on the island. Narciso Hidalgo writes, "There are two seminal models of choteo. One, racist and discriminatory, caricatures and ridicules the black man in teatro bufo and on marquillas cigarreras [colorful papers used to bundle cigarettes in nineteenth-century Cuba, which often featured caricatures of black Cubans], and the reverse, a subversive, anti-hierarchical choteo that mocks the white man to his face, imitating him to the point of caricature" (*Choteo*, 17). In her work on marquillas cigarreras, Agnes

Lugo-Ortíz cites the work of Ada Ferrer and Aline Helg to explain how Cubans of color in the nineteenth century were concerned with the "derisive images and skewed identifications waged against them by racist and pro-colonial forces on the island" ("Material Culture, Slavery, and Governability in Colonial Cuba," 62). Today, television shows in Miami featuring Cuban actors and writers regularly include sketches featuring blackface characters. I will address this in more detail in chapter 4.

20 I have translated this joke and others in this chapter directly into English. I have included particular words and phrases in Spanish when they are relevant to the analysis.

21 The Larry Wilde version is slightly different. It is set in Mississippi and the black victim is described as a "civil rights worker" cornered on a lonely country road. Instead of a lion, a dog is featured in the book. There are some other small embellishments but the premise and the punchline are the same. See *The Official White Folks/Black Folks Joke Book*.

22 A joke from *Alvarez Guedes 7* (1978) about a young black boy who paints himself white can be found in *Truly Tasteless IV* (1984) with only small changes. The form of a joke from *Totally Tasteless* (1983) about British discrimination against Australians corresponds with a joke from *Alvarez Guedes 7* about a black man from Alabama.

23 Ashton Applewhite explains the genesis of her career as "Blanche Knott" and how the early installments of *Truly Tasteless Jokes* were born out of jokes she heard in passing and wrote down on napkins and small slips of paper. In *Truly Tasteless Jokes Two* she included a call for jokes from readers with a notice that "no compensation or credit can be given." The submissions came pouring in. See Applewhite, "Being Blanche."

24 It is no secret that Alvarez Guedes adapted jokes for his acts. In a legal case initiated by Alvarez Guedes about copyright infringement of his material, one of the "uncontested facts" states: "Some of the jokes and stories recited by Alvarez Guedes in his twenty-nine volumes of audio recordings are of his own creation; others are jokes and stories he has heard and adapted for his performances." See *Guillermo Alvarez Guedes v. Hector Luis Marcano Martínez*.

25 Examples include *Last Official Polish Joke Book* (1978), *The Last Official Italian Joke Book* (1978), and *The Official Jewish/Irish Joke Book* (1975).

26 The equivalent in Alvarez Guedes's repertoire would be the many jokes about *gallegos* and their stereotypical stupidity—jokes that have a long history in Cuba. Although *gallego* refers to someone from the autonomous community of Galicia in Spain, *gallego* in Cuba is slang for anyone from that country.

27 Bruce Porter and Marvin Dunn, *Miami Riot*, 18–22. One of the police officers involved, Alex Marrero, was Cuban American.

28 For more on the relationship between Cuban and Miami's black communities, see Alan Aja, "The Intra-Immigrant Dilemma," and N. D. B. Connolly, *A World More Concrete*.

29   See Guillermo Grenier and Max Castro, "Triadic Politics."

30   Guillermo Alvarez Guedes, *Alvarez Guedes 16*.

31   Lane, *Blackface Cuba*, x.

32   The equation of blackness with criminality has a long history in Cuba before and after the Revolution. See Alejandro de la Fuente, *A Nation for All*.

33   There are noteworthy moments when tensions between Cubans and the black community bubbled to the surface in very public ways. The most memorable incident came when Nelson Mandela visited Miami in 1980 and was greeted by Cuban protestors incensed by his approval of Fidel Castro. For a discussion of this incident and others, see Mark Q. Sawyer, *Racial Politics in Post-Revolutionary Cuba*, 154–181.

34   Guillermo Alvarez Guedes, *Alvarez Guedes 22*.

35   Ibid.

36   de la Fuente, *A Nation for All*. Roberto Zurbano, an Afro-Cuban intellectual based in Cuba, wrote an op-ed for the *New York Times* that spoke to the entrenched racism within Cuba after five decades of the Revolution. Soon after, Zurbano was removed from his post at Casa de las Américas. See "For Blacks in Cuba, The Revolution Hasn't Begun," *New York Times*, March 23, 2013.

37   There is certainly evidence within popular culture that Cubans were aware of the ill treatment marielitos were subject to in Miami. A 1985 film written and directed by Iván Acosta called *Amigos* portrayed the difficult experiences and stigma of being a marielito through the lens of humor. Though the film attempts to address the internal conflicts within the community, it never engages race. A white Cuban actor named Ruben Rabasa active in Cuban exile drama and film since the 1970s plays Ramón, the film's protagonist.

38   For an analysis of these attitudes, see Sawyer, *Racial Politics*, 171 and Guillermo Grenier and Lisandro Pérez, *The Legacy of Exile*, chap. 6.

39   Carlos Alberto Montaner, "¿Un Oscar para 'La Otra Cuba?,'" *El Miami Herald*, September 26, 1985. Famed exile poet Heberto Padilla celebrated the film in a column titled "Sobre la conducta impropia de Cuba," *El Miami Herald*, April 30, 1984. Padilla does mention that the film had some detractors within the exile community for showing the human side of some of the officials working at the camp. René Jordan, "Conducta impropia," *El Nuevo Herald*, June 29, 1984, echoes Montaner's sentiment about the film challenging liberal supporters of the Revolution. He reported that the film received a "tremendous ovation" in Miami.

40   Emilio Bejel, *Gay Cuban Nation*, xiii.

41   See Ortíz, *Cultural Erotics*, 73, and Susana Peña, *Oye Loca!*, chap. 5.

42   Peña, *Oye Loca!*, x.

43   To give a sense of the popularity and staying power of these loca jokes, an example is in order. In June 2014, Pedro Sevcec, a television personality based in Miami, interviewed Elsy Alvarez Guedes, the comedian's widow. The celebratory segment revisited the comedian's career on the anniversary of his death and closed with a clip of him telling a joke about "mariconerías" (faggy behavior).

44 Guillermo Alvarez Guedes, *Alvarez Guedes 3*.

45 Susana Peña and José Muñoz have shown how queer artists have used Cuban humor in their performances. See Peña, *Oye Loca!*, chap. 8, "Gay Cuba in Drag," and José Muñoz, "Sister Acts," in *Disidentifications*.

46 Peña's work in *Oye Loca!* is again instructive. In Chapter 8, "Gay Cuba in Drag," she explains how Cuban drag queens (especially those with an anti-Castro position) are popular among heterosexual audiences on the local comic theater circuit in Miami.

47 Ibid., 11.

48 While a large portion of Cubans supported Bryant's initiatives, Cubans also played an important role in the struggle for gay rights in Miami "before, during, and after the 1977 battle" (ibid., 17).

49 See Anita Casavantes Bradford, *The Revolution Is for the Children*.

50 B. Ruby Rich and Lourdes Argüelles suggest that Cubans were inspired to participate in the United States political process in a more intense way because of the Bryant initiative. See "Homosexuality, Homophobia, and Revolution."

51 María del Carmen Martínez references these representations in a broader conversation about the gender politics of the Cuban exile community through a reading of Gustavo Pérez Firmat's creative work. See "Her Body Was My Country."

52 Silvia Pedraza-Bailey, *Political and Economic Migrants in America*.

53 Max Castro, "The Politics of Language in Miami," 115. *El Miami Herald* was an attempt by owners of the dominant newspaper, the *Miami Herald*, to attract a Spanish-language audience. For the most part, the paper was a translated version of material in the English version of the *Miami Herald*. With the readership of *El Miami Herald* declining, the paper was replaced with *El Nuevo Herald* in 1988. *El Nuevo Herald* has its own editorial board functioning independently from the *Miami Herald*. See Portes and Stepick, *City on the Edge*, 15, 175.

54 García, *Havana USA*, 28–30.

55 Pérez, *Cuban Miami*, 91.

56 Portes and Stepick, *City*, 27.

57 For a detailed analysis of the political circumstances that led to Miami's official status as a bilingual and bicultural city in 1973 and the dramatic shift in policy with the anti-bilingual referendum in 1980, see Castro, "Politics of Language."

58 Portes and Stepick, *City on the Edge*, 36–37.

59 Alvarez Guedes, *Alvarez Guedes 2*.

60 Gustavo Pérez Firmat, *Literature and Liminality*, 65.

61 Alvarez Guedes, *Alvarez Guedes 11*.

62 Ibid.

63 Ibid.

64 Freudian conceptualizations of humor certainly ring true when considering Mañach's essay and Alvarez Guedes's choteo. In his essay entitled "Humour," Freud declares, "The grandeur in it [humour] lies in the triumph of narcissism, the victorious assertion of the ego's invulnerability. The ego refuses to be

distressed by the provocations of reality, to let itself be compelled to suffer. . . . Humour is not resigned; it is rebellious. It signifies not only the triumph of the ego but also of the pleasure principle, which is able here to assert itself against the unkindness of real circumstances" (160–166).

65 Choteo is often used to reimagine both the reality of life in exile and the past and present of Cuba in a way that places the exile community on the "righteous" side of history. With that said, there are a number of instances when Alvarez Guedes criticizes the nostalgic impulse that often guides revisionist history of Cuba before Castro. On *Alvarez Guedes 13*, the comedian criticizes the tendency of some to romanticize all things Cuban before the Revolution, as well as the island's natural landscape.

66 Guillermo Alvarez Guedes, *Alvarez Guedes 14*.

67 Portes and Stepick, *City on the Edge*, 31.

68 Robin Moore, *Nationalizing Blackness,* 9.

69 Muñoz, *Disidentifications*, 136.

70 Ibid., 137. Here, Muñoz discusses Carmelita Tropicana's disidentification with the Cuban Revolution. The logic of this insight certainly applies to my thinking about exile cubanía. It is a point that will be developed in more detail in the next chapter.

CHAPTER 2. CUBAN MIAMI ON THE AIR

1 Heberto Padilla, "La radio en Miami," *El Nuevo Herald*, January 2, 1986, 5.

2 For background on the history of radio in Cuba, see Louis A. Pérez, *On Becoming Cuban*, 331–333, and Michael Brian Salwen, *Radio and Television in Cuba*. For studies dedicated to radio and media in Miami more broadly, see Gonzalo Soruco, *Cubans and the Media in South Florida*, and Christine Lohmeier, *Cuban Americans and the Miami Media*.

3 Lars Schoultz provides the details behind the CIA-led operation to destabilize the Cuban government with radio propaganda in *That Infernal Little Cuban Republic*, 117.

4 Howard Frederick, *Cuban American Radio Wars*.

5 For more on the US-Cuba radio conflict over the radio waves, see Frederick, *Radio Wars*; Omar Pérez Salomón, *Terrorismo en el éter*; Daniel C. Walsh, *An Air War with Cuba*.

6 US Congress, Senate, Committee, *Cuba: Immediate Action*.

7 Soruco, *Cubans and the Media*, 36.

8 Ibid., 35.

9 García, *Havana USA*, 106.

10 Susan Douglas, *Listening In*, 29.

11 Torres, *In the Land of Mirrors*, 82.

12 Radio programming sympathetic to the Cuban government does exist but with little reach. Since 2006, Radio Miami has been airing for one hour a day Monday through Friday, positioning itself against the exile ideology. See Fernando Peinado, "La radio rebelde de Miami," *BBC Mundo*, May 3, 2012, www.bbc.com.

13 María Cristina García, "Hardliners v. 'Dialogueros,' " 21.

14 In response to calls for stronger sanctions, Congress enacted the Cuban Democracy Act, which strengthened the embargo against Cuba by prohibiting foreign subsidiaries of US companies from doing business with the Castro government. Four years later, the Helms-Burton Act passed because of fresh international outrage caused by the Cuban military's downing of two civilian planes belonging to a Cuban exile organization called Hermanos al rescate (Brothers to the Rescue). This organization searched the Florida Straits for Cuban rafters and relayed information to the US Coast Guard. The Cuban government claimed that the organization violated Cuban airspace and spread anti-Castro propaganda on the island. The Helms-Burton Act tightened the embargo by including provisions to further discourage foreign investment in Cuba and by making travel to the island more difficult. For a discussion of the Cuban Democracy Act, Hermanos al rescate, and the Helms-Burton Act, see García, "Hardliners v. 'Dialogueros,' " 21.

15 Eckstein, *Immigrant Divide*, 117, and Isabel Molina Guzmán, "Competing Discourses of Community Ideological Tensions."

16 The advertisement can be found in the April 17, 1965 edition of *Zig-Zag Libre*. The program aired on Radio Americas, a station with enough power to transmit its broadcasts into Cuba. The translated text of the advertisement is as follows: "Now, every Sunday at the same time, we will continue to 'infiltrate' the captive fatherland, house by house, radio by radio, for the enjoyment of our compatriots and to enrage the communists. Don't miss it here in Miami either, without having to worry about informants."

17 Ann Louise Bardach, *Cuba Confidential*, 145. For more on the work of Alberto González, see William Labbee "Alberto González—Wild Man at the Plate," *Miami New Times*, January 23, 1991, www.miaminewtimes.com.

18 I detail these demographic and generational shifts in the introduction.

19 Over the years, poll data has demonstrated a drop in support for the exile ideology across generational cohorts but the decline is most stark among US-born Cuban Americans and more recent arrivals from Cuba. The Cuban Research Institute has conducted polls on the Cuban community in South Florida since 1991. The wealth of data produced with each poll provides great insight into Miami's evolution on matters related to Cuba. For poll data, see Florida International University (FIU) Cuba Poll, Cuba Research Institute, 2007, cri.fiu.edu. There are, of course, younger Cuban Americans who continue to hold the hardline. Republican Senator Marco Rubio is an example of the US-born generation taking up the banner of exile politics.

20 For data on US-born attitudes toward Cuba, see Girard, Grenier, and Gladwin, "Declining Symbolic Significance," and FIU Cuba Poll.

21 Vazquez, *Listening in Detail*, 207.

22 Eckstein, *Immigrant Divide*, 57–58.

23 Kapcia, *Island*, 7.

24 This is not to say that US-born Cuban Americans are not active in the politics and issues facing contemporary Cuba. Organizations like Raíces de Esperanza (Roots of Hope) have a strong presence on college campuses with the stated goal of "bridging the gap between Cubans on and off the island and raising awareness about their struggles." See www.rootsofhope.org.

25 The Telecommunications Act of 1996 has had powerful effects on the media landscape in the United States. With its virtual elimination of restrictions on the number of radio and television stations a company can hold, concentration of media outlets into the hands of fewer and increasingly larger media conglomerates like Clear Channel and Univision has risen significantly. See Nicole Serratore, "How Do You Say Big Media in Spanish?," 203.

26 For more scholarship on Spanish-language radio in the United States, see Angharad Valdivia, ed., *Latina/o Communication Studies Today*; Isabel Molina Guzmán, *Dangerous Curves*; Todd Chambers, "The State of Spanish-Language Radio"; Dolores Inés Casillas, *Sounds of Belonging*; Yeidy Rivero and Arlene Dávila, eds., *Contemporary Latina/o Media*.

27 Mari Castañeda, "The Importance of Spanish-Language and Latino Media," 54.

28 Arbitron, "Hispanic Radio Today: How America Listens to Radio," 2011. The file has since been taken down from the Arbitron website. More recent versions of this study are available at www.arbitron.com.

29 Dolores Inés Casillas's work is a notable exception in its analysis of specific show content. See her chapter "Pun Intended" in *Sounds of Belonging*.

30 Enrique Santos and Joe Ferrero got their start together in October 2002 on a show called *El vacilón de la mañana* on El Zol, owned by Spanish Broadcasting System (SBS). After a messy breakup with management there, they signed with Univision radio in 2008 and took over mornings on La Kalle. In late 2009, Santos and Ferrero were split up and given their own shows. The *Enrique Santos Show* took the morning drive slot while *Joe Ferrero y La Animalada* got afternoons. In 2010, Ferrero and Univision parted ways. The *Enrique Santos Show* is still on the air but the format has changed considerably. I will discuss this in more detail later in the chapter.

31 González Echevarría, *Cuban Fiestas*, 138.

32 The prank call, edited down from its original length of twenty-five minutes, has been uploaded to YouTube by different users. See "Prank Call Fidel Castro Hugo Chávez Miami," YouTube video, 11:45, posted by "Robert Pistarino," October 8, 2010, www.youtube.com.

33 Wilfredo Cancio Isla, "Castro responde con insultos a una broma," *El Nuevo Herald*, June 18, 2003.

34 Terms like "intimacy" and "co-presence" are vital to the field of radio studies. In *Key Concepts in Radio Studies,* Hugh Chignell defines co-presence as "the shared experience of radio listening . . . one of the most influential and significant concepts in radio studies" (74–78) and intimacy as "the personal closeness or familiarity that can exist between radio (or its presenters) and listeners" (85–87).

35 Alvarez Guedes released an album called *El día que cayó Fidel Castro* that imagined the final days of the dictatorship through the lens of humor and from the perspective of fictional Cubans on and off the island.

36 See Lohmeier, *Cuban Americans and Miami Media*, 70. For more on this dynamic on the airwaves, see Eckstein, *Immigrant Divide*, 34–35.

37 In June of 2015, Armando Pérez Roura left Radio Mambí. Univision, which owns the station, has been trying to increase its appeal to a broader Spanish-speaking audience in Miami and when Pérez Roura's contract was up, they chose not to renew. He continues to espouse his viewpoints on La Poderosa—one of the few Cuba-centric stations left in Miami.

38 Jordan Levin, "Payola Called Fixture in Latin Music," *Miami Herald*, December 8, 2002.

39 José Sánchez-Boudy, *Diccionario mayor de cubanismos*, 426.

40 Simon Dentith, *Parody*, 32.

41 Geoffrey Baym, "Representation and the Politics of Play," 359.

42 I base this understanding of audience approval on the many reoccurrences of the Radio Maní segment and airtime dedicated to it (about fifteen minutes long) on the *Enrique y Joe Show*.

43 According to the Pew Hispanic Center, Miami-Dade County is home to the largest communities of Colombians, Hondurans, and Peruvians in the country. See Seth Motel and Eileen Patten, "The 10 Largest Hispanic Origin Groups." In addition to these groups, there are smaller migrant populations from all over Latin America. In the 2000s, Venezuelans unhappy with the policies of Hugo Chávez arrived in Miami in large numbers (approximately 70,000 live in South Florida according to the 2010 census). For coverage on the growth of Latino/a populations in South Florida and the influx of Venezuelans in the 2000s, see Kirk Semple, "Rise of Chávez Sends Venezuelans to Florida," *New York Times*, January 23, 2008, www.nytimes.com.

44 For more on this pan-Latina/o narrative in the context of Univision, see Arlene Dávila, *Latinos, Inc.*

45 Ian Hutchby, *Confrontation Talk*, 13.

46 Hidalgo, *Choteo*, 19.

47 Torres, *In the Land of Mirrors*, 100–104.

48 Mikhail Bakhtin, *Rabelais and His World*. For the connection to choteo, see Pérez Firmat, *Literature and Liminality*, 65.

49 Robert Hariman, "Political Parody and Public Culture," 256.

50 See Peter Dale Scott and John Marshall, *Cocaine Politics*, and "Omega-7," National Consortium for the Study of Terrorism and Responses to Terrorism, University of Maryland, www.start.umd.edu.

51 Bardach, *Cuba Confidential*, 119.

52 Robert Hariman, "Political Parody and Public Culture," 253.

53 Eckstein, *Immigrant Divide*, 36. Eckstein uses the term "New Cuban" to describe more recent arrivals from the island "who knew life transformed both by

Revolution and the economic crisis the Soviet Union's dissolution caused" (2). The term "marielito" refers to those Cubans who left the island during the Mariel boat crisis of 1980.

54 According to Miguel Barnet, "Asere y ecobio, also of African roots, have become forms of address, most of all the first [*asere*], among our youth since the 1960s." "La lengua que hablamos," *Granma*, August 20, 2010, 4. A popular arts and culture website called *Generación asere* claims the term *asere* as a move away from the failures of government's "hombre nuevo" project. For the founders of the blog, it is a means to capture the spirit of Cuban revolutionary youth across the decades. See "¿Qué es generación asere?," April 8, 2007, generacionasere.blogspot.com.

55 For a reading of Juanes's celebrity status as it intersects with his international politics and performance of "hegemonic heterosexual masculinity," see Christina Maria Ceisel, "El Rock Star Perfecto?."

56 Radio personalities like Ninoska Pérez and Armando Pérez Roura of Radio Mambí 710 AM slammed Juanes for his performance. Local and national media also picked up the story. See Damien Cave, "Concert Plans in Havana Start Furor in Miami," *New York Times*, September 18, 2009, C1, and Jordan Levin, "Pop Singer Juanes Sparks Furor in Cuban Exile Community with Plans for Havana Concert," *Miami Herald*, August 20, 2009.

57 A recurring issue within Cuban Miami over the years has been the treatment and reception of artists that are aligned with, or construed as being supportive of, the Castro government. On October 9, 1999, Cuban timba group Los Van Van played in Miami amidst community uproar and protests from the exile community. Though Cubans familiar with the group from life in Cuba welcomed the musicians, the exile political machine successfully organized a full-scale media campaign against the concert. The logic guiding this campaign was that any artist from Cuba allowed to travel must be in the good graces of the government. On the day of the concert, a protest of 3,000–4,000 people gathered to hurl insults and throw objects like rocks and eggs at any concertgoers who crossed their path. See Manny García, Jordan Levin and Peter Whorisky, "The Band Plays on as Protest Fails to Deter Van Van's Fans," *Miami Herald*, October 10, 1999. In 2001, organizers of the Latin Grammys moved the event from Miami to Los Angeles out of fear that protesters angry about the attendance of musicians from the island would become violent—a sentiment likely inspired by the reception of Los Van Van just two years earlier. See Katynka Z. Martínez, "American Idols with Caribbean Soul."

58 Viviana Muñoz, "Los ánimos se caldearon en la Calle Ocho," *El Nuevo Herald*, September 29, 2009.

59 By the time the Juanes episode rocked Cuban Miami, Enrique Santos had his own show, *The Enrique Santos Show*, on the same station but rebranded by Univision as Mix 98.3. I discuss the rebranding of the station and Enrique Santos in the concluding section of this chapter.

60 In polls conducted by Bendixen and Associates and the Cuba Study Group (2009), there was a substantial shift in opinion within the Cuban community

regarding the Juanes concert. After the concert, favorable opinions increased across all age groups and generational cohorts but the degree of favorability continued to follow generational patterns. See Jordan Levin, "Poll: Cuban Americans Change Tune about Juanes Concert in Havana," *Miami Herald*, October 1, 2009.

61 Martin Shingler and Cindy Wieringa, *On Air*, 117–122.

62 Earlier in the week, Santos made a number of prank calls to Saavedra asking for tickets to the Juanes concert in Cuba. Saavedra became irate and called the character Santos was playing "an enemy of the Cuban exile community."

63 A sentiment shared by most Cubans in Miami. According to a Bendixen and Associates poll of Cuban Americans from every generational cohort, over 74 percent of those surveyed thought the protest and actions by Vigilia Mambisa had a "negative effect on the image of Cuban exiles in the US." Though many exiles agreed with Vigilia Mambisa's position on the concert, the poll indicates that the means used to convey that message were not favored. See Jordan Levin, "Cuban-American Poll Finds Mixed Emotions on Juanes Show," *Miami Herald*, August 26, 2009.

64 Bendixen and Associates conducted two polls sponsored by the Cuba Study Group, one before and one after the concert, to gauge opinions among Cubans. The percentage of Cubans in favor of the concert rose across generational cohorts after the concert but there was still a dramatic difference between more recent arrivals from the 1990s and 2000s and those Cubans who arrived in the 1960s and 1970s. Only a small part of the sample included US-born Cuban Americans and tellingly, 22 percent opposed the concert, 36 percent supported it, and 42 percent selected "didn't know/no opinion." The fact that the majority of US-born responded "didn't know/no opinion" echoes my arguments about how US-born are less interested and knowledgable about contemporary Cuba-related news. See "Juanes Cuba Concert Study," September 2009, www.cubastudygroup.org.

65 Eckstein speaks to the generational divides within the Cuban community, quoting more recent arrivals who report feeling stigmatized by older exiles who treat them condescendingly because of their "long-time association with the regime the first émigrés abhorred." Eckstein also captures this sentiment from the perspective of older exiles who, like Saavedra, saw these newer arrivals as products of the Revolution and thus tainted. See *Immigrant Divide*, 36–38.

66 Valdivia, "Latinas as Radical Hybrid."

67 Eckstein, *Immigrant Divide*, 88–95, 124–126.

68 Arian Campo-Flores, "Trips Back to Cuba Draw Fire," *Wall Street Journal*, September 17, 2011; Erika Bolstad, "Rivera's Cuban Readjustment Act Reforms Get a Hearing," *Miami Herald Blog*, May 31, 2012, miamiherald.typepad.com; Joe Cardona, "Time to Revisit the Cuban Adjustment Act?" *Miami Herald*, March 9, 2012; Carlos Curbelo, "Keep the Cuban Adjustment Act, But Clamp Down on Its Abusers," *Miami Herald*, November 29, 2015.

69 Enrique Santos and Joe Ferrero created a musical parody of Lynyrd Skynrd's "Sweet Home Alabama" titled "Sweet Home Hialeah," which insists on chusmería as the city's guiding urban and cultural aesthetic.

70 It is important to reiterate that these representations of newer arrivals are not limited to this show. In Chapter 5 I will discuss how US-born Cuban Americans perform and enjoy their cubanía online. There, I perform close readings of memes and videos by US-born Cuban Americans that rely on the figure of the balsero and the refugee to delineate a particular narrative of cubanía.

71 Chignell, *Key Concepts in Radio Studies,* "Radio World."

72 Univision Communications, Inc., "Univision Media Kit," 2012, corporate.univision.com.

73 In an interview that appeared in *People en español* in 2011, there is not a single mention of Santos's Cuban background despite significant attention to where he grew up and other biographical details. Pan-latinidad frames the entire interview. The title, which includes a quote from Santos, captures it best: " 'Ser latino está de moda' " (To Be Latino Is in Style). See Vicglamar Torres, "Enrique Santos: 'Ser latino está de moda,' " *People en español,* May 4, 2011, www.peopleenespanol.com.

74 Syndicated programs featured on Univision radio networks do not always shy away from politics. Univision media, especially radio, played an active role in the 2006 marches for immigrant rights across the country. The difference is that these issues are national and appeal to the majority of Latino/as living in the United States. What is disappearing is a discussion of more local political issues on syndicated radio shows that continue to grow. See Ricardo Ramírez, "Mobilization en Español."

75 The only comparable example to Santos's nationwide reach as a US-born Cuban American is Dan Le Batard on his ESPN show *Highly Questionable.* The show features co-host Bomani Jones, Le Batard, and his Cuban father, Gonzalo, as "Papi." At one point, the set of the show was a "typical" kitchen in Cuban Miami but what has been consistent across the program's life is the guayabera-clad Papi and his Cuban accent as a means to produce comic moments. In this case, the humor is less about diversión as a performance practice and more about the incongruity of Le Batard's "foreign" father on a sports talk show.

76 See Francisco Alvarado, "Cuban Radio Is Dying Because of Aging Hardliners and Miami's Changing Market," *Miami New Times,* August 30, 2012, www.miaminewtimes.com.

CHAPTER 3. NOSTALGIC PLEASURES

1 For US-born and reared Cuban Americans, Tamiami Park has long been an important site for diversión as the home of the Miami Dade Youth Fair since the 1970s. It is fitting to think of Tamiami Park as a site of convergence where Miami youth culture intersects with the hyper-Cuban narrative of the older generation.

2 Past employees of El Encanto formed a group called Asociación de Antiguos Empleados de El Encanto (Association of Former Employees of El Encanto) in order to keep in touch with each other and disseminate the history of the department store. They have produced a documentary on the store's history, photo albums, and even reissued the store's Christmas catalog from 1954–1955.

3 Raúl Rubio, "Discourses of/on Nostalgia," and Ortíz, *Cultural Erotics*, 134–155.

4 Kandiyoti cites authors like Cristina García, Ana Menéndez, Gustavo Pérez Firmat, and Achy Obejas to make this point. She also takes up the relationship between nostalgia and "selling Cuban America," a notion I will consider in detail in this chapter. See Dalia Kandiyoti, "Consuming Nostalgia and the Marketplace," 81.

5 See also Isabel Alvarez Borland, *Cuban-American Literature of Exile*, and Elena Machado Sáez, "The Global Baggage of Nostalgia."

6 Miguel de la Torre, *La Lucha for Cuba*, 32.

7 Svetlana Boym, *The Future of Nostalgia*, xv.

8 This is not to suggest that Cuba was somehow forgotten in the 1980s. But the fall of the Berlin Wall was different from rumors about invasions or assassination attempts against the Castro government. The dissolution of the Soviet bloc put all eyes on Cuba.

9 See Willy Chirino's *Cuba Libre*, an album covering old Cuban standards that featured a who's who of Cuban exile recording artists including Celia Cruz, Jon Secada, and Arturo Sandoval, among others. See also Albita Rodríguez's *No se parece a nada* (1995) featuring "Bolero para nostalgia" and Marisela Verena's "Madre Cuba está de parto" (1990). The best example of this musical manifestation of nostalgia is Gloria Estefan's *Mi Tierra* (1992).

10 Mirta Ojito, "A Nightclub Bottles Cuba, before the Revolution," *New York Times*, October 13, 1998.

11 See Rick Jervis, "South Beach's Hot Havana Nights Party-Goers Drink Up the Atmosphere of Old Cuba at Restaurant's Popular Events," *Miami Herald*, August 15, 1996.

12 See Lynn Carrillo, "Culture Stocked South Beach Store Is about Cuban Heritage, Not Politics," *Orlando Sun Sentinel*, July 4, 1995, and Mirta Ojito, " 'Little Museum' Soothes Pangs of Nostalgia," *Miami Herald*, October 25, 1995.

13 Mirta Ojito, "Longing for the Old Cuba Stirs a Boom in Nostalgia," *New York Times*, June 16, 2002.

14 Marcia Facundo, "¡Ay mi Cuba! Board Game Teaches Culture, History," *Miami Herald*, November 18, 1998. According to an interview with the one of the game's creators, 5,000 copies were sold in two years. See "Interview with Fascinating and Fun Children's Author Martha Rodriguez," by Tim Greaton, July 13, 2012, timgreatonforum.blogspot.com.

15 Frank Davies, "Cuban Finches' Tune a Costly Nostalgia," *Miami Herald*, October 2, 1997.

16 Sociologist Rubén Rumbaut coined the term 1.5 generation to describe immigrant children who arrived in the United States from school age to about twelve years old. This generation would have clear memories of life in the country of origin but would have come of age in the United States.

17 A 1993 article in the *Miami Herald* captures this sentiment well: "A cultural awakening [is] going on among young Cuban Americans, a nostalgia for something they never had, something they know only from their parents' stories, the ones

they always rolled their eyes at" (Lydia Martin, "The Call of Old Cuba," *Miami Herald*, November 9, 1993).

18 Lydia Martin, "Bridging a Cultural Gap: 'Generation ñ' Finds Niche," *Miami Herald*, July 13, 1997.

19 *Generation ñ* 1, no. 1 (April 1996). Joe Cardona's documentary called *Café Con Leche* also focused on the experience of "kids raised in a bilingual and bicultural Miami."

20 Gustavo Pérez Firmat, *The Havana Habit*. See also Louis A. Pérez *Cuba in the American Imagination*. For an excellent reading of the "scramble" to capture Havana through the photographic image in the 1990s, see Ana María Dopico, "Picturing Havana."

21 Frances R. Aparicio and Susana Chávez-Silverman define "tropicalization" as a "means to trope, to imbue a particular space, geography, group or nation with a set of traits, images and values. . . . To tropicalize from a privileged, First World location is undoubtedly a hegemonic move" (*Tropicalizations*, 8).

22 Gloria and Emilio Estefan quickly got involved with the upscale Cuban restaurant trend as early as 1992 with a restaurant called Larios in South Beach. See Nancy Harmon Jenkins, "Putting New Zing into Cuban Food," *New York Times*, February 24, 1991.

23 For a reading of the racial politics of nostalgia and Cuban music around the Buena Vista Social Club, see Tanya Kateri Hernández, "The Buena Vista Social Club." José Quiroga examines the worldwide explosion of interest in Cuban Music in the 1990s in "The Beat of the State" in *Cuban Palimpsests*; for a fantastic analysis of the Buena Vista Social Club, see 159–163.

24 Marilyn Halter, *Shopping for Identity*, 26.

25 For detailed analysis of the events leading up to the rafter crisis and the policies that followed it, see Jorge Duany, *Blurred Borders*, and Ted Henken, "Balseros, Boteros, and El Bombo."

26 Suspicion between Cubans from different migratory waves was also a reality in the 1960s, when those who left first, in 1959–1961, and were often aligned with the Batista dictatorship, questioned the anti-communist credentials of those who left the island during the Freedom Flights of 1965–1973.

27 Boym, *Nostalgia*, 17.

28 Mireya Navarro, "One City, Two Cubas: A Special Report; Miami's Exiles: Side by Side, Yet Worlds Apart," *New York Times*, February 11, 1999.

29 Ivan Karp, "Festivals," 282.

30 Leslie Pantín, interview with author, Miami, Florida, May 14, 2014.

31 Cristina Beltrán, *The Trouble with Unity*, 76.

32 James F. English, "Festivals and the Geography of Culture," 63.

33 It is common to see groups from assisted living facilities and apartment complexes with activities for older populations bussed in to attend on Fridays.

34 In Chapter 4 I discuss how these Cubans imagine the island through their own nostalgic lens. Meanwhile, in Cuba, nostalgia for a time when the Soviet Union

and the island were intertwined politically and culturally is being increasingly felt with restaurants and resurgent interest in Soviet era cultural production such as cartoons. See Jacqueline Loss, *Dreaming in Russian.*

35 Less than 3 percent of Cubans who arrived between 1959 and 1973 were black or mulatto. Between 14 percent and 40 of those who came during the Mariel boatlift were black. See Sawyer, *Racial Politics in Post-Revolutionary Cuba*, 157–159.

36 Alejandro de la Fuente, *A Nation for All*, 3.

37 In an article covering the inaugural Cuba Nostalgia in 1999, Pantín explicitly says that this event is for "the older generation who wants to remember the Cuba they knew and the younger generation, the Generation ñ, who have heard all the stories from their parents" (Fernando González, "The Cuba of Yesteryear," *Miami Herald*, May 12, 1999).

38 Brett Sokol, "A Quick Stop in Old Cuba," *New York Times*, May 12, 2010.

39 Kandiyoti speaks of "codified nostalgia" in the Cuban exile context as intersecting with "anti-Revolutionary politics that repeatedly construct Cuba before Castro as a prelapsarian paradise" ("Consuming Nostalgia," 83).

40 Judith Butler, *Bodies That Matter*, 20.

41 García, *Havana USA*, 91. For a more detailed analysis of Cruzada Educativa Cubana, the most prominent organization for educating children in the exile context, see also Casavantes Bradford *The Revolution Is for the Children*, 193–195.

42 In *Problema del niño cubano*, Ruperto Carmenate writes an impassioned plea to the parents of Cuban American children. He explains that his words "are directed to all Cubans of whatever organization they might be a member of," in an attempt at transcending political differences for the sake of the children. Concerned that this generation will forget or not be interested in eventual return to Cuba, Carmenate outlines strategies for "living" Cuba in exile: "We have to make them live Cuba from here [exile context] and teach them what it is and what it was, and that honorable and dignified work will make you feel happy because it is very beautiful to suffer with honor, because it's very beautiful that our children know that we defend the Fatherland, that we are Cuban and that they too are Cuban and feel for their country" (3). Casavantes Bradford's *The Revolution is for the Children* provides a deep account of the way "the children" were used discursively in Cuba and in exile political rhetoric.

43 Ricardo Ortíz, *Cultural Erotics*, 8.

44 Ibid., 8.

45 Rebecca Schneider, *Performing Remains*, 25.

46 See "Theater Ephemera Collection," Añorada Cuba, Item 15, Cuban Heritage Collection, University of Miami; my translation.

47 Casavantes Bradford, *The Revolution Is for the Children*, 193 The quotation about sports and games comes from a history of the organization released by its members. Although no single author is credited, it was likely written by the founder and secretary of the organization, María Gómez Carbonell.

48 Cruzada Educativa Cubana, *La Escuelita Cubana*, 9.

49 Ibid., 195. The sheer volume of diversión for children speaks to the importance of aligning childhood with exile cubanía. Events like Añorada Cuba and a host of other "cultural pageants" featured children's performances in the form of dances, music, and the recitation of poetry.

50 For a reading of the gendered discourse of Cruzada Educativa Cubana, see Javier A. Fernández, "'The Girl Is Born to Be a Mother. The Boy Is Born to Be a Gentleman.'"

51 The block text in the image reads, "We remember all our young collaborators, who should send their drawings in black ink or dark pencil. Clearly write and send your name, address, and age."

52 Cuban Poster Collection 1959–2012, Drawer 11, Folder 11, Cuban Heritage Collection, University of Miami.

53 In addition to the previously mentioned Añorada Cuba, an event called Feria Nacional de los Municipios de Cuba en el Exilio, held annually since 1983, has marketed itself as a celebration for the entire family.

54 See the organization's official website at www.herenciaculturalcubana.org.

55 For younger Cuban Americans, the organization sponsors the Herencia Kids Art Contest where children are asked to draw how they imagine Cuba. The winning drawings are a mélange of Martís, mangos, and representations of La Caridad del Cobre.

56 The phrase "beauty of noble suffering" is from Carmenate's plea for educating the Cuban children in *Problema del niño cubano*.

57 See Teresa Brennan, *The Transmission of Affect*. Brennan speaks to the ways in which affect can circulate within space, moving between bodies through encounters. Cuba Nostalgia can be understood as an event deeply committed to the transmission of affect through education yes, but also through the atmosphere cultivated in the sounds, smells, and even gestural economy of nostalgia.

58 See Andrew Lynch, "Expression of Cultural Standing in Miami," 26.

59 Patricia L. Price, "Cohering Culture on Calle Ocho," 92.

60 Ana Menéndez, "Nostalgia Is Now for Sale, and It's Costly," *Miami Herald*, May 24, 2006. Menéndez is also a successful fiction writer who has taken up the topic of nostalgia in her own work. See *In Cuba I Was a German Shepherd*.

61 For example, Preferred Care Partners, a "health plan with a Medicare contract," sponsors the Malecón sea wall exhibit pictured earlier in this chapter.

62 In *Shopping for Identity*, 79, Marilyn Halter theorizes the relationship between consumption and ethnic identity. Festivals, cultural spectacles, and ethnic foods constitute modes of consumption through which ethnic subjects can signal and maintain cultural identities.

63 Mirta Ojito counted "at least five stores . . . in the last two years" that had opened selling pre-1959 Cuban memorabilia. See "Longing for the Old Cuba Stirs a Boom in Nostalgia," *New York Times*, June 16, 2002.

64 Gerardo Chávez, interview with author, Miami, Florida, May 2013.

65 There are a number of online retailers that specialize in the nostalgia industry. See www.cubacollectibles.com, www.cubanfoodmarket.com, and www.havanacollectibles.com. For those looking for a more personal touch, businesses like Sentir Cubano have a storefront presence in Little Havana.

66 Arjun Appadurai, *Modernity at Large*, 82.

67 Susan Stewart, *On Longing*, 136.

68 Igor Kopytoff, "The Cultural Biography of Things," 64.

69 Stewart, *On Longing*, 145.

70 Herbert Gans, "Symbolic Ethnicity."

71 Halter, *Shopping for Identity*, 79.

72 Jean Baudrillard, *System of Objects*, 88.

73 For a discussion of the relationship between remittances and small business growth in Cuba, see Manuel Orozco and Katrin Hansing, "Remittance Recipients and the Present and Future of Microentrepeneurship Activities in Cuba."

74 During my conversation with Leslie Pantín, he told me a number of anecdotes illustrating the relative ease with which those with money and an interest in Cuban memorabilia could get very specific items out of the country in a matter of days. María A. Cabrera Arús cites a conversation she had with a collector and seller of antiques who attributed a large part of his collection to Cubans traveling to and from the island transporting goods for a fee. See "Comercio de la nostalgia," *Cuba Material*, May 29, 2014, www.cubamaterial.com.

75 "Cubans are the oldest Hispanic group, with a median age of 40 years, higher than the median age of the U.S. population as a whole" (Pew Research Center, "Median Age for Hispanics is Lower than Median Age for Total U.S. Population"), www.pewresearch.org.

CHAPTER 4. THE TRANSNATIONAL LIFE OF DIVERSIÓN

1 Guillermo Alvarez Guedes, *Alvarez Guedes 30*. It is possible that Alvarez Guedes adapted this joke from another context. I have read similarly structured jokes like "Un salvadoreño en Virginia" and "Un argentino en Toronto." What I do know for sure is that this joke is loved by Cuban humorists and their audiences. In interviews in Cuba and Miami, many artists mentioned this joke in particular when discussing Alvarez Guedes.

2 OnCuba, "Los humoristas cubanos hablan de Alvarez Guedes," YouTube video, 8:41, posted August 5, 2013, www.youtube.com.

3 In Chapter 1, I discussed in detail how Alvarez Guedes is universally loved within the exile community. I found the same to be true among a generation of humorists formed under the Revolution. Poet and humor writer Ramón Fernández-Larrea told me that he considered Alvarez Guedes "the third discoverer of Cuba after Colón and [Alexander von] Humboldt." Zulema Cruz, a well-known comedic actress now based in Miami, dedicated her first standup album in the United States to Alvarez Guedes.

4 Emilio Ichikawa, "Prólogo."

5 See Modesto Arocha, *Chistes de Cuba sobre la revolución* and *Abajo quien tú sabes: humor político en el socialismo*. For a collection of and commentary on political jokes in the Soviet context, see Ben Lewis, *Hammer and Tickle*.

6 Comic content is unique in that it is consumed by a majority Cuban audience. Contemporary musicians from the island travel to the United States regularly, but they often play for much more diverse audiences in and beyond South Florida. While much has been written on the travels of Cuban music internationally, little scholarship has focused on the appeal and work of Cuban humor transnationally.

7 This chapter contributes to the small, yet growing body of work that privileges a transnational frame in a twenty-first-century context. Iraida López considers how the notion of "return" has been taken up in literature produced by the diaspora in *Impossible Returns*. For an examination of religion, see Sarah J. Mahler and Katrin Hansing, "Toward a Transnationalism of the Middle." Significantly more attention has been paid to the circulation of Cuban music. See Nora Gámez Torres, "'La Habana está en todas partes,'" and Cristobal Díaz Ayala, "Yacimientos y explotación de las minas musicales cubanas." See also Damián Fernández, ed., *Cuba Transnational*.

8 During the 1970s and 1980s, the close relationship with the Soviet Union inspired a boom in names that echoed Russian first names and pronunciations: Yuri, Yevgeny, etc. Having a name like Yuliesky or Yamilka marks Cubans of this generation. This trend inspired the title of Cuban dissident Yoani Sánchez's *Generación Y* blog.

9 Alejandro Portes and Aaron Puhrmann point out that although the George W. Bush administration instituted harsh restrictions on travel to Cuba, people were rarely penalized for traveling through third countries. Remittances were also restricted but people found ways around these regulations. With that said, the movement of people and money between the island and the diaspora increased significantly under Obama. See their chapter, "A Bifurcated Enclave," in *Un pueblo disperso*.

10 "Most" is the operative word because the Cuban government can still deny the right to travel to anyone they see fit. In December 2015, Cuba reinstated the need for a travel permit for doctors in an attempt to stem the tide of medical professionals leaving the island. Also, traveling outside of Cuba is expensive. Most Cubans need financial assistance from people or institutions abroad in order to travel. Before this reform, Cubans were allowed to remain outside the island for up to eleven months before losing their privileges—precisely one month short of the year necessary for a Cuban to gain permanent residency in the United States under the Cuban Adjustment Act. Under the new law, Cubans can remain abroad for twenty-four months, plenty of time to secure residency, work legally, and thus contribute to the Cuban economy in the forms of return visits and remittances. See Victoria Burnett, "After Decades, Cuba Eases Travel Rules to Maintain Ties," *New York Times*, January 13, 2013. Cubans who have immigrated permanently to the United States may now visit the island for up to ninety days, up from thirty

days before the reforms. It is possible to argue that these changes take advantage of the Cuban Adjustment Act, despite the government's harsh public criticism of this law as a mechanism for encouraging Cubans to leave the island. Julia Sweig suggests that "allowing Cubans to come and go, keep their property [and] their residences will bring economic benefit to Cuba and dampen the deep unhappiness around the status quo." See Portia Siegelbaum, "Cubans Line Up for Passports after Eased Travel Rules," *CBS News*, January 15, 2013, www.cbsnews.com.

11 Other comedians who acknowledged this strategy were Carlos "Mentepollo" Gonzalvo and Octavio "Churrisco" Rodríguez. Besides their explicit confirmation of their use of nostalgia and memory in their routines, it is, as I will show, a major feature of many of the performances I have studied from a number of comedians.

12 Angel García himself is from Manacas, Cuba. In interviews, he has noted that there is little difference between the character he portrays and his own personality. He proudly performs his identity as "el guajiro de Manacas" to the delight of his audiences. For a biographical sketch that explains the genesis of the character of Antolín in the context of Garcia's broader career, see *El pichón voló*, a 2006 documentary produced by El Centro Promotor del Humor.

13 AmericaTeVeCanal41, "Antolín y Carlos Otero en TN3," YouTube video, 8:57, posted on November 21, 2012, www.youtube.com.

14 "HD: Live En Miami," YouTube video, 14:59, from original live performance on October 28, 2011, posted by 72pantalla2, December 22, 2012, www.youtube.com.

15 Alvarez Guedes would employ similar strategies with his performances but they depended mostly on particular words and idioms that had fallen out of use in the exile context such as "culín culán" (a phrase that communicates astonishment). It would be more difficult for him to refer to a particular social experience given the class differences among his exile audience. For Robertico, making jokes about living in Cuba in the 1990s are less risky given the shared experience of lack on the island.

16 Video no longer available online.

17 Video no longer available online.

18 A quick anecdote about the thirst for the newest gadgets and technology in Cuba is in order. While in a hotel lobby in Havana, my new iPhone 6 slipped out of my pocket without my noticing. A security guard ran after me to return it as I exited the hotel. When the stone-faced guard noticed that it was the new iPhone, his demeanor completely changed. He asked if he could hold it and if we could go back to the lobby to show his friends "que son locos con los productos de Apple" (who are crazy about Apple products). Seconds later I had four hotel staff members asking me a range of technical questions about the phone's hardware specifications that I could barely answer.

19 "ANTOLIN EL PICHON, DE CUBA EL GUAJIRO DE MANACAS, THE PLACE OF MIAMI 2014," YouTube video, 7:14, posted by Ismael Requejo, June 25, 2014, www.youtube.com. Comics like Robertico can be more explicit about the benefits

of life in the United States. In 2012, he toured a show in the United States titled "¡Si el mundo se acaba que me agarre en Miami" (If the End of the World Comes, Let It Catch Me in Miami!).

20 Angel García, interview with author, Havana, Cuba, October 28, 2014.

21 Later in the chapter I will discuss the reasons why these comedians do not just stay in the United States.

22 *Humor Anti Es3: Alexis Valdés con Cristinito y Pánfilo*, Teatro Trail, Alexis Valdés and Luis Silva, Miami, Florida, December 13, 2014.

23 Born in 1978, Luis Silva is the youngest comedian I have discussed in this chapter.

24 A fine example of this is the Pánfilo monologue about bread in Cuba. Silva first performed this is in 2001. In Miami, he included pieces of the old monologue but revamped it to include a comic discussion about US Customs not believing that the bread he brought from the island was in fact bread. When he began his remarks on the sad state of Cuban bread, a woman in the crowd began to yell "El pan, el pan!" in clear recognition of the bit.

25 People I met in Havana could tell me all about episodes and recite lines from the show. My cousin, eleven years old at the time, had an encyclopedic knowledge of the show's characters and what to him were its best moments.

26 There are few Afro-Cuban actors appearing on local Miami channels and national Spanish-language networks more broadly. Conrado Cogle is a notable exception and appears nightly on a show called *TN3* on América Tevé under his stage name Boncó Quiñongo. Alexis Valdés, who has referred to himself as "mulato," often used race as a comic point of departure on his nightly talk show but rarely in the personal way that Cogle does. Because I am primarily considering those who visit and perform from Cuba, I do not address Cogle or Valdés in detail.

27 The legacy of Cuban blackface in Miami extends back to theatrical productions among the first waves of exiles in the 1960s. See *Cuban Theater in Miami: 1960–1980*, scholar.library.miami.edu. But the generation of popular artists in Miami today are a product of later migrations and came of age in revolutionary Cuba. According to Laurie A. Frederik, bufo performances receded in the years after Revolution but began to make a comeback in the 1990s during the Special Period. See *Trumpets in the Mountains*, chap. 1, 7.

28 AmericaTeveCanal41, "Madrina Ondina y su conexión espiritual," YouTube Video, 7:29, posted on July 2, 2013, www.youtube.com.

29 For an analysis of Marrero's character, see Ariana Hernández-Reguant and Jossianna Arroyo, "The Brownface of Latinidad in Cuban Miami."

30 This is not a new character for Doimeadiós. He has performed in Cuba as Mañeña. It is worth noting that Doimeadiós is considered one of the finest artists on the islands for his dramatic and comedic roles. He was also a member of the *Sabadazo* cast.

31 For an excellent reading of the figure of el negro catedrático in Cuban bufo, see Lane, *Blackface Cuba*, 13–17 and chap. 2.

32 Ibid., 13, 72.

33 Lisandro Pérez speaks to segregation in a discussion of racialization in Miami that focuses on Cubans and African Americans in "Racialization among Cubans and Cuban Americans."

34 "Osvaldo Doimeadios como Mañeña en Esta Noche Tu Night 4," YouTube video, 5:15, posted by Rigarm, October 26, 2010, www.youtube.com.

35 Though exact numbers are difficult to pinpoint, the consensus is that the Afro-Cuban population in the United States is small. According to Jorge Duany, "In 2009 almost nine out of ten Cubans in the United States answered that they were white . . . less than 4 percent of the Cubans . . . said they were black" (*Blurred Borders*, 78). Research from the Pew Center puts the number even lower, with reports of 41,000 Afro-Cubans living in the United States as of 2013—less than 3 percent of the Cuban population. These statistics do not take into account that many Afro-Cubans do not live in South Florida. These small numbers can be explained by two major factors. When the Revolution came to power, racial equality and assistance for the island's poorest—many of whom were black—were significant aims of the revolutionary project. Those who left early on were mostly white, with Afro-Cubans only leaving in significant numbers during and after the Mariel boatlift. Migrating to the United States requires familial and economic support. With so few Afro-Cubans living in the United States to provide material assistance to family on the island who want to leave, the numbers have remained small for decades and will remain so into the foreseeable future.

36 Two writers for the channels geared toward Cuban Miami—Iván Camejo and Ramón Fernández-Larrea—cited the powerful role of the ratings in determining programming. Though industry insiders acknowledge that the ratings system is flawed, the numbers are what they can sell to advertisers. Veering away from Cuba-centric programming in the past has led to a negative impact on the ratings.

37 Enrique "Kike" Quiñones, interview with author, Havana, Cuba, October 28, 2014.

38 Ariana Hernandez-Reguant's work on the topic of race and representation on América Tevé speaks to this very point. She spoke with José Carlos Pérez (Carlucho) about his use of blackface on his show, and he laughed at the notion that it might be considered racist, defending blackface as a Cuban theatrical tradition. See Ariana Hernández-Reguant, "Miami Minstrels," unpublished ms. For a discussion of the similarities and differences between blackface performances in Cuba and the United States, see Robin Moore, "The *Teatro Bufo*."

39 Jáuregi performed in 2012 primarily as part of a larger production featuring contemporary Cuban artists staging a version of the legendary comedy show from the 1940s and 1950s called *La tremenda corte* (The Outrageous Court) starring Leopoldo "Tres Patines" Fernández. The name of this reboot was called *Jura decir la verdad?* (Do You Swear to Tell the Truth?) and was very popular in Cuba.

40 "Humorismo: terreno difícil para las mujeres," *Interpress Service en Cuba*, September 14, 2012, www.ipscuba.net. Jáuregui has been very vocal on this topic. For more on her thoughts about sexism in Cuban show business, see "Discriminan en

Cuba a mujeres comediantes," *Cimacnoticias*, October 23, 2012, www.cimacnoti
cias.com.

41 AméricaTeveCanal41, "Carmencita Ruíz en TN3," YouTube video, 5:35 posted on
June 27, 2013, www.youtube.com.

42 Of all the popular culture forms I have come across, women have been most
active in theater. Maribel González continues to write, produce, and direct
comedies in South Florida and Union City. See maribelgonzalez.net. It is also
important to mention the critical work of writer, set designer, and director María
Julia Casanova. Her autobiography, *Mi vida en el teatro*, details her career in
theater in Cuba and in exile. I chose not to write a chapter on theater specifically
because this project is intimately engaged with questions of performance, and I
have been able to find only scripts, playbills, and other theater ephemera in my
archival searches. The most visible women on comic television shows catering to
Cuban audiences in South Florida are Judith González, Zulema Cruz, Ana Lidia
Méndez, Zajaris Fernández, and Ali Sánchez.

43 This strategy is not uncommon in Spanish-language television in the United
States. One need only tune in to the most visible of variety shows, Univision's
recently concluded *Sábado Gigante*, to see this dynamic at work. In the context of
Cuban Miami, Judith González's most famous character, Magdalena la peluda, is
the best example of this grotesque femininity. Literally translated as "Hairy Magdalena," the character features a messy wig, a painted mustache, bad teeth, and a
hairy chest.

44 Maribel González, interview with author, Miami, Florida, February 24, 2015.
González has been writing and performing in her own comic plays since the
1990s.

45 Gayatri Gopinath, *Impossible Desires*, 9.

46 Zulema Cruz, *Malhablando Vol. 2*.

47 See Muñoz, *Disidentifications*, 182.

48 Zulema Cruz, *Malhablando Vol. 3*, 2008, Track 4. Zulema herself is unsure about
what year her third volume was recorded. 2008 is the likeliest year.

49 Ibid.

50 Other Cuban artists and actors based in Miami have appeared in smaller theater
productions in Cuba. See Norge Espino Mendoza, "*Ana en el trópico* de vuelta a
La Habana," *Diario de Cuba*, October 20, 2013, www.diariodecuba.com. Famed
Cuban actor Reynaldo Miravalles returned to play a role in a film called *Esther
en alguna parte* (2013), www.lajiribilla.cu. Those interested in Cuban theater
and exchanges between the United States and the island should see the growing
database of performances and accompanying commentary at cubantheater.org,,
spearheaded by Cuban theater expert Lillian Manzor.

51 For Cruz's comments to the Miami media on her performance in Cuba, see
"Artistas de Miami trabajan en Cuba," *Telemundo 51 Miami* video, 2:31, July 22,
2014, www.telemundo51.com.

52 Zulema Cruz, interview with author, Miami, Florida, February 12, 2015.

53 Ibid.

54 There are notable exceptions. For instance, a well-respected writer and humorist named Pablo Garí, better known as El Pible, is not allowed to travel to the island despite his comedy focusing primarily on wordplay and puns. When I asked him why this was the case, he confessed that he had absolutely no idea.

55 It is important to make a distinction between more recent arrivals from the 1990s and "el exilio historico." Money is not a problem for the likes of Willy Chirino and Gloria Estefan, but it is highly unlikely that the Cuban government would ever allow them to perform because of their high profile and public denunciations of the Castro government. Because of this, many have rightly criticized *el intercambio cultural* as not being a fair exchange, given that the aforementioned Cuban artists are not allowed to perform on the island. For more on this line of argument, see Sarah Moreno, "Cuál intercambio cultural?," *El Nuevo Herald*, October 22, 2010, 3D.

56 Businesses like D'Neme Entertainment, Fuego Media Group, and Blue Night Entertainment have been instrumental in bringing Cuban artists from the island to perform in the United States.

57 Jaime Bayly Show, "Jaime Bayly entrevista a Robertico 10 27 11," YouTube Video, 6:51, posted on November 3, 2011, www.youtube.com.

58 María Elvira Salazar, "Osvaldo Doimeadios entre Miami y La Habana," YouTube video, 10:08, posted on October 23, 2010, www.youtube.com.

59 People I interviewed were quite open about this fact with me, but because it is illegal, they asked me not to publish their names. In fact, when I asked people about whether or not comedians made money from their performances in the United States, each person made a comment suggesting that it was a naive question—*se cae de la mata*! (obviously!).

60 TropicalTel, "TropicalTel y Antolín el pichón VIDEO Llamadas a Cuba," YouTube video, 00:30, posted on June 14, 2014, www.youtube.com.

61 Octavio "Churrisco" Rodríguez, interview with author, Havana, Cuba, October 30, 2014.

62 This sentiment was expressed to me by Manolo Coego, Denise Sánchez, Zulema Cruz, and Iván Camejo. Uncontracted humorists appearing on Cuban variety shows on América Tevé and Mega TV, for example, make only $100 per appearance.

63 It is becoming increasingly more attractive for people to return to Cuba with a planned foreign cash flow. Stories about Cuban Americans "retiring" on the island and using pensions and social security funds to live comfortably on the island are becoming more common. Younger Cubans are taking advantage of training and capital procured in the United States to return to Cuba to set up businesses in a country where there is less competition and still a relatively strong social safety net.

64 People I interviewed were not comfortable discussing the precise terms of the financial arrangements, so it is not possible for me to comment on the question of fairness.

65 For background on Cuban humor in the 1980s and 1990s, see Iván Camejo et al., "El arte de reír."

66 Interview with Quiñones.

67 With that said, island-based artists and playwrights such as Raquel Carrió, Fernando Hechevarría, and Alexis Díaz de Villegas have participated in Miami's theater scene. See "La nostalgia de 'Volver a La Habana' sube a las tablas," *Diario de las Américas*, March 19, 2015, www.diariolasamericas.com. For a more expansive look at the history of cultural exchange since 1959, see Sage Lewis, "It's Sunrise in Cuba. Will the Light Reach the Stage?," April 23, 2015, www.americantheatre.org. Lillian Manzor supplements this article in the comment section by highlighting the roles "Cuban and Latino/a artists living in the US have played in paving the groundwork for these collaborations."

68 In separate interviews with me, both Iván Camejo and Ramón Fernández Larrea communicated a desire to host a Cuban humor festival in Miami that would bring together humorists on and off the island. They explained that they had difficulty finding support for such an endeavor because it would be a gamble for investors.

69 Milena Recio, "Qué Paquete (Semanal)! Diálogo múltiple durante el Ania Pino in Memoriam."

70 See Anna Cristina Pertierra, "Private Pleasures."

71 Recio, "Qué Paquete (Semanal)!."

72 Elio López is the public face of el paquete internationally. The many news articles dedicated to the topic often include interviews with him. Tellingly, others involved in selling and assembling it do not like to be identified in press reports despite the fact that the government has not shut it down.

73 The most thorough investigative report on el paquete comes from Fernando Ravsberg, an Uruguayan journalist who lives in Havana and writes for an online publication called *OnCuba* with offices in Miami and Havana. For a series of articles published on el paquete, see Fernando Ravsberg, "El YouTube Cubano," *OnCuba*, July 7, 2014, oncubamagazine.com.

74 The cost of downloading the entire paquete fluctuates according to when you buy it during the week. The earlier you want the "newest" paquete, the higher the cost. The logic is that those who want the latest updated material the fastest are resellers. In October of 2014, the cost of the entire paquete on a Saturday was fifteen CUC compared to one or two CUC when purchased Wednesday through Friday.

75 Anna Cristina Pertierra captures some of this diversity in her ethnographic research on media consumption in Santiago de Cuba between from 2005 to 2010 in "If They Show *Prison Break* in the United States on Wednesday, by Thursday It Is Here."

76 For coverage of such events, see Madeleine Sautié, "En torno al nuevo consumo cultural"; Recio, "Qué Paquete (Semanal)!." See also Benigno Iglesias et al., "USB," and Aracelys Bedevia, "Poner de moda el conocimiento y la formación cultural," *Juventud Rebelde*, October 31, 2014. *Hurón Azul*, a television show on Cubavisión, aired a conversation entitled "Por una audiencia más crítica frente al paquete de la semana" on June 27, 2014.

77 Though the episode did not air, it quickly leaked out and circulated via hard drives throughout Havana.

78 Fowler's comments to this effect can be found in Recio, "Qué Paquete (Semanal)!" *Temas*. For Gustavo Arcos's commentary see "A Debate." For the insights of the other intellectuals mentioned, see Benigno Iglesias et al., "USB."

79 Leticia Martínez Hernández, "Amplían en Cuba trabajo por cuenta propia," *Cubadebate*, September 24, 2010, www.cubadebate.cu.

80 While the activity of selling media is a recognized and licensed occupation in Cuba, the means by which the content is downloaded is often not legal. For example, having an unapproved satellite connection in Cuba is illegal yet much of the content comes from downloading shows using special software directly from satellite feeds.

81 For more on these reforms, see Carmelo Mesa-Lago and Jorge Pérez-López, *Cuba under Raúl Castro*.

82 Javier Ortíz, "Un servicio a domicilio personalizado," *OnCuba*, July 7, 2014, oncubamagazine.com.

83 Marita Pérez Díaz, "Qué trae un paquete semanal?," *OnCuba*, July 7, 2014, oncubamagazine.com.

84 A commercial for Venus Estudio, a photography studio specializing in "Sweet 15" shoots, was clearly pulling from a US marketing playbook. The commercial begins with a teenaged girl waking up in bed on the morning of her fifteenth birthday. She gets dressed to the sounds of the group One Direction and their 2011 hit song "What Makes You Beautiful." When she arrives at the Venus Estudio, a classic dressing room montage ensues in which the young woman tries on various dresses until her friends help her choose the right one for her photo shoot.

85 This is not the first time advertising has bubbled up in post-revolutionary Cuba. As has been pointed out, advertising returned in the 1990s in the service of state-sponsored initiatives. With that said, the rise of independent business and advertising ventures is certainly a new development. See Ariana Hernández-Reguant, "Socialism with Commercials."

86 AmericaTeveCanal41, "Construyen un parque de diversión infantil al estilo Disney en Cuba," YouTube video, 3:20, posted on Apr 25, 2013, www.youtube.com.

87 Editions of the digital magazine can be downloaded at www.vistarmagazine.com.

88 The most obvious conclusion I can draw is that the growth in advertisements and companies producing them suggests that on some level, featured businesses are seeing an uptick in performance.

89 There is a high concentration of content produced for Spanish-speaking audiences in the United States, with over thirty shows represented from networks like Univision, Telemundo, Televisa, Azteca, and MundoFox.

90 Ashley Carruthers, "National Identity, Diasporic Anxiety, and Music Video Culture in Vietnam," 119. Raúl Castro's reforms have not been as aggressive as Vietnam, but like Vietnam, they have significantly altered the relationship between the diaspora and those living on the island.

91 For an analysis of the *Paris by Night* videos and their content, see Carruthers, "National Identity," and Nhi T. Lieu, "Performing Culture in Diaspora."

92 The phrase "política cultural" is a familiar refrain in talks and articles by those who criticize el paquete. See Recio, "Qué Paquete (Semanal)!"; Sayli Sosa, "'Chacalización' en dos tiempos."

93 The concept of cultural remittances is from Juan Flores's *The Diaspora Strikes Back*, where he defines the term as "the ensemble of ideas, values and expressive forms introduced into societies of origin by remigrants and their families as they return 'home,' sometimes for the first time, for temporary visits or permanent resettlement, and as transmitted through the increasingly pervasive means of telecommunications" (4).

94 Peggy Levitt and Nina Glick Schiller, "Conceptualizing Simultaneity," 1010.

95 Brian Larkin, "Degraded Images, Distorted Sounds," 303.

96 Yasmín Portales explains how she realized this was happening when she compared an American television program aired on Cuban television with a version she downloaded through el paquete. See Benigno Iglesias et al., "USB."

97 Perhaps the best example of this is Ramón Fernández-Larrea, a celebrated poet and comedy writer. He now lives in Miami and writes for comedy shows on Mega TV. Iván Camejo, past director of the Centro Promotor del Humor in Havana, was the head writer for *El show de Alexis Valdés* on Mira TV before going off the air.

98 Susana Méndez, "Alexis Valdés, Public in Cuba Spoiled Me," *OnCuba*, December 15, 2013, oncubamagazine.com.

99 Ravsberg, "El YouTube cubano."

100 As I revise this manuscript in August 2016, reports are circulating that the Cuban government is beginning to crack down on this kind of programming on el paquete as the island braces for a more difficult economic climate in the midst of lower growth and faltering support from Venezuela. See Waldo Fernández Cuenca, "La Seguridad del Estado amenaza a distribuidores del 'paquete,'" *Diario de Cuba*, August 8, 2016, www.diariodecuba.com.

101 See "Humoristas cubanos no se meten con los Castro," *Martí Noticias*, December 9, 2014, www.martinoticias.com. Alejandro "Virulo" García, a celebrated Cuban humorist, is quoted in the article as saying, "Hay un límite que se llaman Fidel Castro y Raúl Castro" (There is a limit and it's called Fidel Castro and Raúl Castro).

102 Iván Camejo, interview with author, Miami, Florida, February, 24, 2015. Ramón Fernández-Larrea, interview with author, Miami, Florida, March 1, 2015.

103 Abel Prieto had this to say about *Caso Cerrado*: "It's difficult to believe that a Cuban formed by the Revolution would believe that people who go on these shows are really talking about real personal problems and not paid to perform, it's all a fraud" ("Abel Prieto se refiere al Paquete Semanal," *OnCuba*, YouTube video, 2:15, posted on July 6, 2014, www.youtube.com).

104 On a case titled "Moringa maravillosa," which aired March 27, 2015, Dr. Polo took up Fidel Castro's celebration of a plant called "moringa" in one of his reflections

published in *Granma*. In addition to mocking his "reflections" on the topic, Dr. Polo brought in experts to debunk Castro's claims about the plant's miraculous health benefits.

CHAPTER 5. DIGITAL DIVERSIÓN

1 I received the email from Alberto Laguna on January 16, 2008, but I have been able to find versions of this "guide" on websites, blogs, and archived emails from the late 1990s until today. See "A Gringos Guide to Cuban Medical Folklore," October 4, 1998, www.mail-archive.com.

2 Of course, not all emails related to Cuba aim to cultivate this playful encounter with cubanía. There are a great deal of forwards that I have seen that speak to the Cuban "tragedy" complete with images that contrast images of contemporary Havana with its pre-1959 past. With that said, scholars have chronicled the prevalence of humor in forwards. See Lillian Boxman-Shabtai and Limor Shifman, "When Ethnic Humor Goes Digital."

3 "Web 2.0 represents a reorganization of the relations between producers and their audiences in a maturing internet market, as well as a set of approaches adopted by companies seeking to harness mass creativity, collectivism, and peer production. . . . The tenets of Web 2.0 entice audience members to join in the building and customizing of services and messages rather than to expect companies to present complete and fully formed experiences" (Henry Jenkins, Sam Ford, and Joshua Green, *Spreadable Media*, 49).

4 Lee Rainie and Barry Wellman, *Networked*, 139.

5 Brenda Danet, *Cyberplay*. For an early look at the role of humor online, see Nancy Baym, "The Performance of Humor in Computer-Mediated Communication."

6 Ana Deumert, "The Performance of a Ludic Self on Social Network(ing) Sites." Deumert borrows the phrase "ludic self construction" from Jos de Mul who uses it in his study of identity and computer games in *The Game of Life.*

7 See Jenkins, Ford, and Green, *Spreadable Media*, 2012; Limor Shifman, *Memes in Digital Culture*; Karine Nahon and Jeff Hemsley, *Going Viral.*

8 Aaron Smith, "6 New Facts about Facebook."

9 See Kristen Purcell, "Online Video 2013."

10 Nicholas A. John, "The Social Logics of Sharing," 116.

11 Henry Jenkins, *The Wow Climax*, 4.

12 Ted Cohen, *Jokes*, 31.

13 Athina Karatzogianni and Adi Kunstman, *Digital Cultures and the Politics of Emotion*, 3.

14 For a book-length study of the Internet and media technologies in Cuba, see Cristina Venegas, *Digital Dilemmas.*

15 See Stefania Vicari, "Exploring the Cuban Blogosphere."

16 Paloma Duong, "Bloggers Unplugged," 377. As Duong points out, the fact that "dissident" blogs have already turned into a subject of discussion on Cuban

mainstream media—as in the TV program *Razones de Cuba*—is evidence that the blogosphere may indeed have potential for offline civic agency and for changes in the country's political culture. Of course, with the state in control of the media, dissident bloggers are at the mercy of how the government chooses to represent them in official media.

17 See Ted Henken and Sjamme van de Voort, "From *Nada* to *Nauta*."

18 Andoni Alonso and Pedro J. Oiarzabal, *Diasporas in the New Media Age*, 11. For other examples of "digital diaspora" scholarship, see Victoria Bernal, *Nation as Network*, and Jennifer M. Brinkerhoff, *Digital Diasporas*.

19 To be sure, people are communicating with friends and family online through email and in some cases, social media, but this is less likely given the difficulty and cost in connecting to the Internet for most Cubans on the island.

20 For insight into the algorithmic dimension of social media content and its circulation, see José van Dijck, *The Culture of Connectivity*; Chapter 1, "Engineering Sociality in a Culture of Connectivity," is particularly relevant.

21 Richard Grusin, *Premediation*, 3–4. Since Grusin published this study and I began writing this chapter, Facebook has changed the ways users can interact with posts. In early 2015, it became possible not only to indicate a "like" but also "love, haha, wow, sad, angry" with emojis. It is also important to note here Facebook's history of manipulating content to better understand emotional responses. See Robinson Meyer, "Everything We Know about Facebook's Secret Mood Manipulation."

22 The Facebook version of "We're Not Yelling, We're Cuban, That's How We Talk" boasted 110,000 members before the page was hacked and taken down. It has reappeared on Instagram and Facebook but has yet to reach its high point of followers. More evidence for the US-born target audience comes from a study from the Pew Research Center, which concludes that among Internet users, 55 percent of those who use Instagram are 18–29 years old, and 28 percent are 30–49. See Maeve Duggan, "The Demographics of Social Media Users."

23 Though Lauzán no longer creates new "editions" of Guamá, the archive is still available at el-guama.blogspot.com. He continues to publish cartoons, many related to Cuban politics. See his most recent work at alen-lauzan.blogspot.com.

24 Kathleen Stewart, *Ordinary Affects*, 27.

25 I interviewed the artist behind Pepe Billete extensively in March of 2015. He asked me not to share any of his biographical details as he believes the popularity of the character relies, in part, on his anonymity. I can share a few pertinent details. The puppeteer was born and raised in South Florida of parents who fled Cuba during the Revolution's early days. His understanding of what it means to be Cuban is drawn primarily from growing up within the Cuban exile community in Miami—a reality that permeates his work.

26 Radio personality Enrique Santos, discussed in Chapter 2, also appeals to this generation but his content is mostly in Spanish and in the 2000s was geared

toward an audience that included US-born Cuban Americans and a younger generation of arrivals from Cuba.

27 Pepe Billete, interview with author, Miami, Florida, March 3, 2015.

28 This is yet another example of Guillermo Alvarez Guedes's comedic influence across generations of humorists on and off the island. See Chapter 1 for a close reading of his career and comedy in Miami during the 1970s and 1980s.

29 Pepe Billete, "Pepe Billete-Mojo," YouTube video, 1:56, December 7, 2014, www.youtube.com.

30 The cross-cultural clashes around holiday celebrations have been consistently tapped for comic material. In a video titled "Thanksgiving when you cuban pero tus suegros son americano" (Thanksgiving When You're Cuban but Your In-Laws Are American), Dairon Vazquez impersonates his mother's critique of American food, especially dry turkey. It has been viewed approximately 600,000 times. See Facebook video, November 25, 2015, www.facebook.com.

31 Christmas often inspires content that combines Cuban cultural signifiers with US holiday traditions. A video called "12 Days of Miami Christmas" combines the melody and structure of the Christmas classic with lyrics that reflect growing up in Cuban Miami. The "partridge in a pear tree" becomes "a Willy Chirino CD." See Hialeah Haikus, "12 Days of Miami Christmas," YouTube video, 3:46, December 12, 2012, www.youtube.com.

32 Pérez Firmat, *Literature and Liminality*, 54–74. Pérez Firmat discusses choteo's scatological mode through a reading of an Alvarez Guedes joke and Jorge Mañach's "Indagación del Choteo."

33 Alvarez Guedes, *Alvarez Guedes 11*.

34 Fusion was originally aimed at young Latino/as who spoke English as a first language, but it quickly shifted its target audience to young viewers broadly conceived. See Ravi Somaiya and Brooks Barnes, "Fusion Media Aims at Millennials, but Struggles to Find Its Identity," *New York Times*, May 24, 2015, B1.

35 Nahon and Hemsley, *Going Viral*, 28.

36 Pepe's creator provided screenshots of these statistics to me directly. "Reach" on Facebook is defined by the number of people who have seen a page's post in their news feed. "Engagement" measures the number of times a post has been clicked, "liked," shared, or commented on. These statistics are integral to the ways in which content producers can sell their services to potential sponsors.

37 Pepe Billete, Twitter, April 15, 2012, twitter.com/PepeBillete.

38 Pepe Billete, Twitter, December 11, 2012, twitter.com/PepeBillete.

39 In one example, Pepe posted an Instagram video of CNN coverage of the Ferguson protests where a reporter on the ground explained, "Obviously there's a smell of marijuana in the air." Pepe took the opportunity to comment on racist character of news coverage during the protests. See instagram.com/pepebilletevplp.

40 I have repeatedly referenced the blackface involved in teatro bufo performances, which can be traced to mid-nineteenth-century Cuba, to illustrate the long relationship between blackness and diversión.

41 See Chapters 1 and 4 specifically, where I address how different generations of Cubans in the United States from the 1960s to the 2000s have represented African Americans in diasporic popular culture.

42 G. Derrick Hodge, "Colonization of the Cuban Body," 21.

43 Pepe Billete, "Banning Same-Sex Marriage Is Tremenda Mariconada," *Miami New Times*, April 1, 2013, www.miaminewtimes.com.

44 Pepe Billete, "Pepe Billete's Open Letter to Lil Wayne," *Miami New Times*, February 20, 2013, www.miaminewtimes.com.

45 There has been a flurry of research dedicated to unraveling the relationship between emotion and language in bilingual and multilingual subjects. For a good start, see Aneta Pavlenko, ed., *Bilingual Minds*.

46 Pepe Billete, "Memories of My Abuela," *Miami New Times,* January 16, 2015, www.miaminewtimes.com.

47 Ibid.

48 Pepe Billete, Facebook photo, March 3, 2015, www.facebook.com. Because of the low resolution of photo, I could not include it above.

49 This is not the only term used to describe a generation of Cuban arrivals in a negative way. Those who came during the Mariel boatlift were called *marielitos*. That term also carried a derogatory connotation because of the narrative of criminalization spread about the newer arrivals. I address this in Chapters 1 and 3. In comments and conversations with US-born Cuban Americans, the Spanish *balsero* is often replaced with *ref* or *refee* to communicate an inability to assimilate and in some contexts, a lack of morals and ethics.

50 Jokes made about "green" immigrants by those who claim the same ethnic ancestry are not new by any means. For an analysis in the Mexican/Chicano context, see José R. Reyna and María Herrera-Sobek, "Jokelore, Cultural Differences, and Linguistic Dexterity."

51 The use of the term *balsero* is flexible. While the term is used here to communicate a lack of refinement, it is also used to index and make fun of young men from Havana who dress in a style that would be considered "in" on the island. One example is what the *New York Times* called the "reggaeton look" after a genre of music popular on the island among the youth, which is often a source of great amusement on Pepe's social media forums. For the article, see Jason Horowitz, "Forget Retro: The Men of Havana Embrace the Reggaeton Look," *New York Times*, August 14, 2015, www.nytimes.com.

52 Muñoz, *Disidentifications*, 182.

53 Muñoz is right to point to the performative dimensions of chusmería and how it is often coded as feminine (there is no word *chusmo* though men can be considered *chusma* as well). The performance of that "over the top" Cubanness is crucial to chusma legibility. In one of the most "chusma" moments of the "Sweet Home Hialeah" video, Santos adopts the exaggerated tone and voice of a chusma Cuban woman who warns, "No te bañe en esa agua que ta contaminada. Mi sobrina se baño allí la semana pasada y está en estado. Vamos a ver si ahora le

nace un cocodrilo" (Don't swim in that water [polluted canals in Hialeah], that water is contaminated. My niece swam in there last week and now she's pregnant. Let's see if she gives birth to a crocodile). See Manny Lara, "Sweet Home Hialeah," YouTube video, 4:15, September 18, 2008, www.youtube.com.

54 For a detailed reading of the figure of the *chonga*, see Jillian Hernández, "'Miss, You Look like a Bratz Doll,'" 68.

55 Mimimimimimimimimo, "Chongalicious," YouTube video, 3:53, April 1, 2007, www.youtube.com. The video is a parody of pop star Fergie's 2006 hit "Fergalicious."

56 This is not to say that growing up or living in Hialeah is not a point of pride for many US-born Cuban Americans. Even in the "Sweet Home Hialeah" parody, there is an affection for the city and its embodiment of a kind of hyper-Cubanness resistant to calls for assimilation. This complex relationship many of this generation have with the city can be best represented by a popular t-shirt with the word "HIA-FUCKING-LEAH" emblazoned on the front.

57 In my interview with the artist behind Pepe, he indicated that he is "constantly" getting images sent to his account related to the balsero theme, suggesting that it is a highly popular form of content and also something his audience is attuned to as they make their way through life in South Florida.

58 Jonathan Gray, *Watching the Simpsons*, 106.

59 I want to stress the popularity of the "balsero" content that Pepe posts. Pepe, with the help of his frequent collaborator, Otto von Schirach, produced a parody of hip-hop star Drake's 2016 hit "Hotline Bling" called "Hotline Balsa." The video, viewed over 400,000 times, features von Schirach dressed in "#BalseroCouture": tight fitting shirt, plucked eyebrows, plenty of jewelry, and ripped jeans. Pepe's lyrics poke fun at this stereotypical "balsero couture" and end with a condemnation of Fidel Castro: "Me cago en Fidel, cojones" (I shit on Fidel, dammit). Much like his article in the *Miami New Times*, the perceived faults of more recent arrivals are attributed to the Castros. See Pepe Billete, "Hotline Balsa," Facebook video, January 10, 2016, www.facebook.com.

60 Sara Ahmed, "Affective Economies," 120.

61 Tomás R. Jiménez, *Replenished Ethnicity*, 102.

62 Ibid. Jiménez's work examines this issue in great detail in the context of Mexican and Mexican Americans in the United States.

63 Though most of their content is online, they have also achieved notoriety in Cuba thanks to the circulation of their content on el paquete semanal.

64 Maikel Rodríguez arrived in 2006 at the age of nineteen. Alejandro González arrived at the age of fourteen in 2001.

65 Los Pichy Boys, interview with author, Miami, Florida, March 2, 2015. If this sounds familiar, biological metaphors suggesting a "natural" Cuban humor were also a prominent feature for how people described Cuban exile comedian Guillermo Alvarez Guedes, as discussed in the first chapter.

66 At the time of our interview, Los Pichy Boys employed ten people. Much of their income comes from sponsorships from companies looking to tap into South Florida's Cuban population such as Estrella Insurance and Rebtel (the latter being a company that offers discounted plans for international calls).

67 As they began to rack up hundreds of thousands of views and became more legitimate in their business practices, Los Pichy Boys moved away from dubbing Hollywood movies because of copyright infringement claims. Fans have posted their old doblajes under their own accounts.

68 Caribe was a brand of television popular throughout Cuba, while the reference to "plasma televisions" is a play on a host of jokes about people traveling to the island loaded with goods like expensive televisions.

69 Los Pichy Boys are not alone in their love of YouTube dubbing. Iranians have dubbed *Shrek*, and Dominican versions of Fox animated sitcom *Family Guy* have been viewed thousands of time. See Chuckstar, "Dominican Family Guy Aventura Peligro (video official)," YouTube video, September 20, 2009, www.youtube.com.

70 Los Pichy Boys furnished this insight in my interview with them. Maikel Rodríguez in particular was clear on the issue: "La mayoría de nuestro publico son muchachos nacidos aquí" (The majority of our audience is made up of kids born here). It would be difficult to confirm these claims, but since they are content producers whose business depends on clicks and an understanding of their audience demographics, I believe it is safe to say that they do have a significant following among the US-born.

71 Jenkins, Ford, and Green, *Spreadable Media*, 201.

72 Ibid., 200.

73 El Pichy Films, "Elpidio se fue," YouTube video, 1:49, May 3, 2011, www.youtube.com.

74 See Jenkins, Ford, and Green, *Spreadable Media*, 207.

75 For a short, yet thorough explanation of Che Guevara's formulation of "The New Man," see Peña, *Oye Loca!*, 3.

76 Gray, *Watching with the Simpsons*, 105.

77 El Pichy Films, "Elpidio."

78 Jonathan Gray, Jeffrey P. Jones, and Ethan Thompson, *Satire TV*, 18.

79 In my interview with them, González explained that filtering "first world problems" through a Cuban comic lens has been a fertile approach to producing their content.

80 El Pichy Films, "Iphone Cubano Asiri Siri Parody," YouTube video, 1:56, December 7, 2011, www.youtube.com. It is important to note that they were not the first to create a parody of Siri. Los Pichy Boys often draw on parodic approaches popular on YouTube for inspiration.

81 The video was so popular that they created a video that featured Dominican, Argentinean, and Puerto Rican accents. See El Pichy Films, "Iphone Cubano, Boricua, Dominicano y Argentino Asiri 2.0," YouTube video, 2:24, January 16, 2012, www.youtube.com.

82 Joseph Roach, *Cities of the Dead*, 27.

83 As a star for the hometown Miami Heat basketball team, James featured prominently in many videos by Los Pichy Boys. In some he is represented as practitioner of Afro-Cuban religions. Tellingly, when the news about James leaving the
Heat for his hometown Cleveland Cavaliers broke, he is referred to in a video as
"negro singao" (fucking negro). The phrase is extremely derogatory but I do not
wish to translate negro to "nigger" in this context. Doing so would combine racial
legacies across two very different contexts in a manner that obfuscates historical complexity. See Los Pichy Boys TV, "Lebron se va de Miami a Lo Cubano,"
YouTube video, July 11, 2014, 1:43, www.youtube.com.

84 See Chapters 1 and 4 of this book.

85 Anett Rios, "La reapertura crea ola de sarcasmo," *El Nuevo Herald*, December 19,
2014, www.elnuevoherald.com.

86 Alan Gross was a subcontractor for a US program promoting democracy in Cuba
and was arrested on the island in Havana in 2009 for bringing illegal telecommunications equipment to the island. He was released on December 17, 2014, in
an agreement that also brought the freedom of the remaining members of the
Cuban Five, members of a spy ring active in South Florida in the 1990s: Gerardo
Hernández, Antonio Guerrero, and Ramón Labañino.

87 The phrase "recarga doble lo que toca" refers to deals offered periodically by the
Cuban telecommunications service ETECSA. Under these deals, it is possible
to add two minutes for the price of one. It is very much a part of the diasporic
imagination because people abroad can "recharge" the cell phone minutes of
people on the island. In this *doblaje*, Castro is looking for a similar "discounted"
deal from Obama.

88 Lane, *Blackface Cuba*, ix.

89 I have had little luck unraveling the reason why the term *chino*, which literally
translates to Chinese person or man, is also utilized as a term of endearment and
affection. This is just one of the many ways in which *chino* is invoked in Cuban
vernacular speech. For more meanings, see José Sánchez-Boudy, *Diccionario
mayor de Cubanismos*.

90 Alvarez Guedes, *Alvarez Guedes 8*. The translation of the song lyrics is as follows:
"Damn how great / Damn how crazy / If you want to laugh a little, just wait a
moment / Because the play of comedy is better than seriousness."

WORKS CITED

Abreu, Christina D. *Rhythms of Race: Cuban Musicians and the Making of Latino New York City and Miami, 1940–1960.* Chapel Hill: University of North Carolina Press, 2015.

Aching, Gerard. *Masking and Power: Carnival and Popular Culture in the Caribbean.* Minneapolis: University of Minnesota Press, 2002.

Aguilar, Juan Zevallos. "Latino Cultural Studies." In *Critical American and Latino Studies*, edited by Juan Poblete, 3–31. Minneapolis: University of Minnesota Press, 2003.

Aguiliú de Murphy, Raquel. *Los textos dramáticos de Virgilio Piñera y el teatro del absurdo.* Madrid: Editorial Pliegos, 1989.

Ahmed, Sara. "Affective Economies." *Social Text* 22, no. 2 (2004): 117–139.

Aja, Alan. "The Intra-Immigrant Dilemma." *New Politics* 10, no. 4 (Winter 2006).

Almaguer, Tomás. "Race, Racialization, and Latino Populations in the United States." In *Racial Formation in the 21st Century*, edited by Daniel Martinez HoSang, Oneka LaBennett, and Laura Pulido, 143–161. Berkeley: University of California Press, 2012.

Alonso, Andoni, and Pedro J. Oiarzabal. *Diasporas in the New Media Age: Identity, Politics, and Community.* Reno: University of Nevada Press, 2010.

Alvarez Borland, Isabel. *Cuban-American Literature of Exile: From Person to Persona.* Charlottesville: University Press of Virginia, 1998.

Alvarez Guedes, Guillermo. *El día que cayó Fidel Castro.* Santurce, Puerto Rico: Gema Records, 1975, LP.

———. *Alvarez Guedes 2.* Miami: AG Enterprises, 1996, compact disc. Originally released 1974.

———. *Alvarez Guedes 3.* Miami: AG Enterprises, 1996, compact disc. Originally released in 1975.

———. *Alvarez Guedes 4.* Miami: AG Enterprises, 1996, compact disc. Originally released 1976.

———. *Alvarez Guedes 8.* Miami: AG Enterpreises, 1996, compact disc. Originally released 1979.

———. *Alvarez Guedes 11.* Miami: AG Enterprises, 1996, compact disc. Originally released 1980.

———. *Alvarez Guedes 14: How to Defend Yourself from the Cubans.* Miami: AG Enterprises, 1996, compact disc. Originally released 1982.

———. *Alvarez Guedes 16.* Miami: AG Enterprises, 1996, compact disc. Originally released 1984.

———. *Alvarez Guedes 22.* Miami: AG Enterprises, 1996, compact disc. Originally released 1991.

————. *Alvarez Guedes 30*. Miami: AG Enterprises, 2000, compact disc.

Aparicio, Frances R. *Listening to Salsa: Gender, Latin Popular Music, and Puerto Rican Cultures*. Middletown, CT: Wesleyan University Press, 1998.

Aparicio, Frances R., and Susana Chávez-Silverman, eds. *Tropicalizations: Transcultural Representations of Latinidad*. Hanover, NH: Dartmouth College University Press of New England, 1997.

Appadurai, Arjun. *Modernity at Large: Cultural Dimensions of Globalization*. Minneapolis: University of Minnesota Press, 1996.

Applewhite, Ashton. "Being Blanche: Coming Clean about *Truly Tasteless Jokes*." *Harper's Magazine*, June 2011. www.harpers.org.

Arcos, Gustavo. "Cómo acabar de una vez y por todas con el paquete." *Café Fuerte*, November 5, 2014. www.cafefuerte.com.

Arocha, Modesto. *Chistes de Cuba sobre la revolución*. Miami: Alexandria Library, 1997.

————. *Abajo quien tú sabes: humor político en el socialismo*. Miami: Alexandria Library, 2014.

Bakhtin, Mikhail. *Rabelais and His World*. Bloomington: Indiana University Press, 1984.

Bardach, Ann Louise. *Cuba Confidential: Love and Vengeance in Miami and Havana*. New York: Vintage, 2002.

Barradas, Efraín. "Cursi, choteo, guachafita: Propuesta para una historia del humor caribeño." *Casa de las Américas* 230 (January–March 2003): 101–107.

Baudrillard, Jean. *System of Objects*, translated by James Benedict. New York: Verso, 1996.

Baym, Geoffrey. "Representation and the Politics of Play: Stephen Colbert's Better Know a District." *Political Communication* 24, no.4 (2007): 359–376.

Baym, Nancy. "The Performance of Humor in Computer-Mediated Communication." *Journal of Computer-Mediated Communication* 1, no.2 (September 1995). doi:10.1111/j.1083–6101.1995.tb00327.x.

Beaupied, Aída. "Libertad con minúscula y el choteo de los jueces en el cine de Gutiérrez Alea." *Ciberletras: Revista de crítica literaria y de cultura* 13, no.7 (2005).

Bejel, Emilio. *Gay Cuban Nation*. Chicago: University of Chicago Press, 2011.

Beltrán, Cristina. *The Trouble with Unity: Latino Politics and the Creation of Identity*. New York: Oxford University Press, 2010.

Beltrán, Mary. *Latina Stars in US Eyes: The Makings and Meanings of Film and TV Stardom*. Urbana: University of Illinois Press, 2009.

Bernal, Victoria. *Nation as Network: Diaspora, Cyberspace, and Citizenship*. Chicago: University of Chicago Press, 2014.

Boym, Svetlana. *The Future of Nostalgia*. New York: Basic Books, 2001.

Boxman-Shabtai, Lillian, and Limor Shifman. "When Ethnic Humor Goes Digital." *New Media and Society* 17, no. 4 (2015): 1–20.

Brennan, Teresa. *The Transmission of Affect*. Ithaca, NY: Cornell University Press, 2004.

Brewer Current, Cheris. "Normalizing Cuban Refugees: Representations of Whiteness and Anti-Communism in the USA during the Cold War." *Ethnicities* 8, no. 1 (2008): 42–67.

Brinkerhoff, Jennifer M. *Digital Diasporas: Identity and Transnational Engagement.* Cambridge, MA: Cambridge University Press, 2009.

Brown, Anna, and Mark Hugo López. "Mapping the Latino Population, by State, County and City." Pew Research Center. August 29, 2015. www.pewhispanic.org.

Bureau of Western Hemisphere Affairs. "US Relations with Cuba Fact Sheet." US Department of State. July 21, 2015. www.state.gov.

Bustamante, Michael. "¿Qué Pasa, U.S.A.?: Una Comedia Bilingüe Cubano-Americana Entre lo Nacional y lo Particular, la Parodia y el Silencio." In *Latinidad en Encuentro: Experiencias Migratorias en los Estados Unidos,* edited by Ana Niria Albo Díaz and Antonio Aja. Havana: Casa de las Américas, 2014.

Butler, Judith. *Bodies That Matter: On the Discursive Limits of "Sex."* New York: Routledge, 1993.

Camejo, Iván, Osvaldo Doimeadiós, Carlos Fundora, Gustavo Garrincha, and Rafael Hernández. "El arte de reír: el humor en la cultura." *Temas* 52 (October–December 2007): 96–107.

Carmenate, Ruperto. *Problema del niño cubano.* Brooklyn, NY: Editorial Ebenézer, 1971.

Carpio, Glenda. *Laughing Fit to Kill: Black Humor in the Fictions of Slavery.* New York: Oxford Press, 2008.

Carruthers, Ashley. "National Identity, Diasporic Anxiety, and Music Video Culture in Vietnam." In *House of Glass: Culture, Modernity, and the State in Southeast Asia,* edited by Yao Souchou, 119–149. Singapore: Institute of Southeast Asian Studies, 2001.

Casanova, María Julia. *Mi vida en el teatro: El teatro como culto y profesión: Autobiografía de una teatrista en Cuba y en el exilio.* Miami: Ediciones Universal, 2001.

Casavantes Bradford, Anita. *The Revolution Is for the Children: The Politics of Childhood in Havana and Miami, 1959–1962.* Chapel Hill: University of North Carolina Press, 2014.

Casillas, Dolores Inés. *Sounds of Belonging: US Spanish-Language Radio and Public Advocacy.* New York: New York University Press, 2014.

Castañeda, Mari. "The Importance of Spanish-Language and Latino Media." In *Latina/o Communication Studies Today,* edited by Angharad N. Valdivia, 51–68. New York: Peter Lang, 2008.

Castro, Max. "The Politics of Language in Miami." In *Miami Now!: Immigration, Ethnicity and Social Change,* edited by Guillermo J. Grenier and Alex Stepick, 109–132. Gainesville: University of Florida Press, 1992.

Catalá Carrasco, Jorge L. "From Suspicion to Recognition? 50 years of Comics in Cuba." *Journal of Latin American Cultural Studies* 20, no. 2 (2011): 139–160.

Ceisel, Christina Maria. "El Rock Star Perfecto? Theorizing Juanes and New Directions in Cross-Over Celebrity," *Communication Theory* 21 no.4 (2011): 413–435.

Chambers, Todd. "The State of Spanish-Language Radio." *Journal of Radio Studies* 13, no.1 (2006): 34–50.

Chignell, Hugh. *Key Concepts in Radio Studies.* London: Sage, 2009.

Cohen, Ted. *Jokes: Philosophical Thoughts on Joking Matters*. Chicago: University of Chicago Press, 1999.

Connolly, N. D. B. *A World More Concrete: Real Estate and the Remaking of Jim Crow South Florida*. Chicago: University of Chicago Press, 2014.

Cooper, Sara E. "Irreverent Humor in Postrevolutionary Cuban Fiction: The Case of Mirta Yáñez." *Cuban Studies* 37 (2006): 33–55.

Cruz, Zulema. *Malhablando Vol 2*. Miami: Reyes Music, 2007, compact disc.

———. *Malhablando Vol. 3*. Miami: Reyes Music, 2008, compact disc.

Cruzada Educativa Cubana. *La escuelita cubana: Homenaje a los próceres de 1869*. Miami, 1968?.

Cumber Dance, Daryl. *Honey, Hush!: An Anthology of African American Women's Humor*. New York: W. W. Norton, 1998.

Cvetkovich, Ann. *An Archive of Feelings*. Durham, NC: Duke University Press, 2003.

Danet, Brenda. *Cyberplay: Communicating Online*. New York: Berg, 2001.

Dávila, Arlene. *Latinos, Inc.: The Marketing and Making of a People*. Berkeley: University of California Press, 2012.

de la Campa, Román. "Resistance and Globalization in Caribbean Discourse: Antonio Benítez-Rojo and Edouard Glissant." In *A History of Literature in the Caribbean: Cross-Cultural Studies 3*, edited by A. James Arnold, 87–116. Philadelphia: John Benjamins, 1997.

de la Fuente, Alejandro. *A Nation for All: Race, Inequality, and Politics in Twentieth Century Cuba*. Chapel Hill: University of North Carolina Press, 2001.

de la Torre, Miguel. *La Lucha for Cuba: Religion and Politics on the Streets of Miami*. Berkeley: University of California Press, 2003.

de Mul, Jos. *The Game of Life: Narrative and Ludic Identity Formation in Computer Games*. Cambridge, MA: MIT Press, 2005.

Dentith, Simon. *Parody*. London: Routledge, 2000.

Deumert, Ana. "The Performance of a Ludic Self on Social Network(ing) Sites." In *The Language of Social Media: Identity and Community on the Internet*, edited by Philip Seargeant and Caroline Tagg, 23–45. New York: Palgrave Macmillan, 2014.

Díaz Ayala, Cristobal. "Yacimientos y explotación de las minas musicales cubanas." In *Un pueblo disperso: Dimensiones sociales y culturales de la diáspora cubana*, edited by Jorge Duany, 182–189. Valencia: Aduana Vieja, 2013.

Dickson-Carr, Darryl. *African American Satire: The Sacredly Profane Novel*. Columbia: University of Missouri Press, 2001.

Dopico, Ana María. "Picturing Havana: History, Vision, and the Scramble for Cuba." *Nepantla: Views from the South* 3, no. 3 (2002): 451–593.

Douglas, Susan. *Listening In: Radio and the American Imagination*. New York: Times Books Random House, 1999.

Duany, Jorge. "Reconstructing Cubanness: Changing Discourses of National Identity on the Island and in the Diaspora during the Twentieth Century." In *Cuba, the Elusive Nation: Interpretations of National Identity*, edited by Damián J. Fernández and Madeline Cámara Betancourt. Gainesville: University Press of Florida, 2000.

———. *Blurred Borders: Transnational Migration between the Hispanic Caribbean and the United States*. Chapel Hill: University of North Carolina Press, 2011.

Duggan, Maeve. "The Demographics of Social Media Users." Pew Research Center: Internet, Science, Tech, August 19, 2015. www.pewinternet.org.

Duong, Paloma. "Bloggers Unplugged: Amateur Citizens, Cultural Discourse, and Public Sphere in Cuba." *Journal of Latin American Cultural Studies: Travesia* 22, no. 4 (2013): 375–397.

Eckstein, Susan. *The Immigrant Divide: How Cuban Americans Changed the US and Their Homeland*. New York: Routledge, 2009.

English, James F. "Festivals and the Geography of Culture: African Cinema in the 'World Space' of Its Public." In *Festivals and the Cultural Public Sphere*, edited by Liana Giorgi, Monica Sassatelli, and Gerard Delanty, 63–78. New York: Routledge, 2011.

Evora, José Antonio. "Guillermo Alvarez Guedes, El Natural." *Encuentro de la cultura cubana* 44 (2007): 171–180.

Fernández, Damián J. *Cuba and the Politics of Passion*. Austin: University of Texas Press, 2000.

———, ed. *Cuba Transnational*. Gainesville: University Press of Florida, 2005.

Fernández, Javier A. "'The Girl Is Born to Be a Mother. The Boy Is Born to Be a Gentleman': Gender and National Identity in a Cuban Exile Cultural Organization, 1962–1974." MA thesis, University of Georgia, 2004.

Fernández, Roberto. *Raining Backwards*. Houston: Arte Público Press, 1988.

Flores, Juan. *From Bomba to Hip Hop: Puerto Rican Culture and Latino Identity*. New York: Columbia University Press, 2000.

———. *The Diaspora Strikes Back: Caribeño Tales of Learning and Turning*. New York: Routledge, 2009.

Frederick, Howard. *Cuban American Radio Wars: Ideology in International Telecommunications*. New York: Ablex, 1986.

Frederik, Laurie A. *Trumpets in the Mountains: Theater and the Politics of National Culture in Cuba*. Durham, NC: Duke University Press, 2012.

Freud, Sigmund. "Humor." In *The Standard Edition of the Complete Psychological Works of Sigmund Freud*, translated and edited by James Strachey, 21:160–166. London: Hogarth, 1961.

Gámez Torres, Nora. "'La Habana está en todas partes': Young Musicians and the Symbolic Redefinition of the Cuban Nation." In *Un pueblo disperso: Dimensiones sociales y culturales de la diáspora cubana*, edited by Jorge Duany, 190–216. Valencia: Aduana Vieja, 2013.

Gans, Herbert. "Symbolic Ethnicity: The Future of Ethnic Groups and Cultures in America." *Ethnic and Racial Studies* 2, no.1 (1979): 1–20.

García, María Cristina. *Havana USA: Cuban Exiles and Cuban Americans in South Florida, 1959–1994*. Berkeley: University of California Press, 1996.

———. "Hardliners v. 'Dialogueros': Cuban Exile Political Groups and United States–Cuba Policy." *Journal of American Ethnic History* 17, no.4 (1998): 3–28.

García Borrero, Juan Antonio. "Invitación al choteo." *Casa de las Américas* 234 (January–March 2004): 75–84.

Girard, Chris, Guillermo Grenier, and Hugh Gladwin. "The Declining Symbolic Significance of the Embargo for South Florida's Cuban Americans." *Latino Studies* 8, no.1 (2010): 4–22.

Glissant, Edouard. *Caribbean Discourse*. Translated by J. Michael Dash. Charlottesville: University Press of Virginia, 1989.

Gómez, Pablo. "Su artista favorite puede ser un comunista." *Espectaculos*, February 2, 1967.

González, Tanya, and Eliza Rodriguez y Gibson. *Humor and Latina/o Camp in Ugly Betty: Funny Looking*. Lanham, MD: Lexington Books, 2015.

González Echevarría, Roberto. *Cuban Fiestas*. New Haven, CT: Yale University Press, 2010.

Gopinath, Gayatri. *Impossible Desires: Queer Diasporas and South Asian Public Cultures*. Durham, NC: Duke University Press, 2005.

Gray, Jonathan. *Watching with the Simpsons: Television, Parody, and Intertextuality*. New York: Routledge, 2006.

Gray Jonathan, Jeffrey P. Jones, and Ethan Thompson. *Satire TV: Politics and Comedy in the Post-Network Era*. New York: New York University Press, 2009.

Grenier, Guillermo, and Lisandro Pérez. *The Legacy of Exile: Cubans in the United States*. Boston: Allyn & Bacon, 2003.

Grenier, Guillermo J., Lisandro Pérez, Sung Chang Chun, and Hugh Gladwin. "There Are Cubans, There Are Cubans, and There Are Cubans: Ideological Diversity among Cuban Americans in Miami." In *Latinos in a Changing Society*, edited by Martha Montero-Sieburth and Edwin Meléndez, 93–111. Westport, CT: Praeger, 2007.

Grenier, Guillermo, and Max Castro. "Triadic Politics: Ethnicity, Race, and Politics in Miami, 1959–1998." *Pacific Historical Review* 68, no. 2 (1999): 273–292.

Grusin, Richard. *Premediation: Affect and Mediality after 9/11*. New York: Palgrave Macmillan, 2010.

Guillermo Alvarez Guedes v. Hector Luis Marcano Martínez, United States District Court, D, Puerto Rico, February 12, 2001. www.leagle.com.

Gutiérrez-Jones, Carl Scott. "Humor, Literacy and Chicano Culture." *Comparative Literature Studies* 40, no. 2 (2003): 112–126.

Habell-Pallán, Michelle. *Loca Motion: The Travels of Chicana and Latina Popular Culture*. New York: New York University Press, 2005.

Haggins, Bambi. *Laughing Mad: The Black Comic Persona in Post-Soul America*. New Brunswick, NJ: Rutgers University Press, 2007.

Hall, Stuart. "Notes on Deconstructing the Popular." In *People's History and Socialist Theory*, edited by Raphael Samuel, 227–240. London: Routledge and Kegan Paul, 1981.

Haller, William, and Patricia Landolt. "The Transnational Dimensions of Identity Formation: Adult Children of Immigrants in Miami." *Ethnic and Racial Studies* 28, no.6 (2005): 1182–1214.

Halter, Marilyn. *Shopping for Identity: The Marketing of Ethnicity*. New York: Random House, 2000.

Hariman, Robert. "Political Parody and Public Culture." *Quarterly Journal of Speech* 94, no.3 (2008): 247–72.

Henken, Ted. "Balseros, Boteros, and El Bombo: Post-1994 Cuban Immigration to the United States and the Persistence of Special Treatment." *Latino Studies* 3, no. 3 (2005): 393–416.

Henken, Ted, and Sjamme van de Voort. "From *Nada* to *Nauta*: Internet Access and Cyber-Activism in a Changing Cuba." *Cuba in Transition: Association for the Study of the Cuban Economy* 23 (2013): 341–350. www.ascecuba.org.

Hernández, Arístides Esteban, and Jorge Alberto Piñero. *Historia del humor gráfico en Cuba*. Lleida, Spain: Editorial Milenio, 2007.

Hernández, Guillermo. *Chicano Satire: A Study in Literary Culture*. Austin: University of Texas Press, 2014.

Hernández, Jillian. "'Miss, You Look like a Bratz Doll': On Chonga Girls and Sexual-Aesthetic Excess." *National Women's Studies Association Journal* 21, no.3 (2009): 63–90.

Hernández-Reguant, Ariana. "Socialism with Commercials: Consuming Advertising in Today's Cuba." *ReVista: Harvard Review of Latin America* (Winter 2000), 12–14. www.revista.drclas.harvard.edu.

Hernández-Reguant, Ariana, and Jossianna Arroyo. "The Brownface of Latinidad in Cuban Miami." *CubaCounterpoints*, July 13, 2015. www.cubacounterpoints.com.

Hidalgo, Narciso J. *Choteo: Irreverencia y humor en la cultural cubana*. Bogotá: Siglo del Hombre Editores, 2012.

Hodge, G. Derrick. "Colonization of the Cuban Body: The Growth of Male Sex Work in Havana." *North American Congress on Latin America Report on the Americas* 34, no. 5 (2001): 20–28.

Hutchby, Ian. *Confrontation Talk: Arguments, Asymmetries, and Power on Talk Radio*. New York: Routledge, 2013.

Ichikawa, Emilio. "Prólogo: Alvarez Guedes: La alegría como misión." In *Cadillac 59* by Guillermo Alvarez Guedes. Twickenham, UK: Athena Press, 2001.

Iglesias, Benigno, Cecilia Linares, Mario Masvidal, Irina Pacheco, and Rafael Hernández. "USB: El consume audiovisual informal." *Temas* 70 (April–June 2012): 81–91.

Iton, Richard. *In Search of the Black Fantastic: Politics and Popular Culture in the Post–Civil Rights Era*. New York: Oxford University Press, 2008.

Jenkins, Henry. *The Wow Climax: Tracing the Emotional Impact of Popular Culture*. New York: New York University Press, 2006.

Jenkins, Henry, Sam Ford, and Joshua Green. *Spreadable Media: Creating Value and Meaning in a Networked Culture*. New York: New York University Press, 2013.

Jenkins, Henry, Tara McPherson, and Jane Shattuc. "The Cultural That Sticks to Your Skin: A Manifesto for a New Cultural Studies." In *Hop on Pop: The Politics and Pleasures of Popular Culture*, edited by Henry Jenkins, Tara McPherson, and Jane Shattuc, 3–26. Durham, NC: Duke University Press, 2002.

Jiménez, Tomás R. *Replenished Ethnicity: Mexican Americans, Immigration, and Identity*. Berkeley: University of California Press, 2010.

Jiménez Román, Miriam, and Juan Flores, eds. *The Afro-Latin@ Reader*. Durham, NC: Duke University Press, 2010.

John, Nicholas A. "The Social Logics of Sharing." *Communication Review* 16, no. 3 (2013): 113–131.

Kandiyoti, Dalia. "Consuming Nostalgia and the Marketplace in Cristina García and Ana Menéndez." *MELUS* 31, no. 1 (Spring 2006): 81–97.

Kanellos, Nicolás. *A History of Hispanic Theatre, Origins to 1940*. Austin: University of Texas Press, 1990.

Kapcia, Antoni. *Cuba: Island of Dreams*. Oxford: Berg, 2000.

Karp, Ivan. "Festivals." In *Exhibiting Cultures: The Poetics and Politics of Museum Display*, edited by Ivan Karp and Steven D. Lavine, 279–287. Washington, DC: Smithsonian Institution Press, 1991.

Karatzogianni, Athina, and Adi Kunstman. *Digital Cultures and the Politics of Emotion: Feelings, Affect and Technological Change*. New York: Palgrave Macmillan, 2012.

Katerí Hernández, Tanya. "The Buena Vista Social Club: The Racial Politics of Nostalgia." In *Latina/o Popular Culture*, edited by Michelle Habell-Pallán and Mary Romero, 61–72. New York: New York University Press, 2002.

———. "'Too Black to Be Latino/a': Blackness and Blacks as Foreigners in Latino Studies." *Latino Studies* 1, no.1 (2003): 152–159.

Kopytoff, Igor. "The Cultural Biography of Things: Commoditization as Process." In *The Social Life of Things: Commodities in Cultural Perspective*, edited by Arjun Appadurai, 64–94. Cambridge: Cambridge University Press, 1986.

Krogstad, Jens Manuel. "Cuban Immigration to U.S. Surges as Relations Warm." Pew Research Center. December 10, 2015. www.pewresearch.org.

Laguna, Albert Sergio. "Aquí Está Alvarez Guedes: Cuban Choteo and the Politics of Play." *Latino Studies* 8, no. 4 (2010): 509–531.

———. "Cuban Miami on the Air: Narratives of Cubanía." *Journal of Latin American Cultural Studies* 23, no. 1 (2014): 87–110.

Lane, Jill. *Blackface Cuba: 1840–1895*. Philadelphia: University of Pennsylvania Press, 2005.

Larkin, Brian. "Degraded Images, Distorted Sounds: Nigerian Video and the Infrastructure of Piracy." *Public Culture* 16, no. 2 (2004): 289–314.

Lazo, Rodrigo. *Writing to Cuba: Filibustering and Cuban Exiles in the United States*. Chapel Hill: University of North Carolina Press, 2005.

Levitt, Peggy, and Nina Glick Schiller. "Conceptualizing Simultaneity: A Transnational Social Field Perspective on Society." *International Migration Review* 38, no. 3 (September 2004): 1002–1039.

Lewis, Ben. *Hammer and Tickle: A History of Communism Told through Communist Jokes*. London: Weidenfeld & Nicolson, 2009.

Lieu, Nhi T. "Performing Culture in Diaspora: Assimilation and Hybridity in *Paris by Night* Videos and Vietnamese American Niche Media." In *Alien Encounters, Popular Culture in Asian America*, edited by Mimi Thi Nguyen and Thuy Linh Nguyen Tu, 194–220. Durham, NC: Duke University Press, 2007.

Lima, Lázaro. "The King's Toilet: Cruising Literary History in Reinaldo Arenas' *Before Night Falls*." *A contra corriente: A Journal on Social History and Literature in Latin America* 10, no.1 (2012): 198–225.

Lincoln, Kenneth. *Indi'n Humor: Bicultural Play in Native America*. New York: Oxford University Press, 1993.

Lohmeier, Christine. *Cuban Americans and the Miami Media*. Jefferson, NC: McFarland, 2014.

López, Ana M. "Memorias of a Home: Mapping the Revolution (and the Making of Exiles?)." *Revista Canadiense de Estudios Hispánicos* 20, no. 1 (1995): 5–17.

———. "Greater Cuba." In *The Ethnic Eye: Latino Media Arts*, edited by Chon A. Noriega and Ana M. López, 38–58. Minneapolis: University of Minnesota Press, 1996.

López, Antonio. *Unbecoming Blackness: The Diaspora Cultures of Afro-Cuban America*. New York: New York University Press, 2012.

López, Iraida. *Impossible Returns: Narratives of the Cuban Diaspora*. Gainesville: University Press of Florida, 2015.

Loss, Jacqueline. *Dreaming in Russian: The Cuban Soviet Imaginary*. Austin: University of Texas Press, 2013.

Lugo-Ortíz, Agnes. "Material Culture, Slavery, and Governability in Colonial Cuba: The Humorous Lessons of the Cigarette *Marquillas*." *Journal of Latin American Cultural Studies* 21, no. 1 (2012): 61–85.

Lynch, Andrew. "Expression of Cultural Standing in Miami: Cuban Spanish Discourse about Fidel Castro and Cuba." *Revista Internacional de Lingüística Iberoamericana* 7, no. 2 (2009): 21–48.

Machado Sáez, Elena. "The Global Baggage of Nostalgia in Cristina García's *Dreaming in Cuban*." *MELUS* 30, no.4 (Winter 2005): 129–147.

Maguire, Emily A. *Racial Experiments in Cuban Literature and Ethnography*. Gainesville: University Press of Florida, 2011.

Mahler, Sarah J., and Katrin Hansing. "Toward a Transnationalism of the Middle: How Transnational Religious Practices Help Bridge Divides between Cuba and Miami." *Latin American Perspectives* 32, no.1 (2005): 121–146.

Mañach, Jorge. *Indagación del choteo*. Miami: Ediciones Universal, 1991. Originally published in 1928.

Martínez, Katynka Z. "American Idols with Caribbean Soul: Cubanidad and the Latin Grammys." *Latino Studies* 4, no. 4 (2006): 381–400.

Martínez, María del Carmen. " 'Her Body Was My Country': Gender and Cuban-American Exile-Community Nationalist Identity in the Work of Gustavo Pérez Firmat." *Latino Studies* 7, no. 3 (2009): 295–316.

McPherson, Tara. *Reconstructing Dixie: Race, Gender, and Nostalgia in the Imagined South*. Durham, NC: Duke University Press, 2003.

Mendible, Myra, ed. *From Bananas to Buttocks: The Latina Body in Popular Film and Culture*. Austin: University of Texas Press, 2010.

Menéndez, Ana. *In Cuba I Was a German Shepherd*. New York: Grove Press, 2001.

Mesa-Lago, Carmelo, and Jorge Pérez-López. *Cuba under Raúl Castro: Assessing the Reforms*. Boulder, CO: Lynne Rienner, 2013.

Meyer, Robinson. "Everything We Know about Facebook's Secret Mood Manipulation." *Atlantic*, June 28, 2014. www.theatlantic.com.

Mirabal, Nancy Raquel. *Suspect Freedoms: The Racial and Sexual Politics of Cubanidad in New York, 1823–1957*. New York: New York University Press, 2017.

Molina Guzmán, Isabel. "Competing Discourses of Community: Ideological Tensions between Local General-Market and Latino News Media." *Journalism* 7, no. 3 (2006): 281–298.

Molina Guzmán, Isabel. *Dangerous Curves: Latina Bodies in the Media*. New York: New York University Press, 2010.

Moore, Robin. *Nationalizing Blackness: Afrocubanismo and Artistic Revolution in Havana, 1920–1940*. Pittsburgh, PA: University of Pittsburgh Press, 1998.

———. "The *Teatro Bufo*: Cuban Blackface Theater of the Nineteenth Century." In *Soundscapes from the Americas: Ethnomusicological Essays on the Power, Poetics, and Ontology of Performance*, edited by Donna A. Buchanan, 25–42. Burlington, VT: Ashgate, 2014.

Motel, Seth, and Eileen Patten. "The 10 Largest Hispanic Origin Groups: Characteristics, Rankings, Top Counties." June 27, 2012. www.pewhispanic.org.

Muñoz, José Esteban. *Disidentifications: Queers of Color and the Performance of Politics*. Minneapolis: University of Minnesota Press, 1999.

———. "Feeling Brown: Ethnicity, and Affect in Ricardo Bracho's *The Sweetest Hangover and Other STDs*." *Theatre Journal* 52, no.1 (2000): 67–79.

———. "The Onus of Seeing Cuba: Nilo Cruz's Cubanía." *South Atlantic Quarterly* 99, nos. 2–3 (2000): 455–459.

Nahon, Karine, and Jeff Hemsley. *Going Viral*. Malden, MA: Polity, 2013.

Negrón-Muntaner, Frances. *Boricua Pop: Puerto Ricans and the Latinization of American Culture*. New York: New York University Press, 2004.

Nguyen, Mimi Thi, and Thuy Linh Nguyen Tu, eds. *Alien Encounters: Popular Culture in Asian America*. Durham, NC: Duke University Press, 2007.

Noel, Urayoán. *In Visible Movement: Nuyorican Poetry from the Sixties to Slam*. Iowa City: University of Iowa Press, 2014.

Orozco, Manuel, and Katrin Hansing. "Remittance Recipients and the Present and Future of Microentrepeneurship Activities in Cuba." In *A Contemporary Cuba Reader*, edited by Philip Brenner, Marguerite Rose Jiménez, John M. Kirk, and William M. LeoGrande, 183–190. Lanham, MD: Rowman & Littlefield, 2015.

Ortíz, Fernando. *Nuevo catauro de cubanismos*. Havana, Cuba: Editorial Ciencias Sociales, 1985. Originally published in 1923.

———. *Entre cubanos: psicología tropical*. Havana, Cuba: Editorial de Ciencias Sociales, 1986. Originally published in 1913.

Ortíz, Ricardo L. *Cultural Erotics in Cuban America*. Minneapolis: University of Minnesota Press, 2007.

Parvulescu, Anca. *Laughter: Notes on a Passion*. Cambridge, MA: MIT Press, 2010.

Pavlenko, Aneta, ed. *Bilingual Minds: Emotional Experience, Expression, and Representation*. Tonawanda, NY: Multilingual Matters, 2006.

Pedraza, Silvia. *Political Disaffection in Cuba's Revolution and Exodus*. New York: Cambridge University Press, 2007.

Pedraza-Bailey, Silvia. *Political and Economic Migrants in America*. Austin: University of Texas Press, 1985.

Peña, Susana. *Oye Loca! From the Mariel Boatlift to Gay Cuban Miami*. Minneapolis: University of Minnesota Press, 2013.

Pérez, Lisandro. "Cuban Miami." In *Miami Now! Immigration, Ethnicity, and Social Change*, edited by Guillermo Grenier and Alex Stepick, 83–108. Gainesville: University of Florida Press, 1992.

———. "Racialization among Cubans and Cuban Americans." In *How the United States Racializes Latinos: White Hegemony and Its Consequences*, edited by José A. Cobas, Jorge Duany, and Joe R. Feagin, 134–148. Boulder, CO: Paradigm Publishers, 2009.

Pérez, Louis A. *On Becoming Cuban: Identity, Nationality, and Culture*. Chapel Hill: University of North Carolina Press, 2009.

———. *Cuba in the American Imagination: Metaphor and the Imperial Ethos*. Chapel Hill: University of North Carolina Press, 2011.

Pérez Firmat, Gustavo. *Literature and Liminality: Festive Readings in the Hispanic Tradition*. Durham, NC: Duke University Press, 1986.

———. *The Cuban Condition: Translation and Identity in Modern Cuban Literature*. New York: Cambridge University Press, 1989.

———. "A Willingness of the Heart: Cubanidad, Cubaneo, Cubanía." *Cuban Studies Association Occasional Papers Series* 2, no. 7 (1997): 1–11.

———. *The Havana Habit*. New Haven, CT: Yale University Press, 2010.

Pérez Salomón, Omar. *Terrorismo en el éter: Agresión radio televisa contra Cuba*. Havana, Cuba: Editora Política, 2004.

Pertierra, Anna Cristina. "Private Pleasures: Watching Videos in Post-Soviet Cuba." *International Journal of Cultural Studies* 12, no. 2 (2009): 113–130.

———. "If They Show *Prison Break* in the United States on Wednesday, by Thursday It Is Here: Mobile Media Networks in 21st-Century Cuba." *Television and New Media* 13, no. 5 (2012): 399–414.

Pew Research Center. "Median Age for Hispanics Is Lower than Median Age for Total U.S. Population." July 2, 2012. www.pewresearch.org.

Porter, Bruce, and Marvin Dunn. *The Miami Riot of 1980*. Lexington, MA: Lexington Books, 1984.

Portes, Alejandro. "La máquina política cubano-estadounidense: Reflexiones sobre su origen y permanencia." *Foro Internacional* 43, no. 3 (2003): 608–626.

———. "The Cuban-American Political Machine: Reflections on its Origins and Perpetuation," In *Debating Cuban Exceptionalism*, edited by Bert Hoffman and Laurence Whitehead, 123–137. New York: Palgrave Macmillan, 2007.

Portes, Alejandro, and Aaron Puhrmann. "A Bifurcated Enclave: The Peculiar Evolution of the Cuban Immigrant Population in the Last Decades." In *Un pueblo disperso: Dimensiones sociales y culturales de la diáspora cubana*, edited by Jorge Duany, 122–149. Valencia: Aduana Vieja, 2013.

Portes, Alejandro, and Alex Stepick. *City on the Edge: The Transformation of Miami.* Berkeley: University of California Press, 1993.

Price, Patricia L. "Cohering Culture on Calle Ocho: The Pause and Flow of Latinidad." *Globalizations* 4, no. 1 (2007): 81–99.

Purcell, Kristen. "Online Video 2013." Pew Internet and American Life Project. www.pewinternet.org.

Quiroga, José. *Cuban Palimpsests.* Minneapolis: University of Minnesota Press, 2005.

Rainie, Lee, and Barry Wellman. *Networked: The New Social Operating System.* Cambridge, MA: MIT Press, 2012.

Ramírez, Ricardo. "Mobilization en Español: Spanish-Language Radio and the Activation of Political Identities." In *Rallying for Immigrant Rights: The Fight for Inclusion in 21st Century America*, edited by Kim Voss and Irene Bloemraad, 63–81. Berkeley: University of California Press, 2011.

Ramos, José Antonio. *El manual del perfecto fulanista.* Miami: Editorial Cubana, 1995. Originally published in 1916.

Recio, Milena. "Qué Paquete (Semanal)! Diálogo múltiple durante el Ania Pino in Memoriam." *Catalejo: El blog de Temas.* December 3, 2014. www.temas.cult.cu/.

Reyes, Israel. *Humor and the Eccentric Text in Puerto Rican Literature.* Gainesville: University Press of Florida, 2005.

Reyna, José R., and María Herrera-Sobek. "Jokelore, Cultural Differences, and Linguistic Dexterity: The Construction of the Mexican Immigrant in Chicano Humor." In *Culture across Borders: Mexican Immigration and Popular Culture*, edited by David R. Maciel and María Herrera-Sobek, 203–226. Tucson: University of Arizona Press, 1998.

Rich, B. Ruby, and Lourdes Argüelles. "Homosexuality, Homophobia, and Revolution: Notes toward an Understanding of the Cuban Lesbian and Gay Male Experience, Part II." *Signs: Journal of Women in Culture and Society* 11, no. 1 (1985): 120–136.

Rivero, Yeidy. "Interpreting Cubanness, Americanness, and the Sitcom: WPBT-PBS's *¿Qué Pasa, USA?*, (1975–1980)." In *Global Television Formats: Understanding Television across Borders*, edited by Tasha Oren and Sharon Shahaf, 90–108. New York: Routledge, 2012.

———. *Broadcasting Modernity: Cuban Commercial Television 1950–1960.* Durham, NC: Duke University Press, 2015.

Rivero, Yeidy, and Arlene Dávila, eds. *Contemporary Latina/o Media: Production, Circulation, Politics.* New York: New York University Press, 2014.

Roach, Joseph. *Cities of the Dead: Circum-Atlantic Performance.* New York: Columbia University Press, 1996.

Rubio, Raúl. "Discourses of/on Nostalgia: Cuban America's Real and Fictional Geographies." *Letras Hispanas* 3, no. 1 (2006): 13–24.

Salwen, Michael Brian. *Radio and Television in Cuba: The Pre-Castro Era.* Iowa City: Iowa State University Press, 1994.

Sánchez-Boudy, José. *Diccionario mayor de cubanismos*. Miami: Ediciones Universal, 1999.

Santí, Enrico Mario. "Cabrera Infante: El estilo de la nación." *Letras Libres no.76* (April 2005): 21–24.

Sawyer, Mark Q. *Racial Politics in Post-Revolutionary Cuba*. New York: Cambridge University Press, 2006.

Schneider, Rebecca. *Performing Remains: Art and War in Times of Theatrical Reenactment*. New York: Routledge, 2011.

Schoultz, Lars. *That Infernal Little Cuban Republic: The United States and the Cuban Revolution*. Chapel Hill: University of North Carolina Press, 2009.

Scott, Peter Dale, and John Marshall. *Cocaine Politics: Drugs, Armies, and the CIA in Central America*. Berkeley: University of California Press, 1998.

Serratore, Nicole. "How Do You Say Big Media in Spanish? Spanish-Language Media Regulation and the Implications of the Univision-Hispanic Broadcasting Merger on the Public Interest." *Fordham Intellectual Property, Media & Entertainment Law Journal* 15 (Autumn 2004): 203–272.

Shifman, Limor. *Memes in Digital Culture*. Cambridge, MA: MIT Press, 2014.

Shingler, Martin, and Cindy Wieringa. *On Air: Methods and Meanings of Radio*. New York: Oxford University Press, 1998.

Smith, Aaron. "6 New Facts about Facebook." Pew Internet and American Life Project. February 3, 2014. www.pewresearch.org.

Soruco, Gonzalo. *Cubans and the Media in South Florida*. Gainesville: University Press of Florida, 1996.

Sosa, Sayli. "'Chacalización' en dos tiempos." *La plaza de Sayli*, November 10, 2014. plazadesayli.wordpress.com.

Stewart, Kathleen. *Ordinary Affects*. Durham, NC: Duke University Press, 2007.

Stewart, Susan. *On Longing: Narratives of the Miniature, the Gigantic, the Souvenir, the Collection*. Durham, NC: Duke University Press, 1993.

Torres, María de los Angeles. *In the Land of Mirrors: Cuban Exile Politics in the United States*. Ann Arbor: University of Michigan Press, 2001.

Torres-Saillant, Silvio. "Inventing the Race: Latinos and the Ethnoracial Pentagon." *Latino Studies* 1, no. 1 (2003): 123–151.

U.S. Congress. Senate. Committee on Foreign Relations. *Cuba: Immediate Action Is Needed to Ensure Survivability of Radio and TV Martí*. 111th Cong., 2d sess., 2010. S. Prt 111-46.

Valdés García, Félix. "El Caribe: Integración, identidad, y choteo." *Utopía y Praxis Latinoamericana: Revista Internacional de Filosofía Iberoamericana y Teoría Social* 9, no. 27 (2004): 49–60.

Valdivia, Angharad. "Latinas as Radical Hybrid: Transnationally Gendered Traces in Mainstream Media." *Global Media Journal* 3, no. 4. (2004): 1–21.

——— ed. *Latina/o Communication Studies Today*. New York: Peter Lang, 2008.

van Dijck, José. *The Culture of Connectivity: A Critical History of Social Media*. New York: Oxford University Press, 2013.

Vazquez, Alexandra T. *Listening in Detail: Performances of Cuban Music*. Durham, NC: Duke University Press, 2013.

Vega, Bernardo. *Memoirs of Bernardo Vega: A Contribution to the History of the Puerto Rican Community in New York*. Edited by César Andreu Iglesias and translated by Juan Flores. New York: Monthly Press, 1984.

Venegas, Cristina. *Digital Dilemmas: The State, the Individual, and Digital Media in Cuba*. New Brunswick, NJ: Rutgers University Press, 2010.

Vicari, Stefania. "Exploring the Cuban Blogosphere: Discourse Networks and Informal Politics." *New Media & Society* (2014): 998–1015.

Walsh, Daniel C. *An Air War with Cuba: The United States Radio Campaign against Castro*. Jefferson, NC: McFarland, 2011.

Warner, Sara. *Acts of Gaiety: LGBT Performance and the Politics of Pleasure*. Ann Arbor: University of Michigan Press, 2012.

Watkins, Mel. *On The Real Side: A History of African American Comedy*. Chicago: Chicago Review Press, 1999.

Wilde, Larry. *The Official White Folks/Black Folks Joke Book*. New York: Pinnacle, 1975.

Zupančič, Alenka. *The Odd One In: On Comedy*. Cambridge, MA: MIT Press, 2008.

INDEX

Page numbers in italic indicate illustrations.

Albert Sergio Laguna is Assistant Professor of American Studies and of Ethnicity, Race, and Migration at Yale University. His work has appeared in *Latino Studies*, the *Journal of Latin American and Caribbean Studies*, the *Miami Herald*, the *Washington Post*, and CNN. He is originally from New Jersey.